1989

Democracy
in the
Americas

Democracy
in the
Americas

STOPPING THE PENDULUM

Edited by
ROBERT A. PASTOR

HM HOLMES
& MEIER   New York   London

Published in the United States of America 1989 by
  Holmes & Meier Publishers, Inc.
  30 Irving Place
  New York, N.Y. 10003

BOOK DESIGN BY DALE COTTON

The paper used in this publication meets the requirements of the American
National Standard for Permanence of Paper for printed Library Materials,
Z39.48-1984.

Library of Congress Cataloging-in-Publication Data

Democracy in the Americas : stopping the pendulum / edited by Robert
    Pastor.
        p. cm.
      Bibliography: p.
      Includes index.
      ISBN 0-8419-1182-7.—ISBN 0-8419-1183-5 (pbk.)
        1. Political participation—Latin America.   2. Latin America—
    Politics and government—1948–   3. Democracy.   I. Pastor, Robert
    A.
      JL966.D455   1989
    321.8'098—dc19   89-1781
                                                                      CIP

MANUFACTURED IN THE UNITED STATES OF AMERICA

To the memory of
Errol Barrow (1920–1987)
for his defense and promotion of democracy

Contents

CONTENTS

Abbreviations

AP	Acción Popular (Popular Action Party) of Peru
AD	Acción Democrática (Democratic Action) of Venezuela
ANAPO	Alianza Nacional Popular (National Popular Alliance) of Colombia
APRA	Alianza Popular Revolucionario Americano (American Popular Revolutionary Alliance) of Peru
ARENA	Alianza Republicana Nacional (National Republican Alliance) of El Salvador
CAPEL	Centro Interamericano de Asesoría y Promoción Electoral (Interamerican Center for Electoral Promotion and Assistance)
COPEI	Comité de Organización Política Electoral Independiente (Social Christian Party) of Venezuela
ETA	Euzkadi ta Azkatazana (Basque Nation and Liberty) of Spain
FMLN	Frente Farabundo Martí de Liberación Nacional (Farabundo Martí National Liberation Front) of El Salvador
GAOR	General Assembly Official Records
OAS	Organization of American States
ORDEN	Organización Democrática Nacionalista (Nationalist Democratic Organization) of El Salvador
PDC	Partido Demócrata Cristiano (Christian Democratic Party) of El Salvador
PLN	Partido Liberación Nacional (National Liberation Party) of Costa Rica
PMDB	Partido Movimiento Democrático Brasiliero (Brazilian Democratic Movement Party)
PRD	Partido Revolucionario Dominicano (Dominican Revolutionary Party)
PRI	Partido Revolucionario Institucional (Institutional Revolutionary Party) of Mexico
UCR	Unión Cívica Radical (Radical Civic Union) of Argentina

Preface

Beginning in the mid-1970s, one Latin American military government after another relinquished power to civilian democratic rulers. Within a decade, elections had been held and civilian governments had taken office in all of Central America, in all but two governments in South America, and all but two regimes in the Caribbean. Still, democracy was secure in few places and often civilian presidents served at the pleasure of the generals rather than the other way around. All democrats feared that the pendulum that had swung toward democracy could swing back toward dictatorship, as it had done before in Latin America. This book is a multinational effort to understand why Latin America and the Caribbean have become democratic and why many previous such experiments have failed.

The research project that led to this book originated in a series of discussions that former United States President Jimmy Carter, Rosalynn Carter, and I had during two visits to Latin America in October 1984 and February 1986. We met with current and former presidents from Venezuela, Peru, Brazil, Argentina, Panama, Costa Rica, Nicaragua, El Salvador, and Mexico. All insisted that the time to study the success and failure of past democratic experiments was now—as democracy seemed to be in full flower.

We commissioned papers from some of the foremost scholars of democracy in the world and asked them to identify the policy implications of democracy's experience in Latin America and the Caribbean. From the beginning, we intended for the research to be policy-oriented, and the papers were reviewed with that in mind in two stages. First, over thirty scholars and experts from throughout the hemisphere attended a one-day workshop to discuss the papers and the issues and to propose specific recommendations on what needed to be done. In preparation for the workshop, we also commissioned eighteen case studies (see the Appendix), each of which succinctly describes the key decisions that were made or in certain cases were not made that resulted in the breakdown of, transition to, or consolidation of democracy. Each case study also includes a brief chronology and bibliography. Surprisingly, nothing like this had been done before. Because of the brevity of the cases—fourteen countries at eighteen points in time—they serve as a useful compass for locating the key variables to explain the swing of the pendulum.

A second way to ensure the policy relevance of the papers was to have them presented to leading politicians and statesmen throughout the hemisphere, including Jimmy Carter, Gerald Ford, Raúl Alfonsín, Vinicio Cerezo, Rafael Caldera, Pierre Elliott Trudeau, and eight other former and current presidents and prime ministers from the Americas, the former Speaker of the House Jim Wright, and former Chairman of the Senate Foreign Relations Committee Richard Lugar. Convened in November 1986, the conference was the first one at the newly completed Carter Center of Emory University. The statesmen drew on their own experiences in commenting on the papers, which were subsequently revised for this book. In addition, the commentaries were transcribed and edited and these are listed in the bibliography at the end of the book together with twenty-two memoranda on specific countries or issues that were prepared for the conference.

The first part of this book is a discussion of the previous swings of the democratic pendulum in Latin America and the different ways that democracy has been defined. Lorenzo Meyer evaluates several key propositions on democratization from the perspective of three distinct Latin American groups: authoritarians, opportunists, and democrats. In Part II, the authors explore the policy implications of three phases in the political process of democratization: breakdown of democracy, transition toward democracy, and consolidation of the democratic experience. Osvaldo Hurtado analyzes recent changes in Latin American attitudes—or political culture—and asserts that these changes have increased the chances that democracy will prevail in the region's future. Nicolás Ardito Barletta assesses the political implications for democracy of economic policy during a period of austerity and recession. Part III includes a summary and analysis of the major themes of the book by Thomas Skidmore and a series of specific recommendations by Tom Farer and myself on ways that the inter-American community can reinforce democracy in the region.

To organize a research and policy project on this scale required the support and assistance of many people and organizations. Eric Bord, who served as the associate director of the Latin American Program, provided invaluable assistance in organizing the conference and compiling the revised papers. I would also like to thank Jennifer McCoy, who is a scholar of democratization in Latin America and who succeeded Eric as associate director, for her comments on several of the chapters. Tim Johnson assisted in the transcribing and editing of the commentaries and Pat Kent and Diane Diaz helped in typing the papers. Linda Helms helped teachers who attended the program to turn the research into lessons for secondary school students.

The conference was co-sponsored by the Institute of the Americas. We would have been unable to organize as unique a conference as came about without the constant flow of advice and ideas of Joseph Grunwald and Richard Sinkin, who were president and vice president of the Institute at that time. The two of them were especially helpful in making the workshop a success. We are also very grateful for the generous support of the Ford Foundation, the National Endowment for Democracy, and the Arca Foundation, and to contributions by the Southeast Bank of Miami, Juan Yañes and the Exxon Education Foundation, and E. I. du Pont.

Although the focus of much of this book is on Latin America, we deliberately widened our area of inquiry to include all of the Americas. There is much that can be learned from the vigorous democracies in the Caribbean, and Errol Barrow together with George Price helped us to understand those lessons. Errol Barrow led Barbados to independence in 1966 and served as prime minister there for a decade. After leading the opposition during most of the next decade, he and his party won a landslide electoral victory in 1986. Barbados is a small country, but it is a spirited democracy with one of the best health and educational systems in the developing world.

At the conference, Errol Barrow encouraged the statesmen to adopt a proposal to use their individual and collective influence to reinforce democracy in the Americas. He called the idea a Council of Freely Elected Heads of Government, and the name and his proposal were adopted unanimously by the leaders and were one of several specific recommendations accepted at the meeting. Just one month before his tragic death on 1 June 1987, he wrote to Jimmy Carter urging the council to play a leadership role in assisting the Haitian people in their effort to move from Duvalier's dictatorship to democracy. This book and the council's efforts are dedicated to his memory and to his tireless devotion to democracy.

Robert A. Pastor
Atlanta, Georgia

Foreword
Human Rights and Democracy

JIMMY CARTER

Human rights and democracy are intimately related. The global movement to defend human rights has made possible the spread of democracy in the western hemisphere, and democratic governments have proven the best means of defending human rights.

Human rights have become a standard by which the world judges individual governments. Because no country has a perfect human rights record, all countries should respond positively to criticism from the international community. Nevertheless, as one compares the human rights practices around the world, democracies—despite flaws—have much better records for respecting the rights of their citizens than other governments. Winston Churchill was at once a critic of democracy's failings and its most eloquent spokesman. He captured both sides in his apt description of democracy as the worst form of government in the world—except for all the others.

When people can choose their leaders, governments violate human rights at the risk of losing power, and politicians do not run for office in order to lose. Elections keep governments accountable to their people. Those leaders who claim to speak for the people but do not permit free elections almost inevitably become oppressors. Octavio Paz, the great Mexican philosopher, once wrote: "A country without free elections is a country without a voice, without eyes, and without arms." An election is the means by which the governed either give their consent or withdraw it; it is the connection between the people and their leaders.

But a free election alone does not make a democracy any more than a democracy automatically guarantees human rights. Let me first discuss the relationship between democracy and human rights and then between democracy and economic and social rights.

Human Rights and Democracy

Since the proclamation of the Universal Declaration of Human Rights in 1948, human rights have been on the international agenda, with the protection and promotion of human rights a responsibility shared by all the world's citizens and governments. The American Convention on Human Rights signed in 1969 in Costa Rica gave additional strength to the rights of the people of the

Americas by recommending that they be defended by two new institutions. The convention provided a legal mandate for the Inter-American Commission on Human Rights, and it recommended the establishment of the Inter-American Court on Human Rights once the convention came into force.

Today, no government in this hemisphere can claim that mistreatment of its citizens is solely its own business. Silence—the accomplice of terror—is no longer acceptable; loud voices and determined actions should be heard and felt when a government violates its citizens' human rights.

When I took office in 1977, a plague of repression had descended upon Latin America. People were being tortured or "disappeared"—a grisly euphemism for murder—for their political beliefs in Argentina, Chile, Uruguay, Paraguay, Brazil, Bolivia, Haiti, Cuba, Nicaragua, El Salvador, and Guatemala. Military governments ruled in all but two Latin countries in South America.

Our first task was to expose and try to stop the abuses of the first and most important category of human rights—the respect for the integrity of the person. We did not ignore the second category of human rights—civil and political liberties—or the third category—social and economic rights—but we were compelled to give highest priority to the victims of arbitrary arrest, torture, and murder by death squads associated with military governments.

As the most powerful democracy in the hemisphere, the United States had a special responsibility to defend human rights, but we wanted to work with other democratic governments to strengthen regional norms and institutions. I signed the American Convention on Human Rights in June 1977 and encouraged other governments to sign and ratify it too. At the time, only two governments had ratified the convention, but within a year fourteen governments had ratified it and brought it into effect.

We quadrupled the budget of the Inter-American Commission on Human Rights, and we put the weight of the United States behind the organization's efforts to get their reports considered and approved by the Organization of American States. As president, I also personally wrote to many leaders in the region urging them to invite the commission to investigate charges that had been made of human rights violations. Moreover, the United States conditioned its relations with each government on the way it treated its own citizens. Together with our democratic friends, we piqued the hemisphere's conscience and raised everyone's consciousness: human rights was not just a slogan but a legitimate and universal responsibility.

By joining together with other human rights defenders throughout the hemisphere, we gave strength to those who wanted to institutionalize respect for humanity with democratic governments. We also worked directly to promote democracy by encouraging military governments to open up the political system, to permit free speech, and to hold free elections. In the first major trip to the region during my administration, my wife Rosalynn visited Brazil, Peru, and Ecuador to encourage these three military governments that had pledged to transfer power to civilians to fulfill their promises. We did not stop our efforts with this visit; we began them. Working again with Venezuela, Costa

Rica, and Colombia, we used every opportunity to demonstrate to the military leaders that their efforts to continue the transition toward democracy would win their countries new respect. Ecuador and Peru elected civilian presidents in 1979 and 1980, and Rosalynn returned, as she promised, for the inaugurations.

When President Reagan entered office, many in his administration wanted to reverse course on human rights and democracy. The secretary of state said that a concern for human rights would be replaced with a policy on terrorism; the U.S. ambassador to the United Nations visited Chile and Argentina and had cordial meetings with the military dictators while shunning human rights activists; and the first Latin leader invited to the White House was General Roberto Viola of Argentina. Fortunately, the policy changed direction after a few years, and the administration became a strong supporter of democracy in the region.

Today, there is a bipartisan consensus in the United States for supporting democracy in Latin America, and the spread of democracy is breathtaking. As democracy has expanded so too has respect for human rights, and indeed, many human rights leaders, including Raúl Alfonsín of Argentina, have become elected leaders in the newly emerging or restored democracies. The democratic leaders who had struggled during the military dictatorships remember well the support they received from the United States.

Democracy and Economic and Social Rights

Free elections are the foundation, but a democratic building will remain a shell unless the elected governments are responsive to the social and economic concerns and rights of their constituents. There are, however, no simple formulas for respecting social and economic rights. Most governments, for example, acknowledge the right to a job as a human right, and yet few governments guarantee this right. The Communist governments that do guarantee the right to employment violate political rights more than some of those that do not.

Human rights are not a static concept; they have evolved and expanded over time. Today, no democratic government would exclude women from voting, although this was the norm in the nineteenth century. Today, people expect their governments to protect them from unsafe drugs, pollution, or misleading advertising. Countries also differ as to what constitutes a right. Some governments consider a death sentence a crime, and some consider it a justifiable punishment. Democracy is not just a mechanism for protecting human rights; it is also a framework to permit people to decide which economic and social rights should be protected and how.

All democratic governments do not have the same amount of resources to fulfill the human rights of their citizens. The United States can and should do more for its poor and disadvantaged than Bolivia. But even in this world of sovereignty and nation-states, the United States and other richer countries should do more for needy people in poor countries. Today, the debt crisis in

Latin America is probably the single most important reason why democratic governments cannot meet the human needs of their citizens. Because of this crisis, Latin American governments must send scarce foreign exchange abroad to service their debt rather than invest in the education, health, or welfare of their peoples. Because of the crisis, many people do not have access to clean water, schools are not built, jobs are not created, hospitals are not maintained, medicines are not available, forests are decimated, fertile land erodes, and the future looks ever more bleak.

In failing to alleviate this crisis, the United States and other industrial countries have made it difficult for these debtor governments to meet the human rights and needs of their people. Unless new democratic governments can demonstrate to their people that they can better meet their needs than the military governments that preceded them, people will become disillusioned with democracy. Solving the debt crisis is therefore a key to preserving human rights and maintaining democracy in Latin America and the Caribbean.

Cooperation Among Democracies

The greatest challenge facing the hemisphere today is to maintain and expand democracy. To meet this challenge, all the democracies in the hemisphere need to cooperate to ensure that democracy does not fail anywhere. This book provides an essential road map describing how that goal can be achieved. If we succeed, the hemisphere will not only be freer, it will also be more peaceful, because as Harry S. Truman once said, "The attainment of worldwide respect for essential human rights is synonymous with the attainment of world peace." In this hemisphere, we can begin by taking the first step. The yearning for freedom and peace cuts across all artificial boundaries and unites the human family. It is time to concentrate on our unity and not our differences; it is time to reinforce democracy as the best way to defend human rights.

Foreword
Consolidating Democracy

RAÚL ALFONSÍN

The conference on democracy at the Carter Center in November 1986 had a special significance for me. It gave me the opportunity to express my ideas on a subject that is a central concern for millions of my fellow citizens: the consolidation of democracy and the transformation of our social structures so as to guarantee pluralism, promote tolerance, and permit an equitable distribution of wealth.

Serious obstacles have had to be overcome in the effort to consolidate democracy in Argentina. There has been an unfortunate tendency in our past to blame current problems on countries that used their relative power to their advantage, on some inherent flaw in our people, or on a particular group. These oversimplifications have been harmful and have caused us either to underestimate the obstacles to progress or to isolate ourselves in our own backwardness. These views are now disappearing from Argentine society as we begin to understand that the problems we must confront are so complex that simple answers become demagogic and part of the problem. Moreover, Argentines are conscious that our present backwardness is largely due to the attempt by some to impose their narrow self-interest at the expense of others. In that game, the end justified the means and the entire society became engulfed in conflicts that were often violent.

Political and social conflicts usually are the result of low levels of economic growth and consequently result from powerful struggles over the distribution of scarce resources. In order to develop the country today, it is necessary to guarantee respect for individual rights and accept procedural rules for the resolution of conflicts of ideas and interests. The democratic system provides the rules and the forum for an organized discussion about the preferred model of society and about the most effective way to implement it. This process assumes that there are many valid ideas and interests, and the way to test these ideas is in open and rational debate.

Debates do not involve confrontations among established interests, but rather a competition of arguments over which of these interests are legitimate. The decision of the majority grants a prima facie validity to the solution and requires us to accept it, even though we retain the right to try to reverse it peacefully at some future time.

The functioning of democracy implicitly carries with it a respect for the rights that sustain human dignity. This concept is solidly anchored in Argentine society. The protection of basic rights does not mean simply the avoidance of state intervention in individual lives. Indeed, it is of little use to guarantee the right to express ideas freely if people cannot count on an education to develop those ideas. Freedom of action must be balanced by helping those who are disadvantaged. This requires concrete actions by society and the state to avoid a situation in which the freedom of some diminishes the freedom of others. In sum, what is required for democracy is a vision of solidarity.

This means that participation is an essential component of democracy. Some argue that the survival of democracy is at risk when there is a high level of participation and a low level of institutionalization—if the system is incapable of channeling demands and satisfying them. This idea is not unknown in the more developed countries with established democracies; it was called the "crisis of democracy," and some advocated a restriction of participation as the way to deal with the problem until adequate institutions had been established. But in my opinion, to give democracy such a restricted meaning would devalue it. On the contrary, democracy requires the highest levels of participation in order to enrich the collective debate and to assure that each citizen is both a part of the system and a promoter of the ethic of solidarity that is the foundation of the system. Despite the inconvenience of participatory democracy, we must seek solutions that strengthen participation rather than limit it.

Democratic participation requires broad and flexible institutional designs that can channel the uncertainties of the people. Argentina, for several reasons, has not yet modified its institutional framework either to maintain, strengthen, or advance its democratic system. We are now, however, in the process of developing important mechanisms, including opening channels of participation, rendering the political system more flexible, promoting more fairness in the administration of justice, and making the state more efficient in providing public services.

Societywide political participation necessarily implies the decentralization of decision making. In Latin America that requires a profound redistribution of power that would modify norms that have been entrenched during recurrent authoritarian periods. Participation, entailing an open rather than closed society, also generates modernization. For many years, some assumed that modernization consisted of technological development, excluding any concern with how this type of development would affect social organization. The task of modernization was frequently associated with authoritarian regimes. But this was a mirage. Today we know that participation is the indispensable instrument for national modernization.

It is no longer possible to continue believing that the solution to all problems can be handled by a few. On the contrary, in so far as more people participate in the decision-making process, the greater the possibility becomes of success and impartiality. Modernization will thus be the result of a process of wide discussion that will determine the most likely means to success. The distribution of costs and benefits can only be a product of democratic debate.

Let me add that participation is no less important for the consolidation of peace in the entire world. The name for participation at the international level is multilateralism. Just as with the problems of the world economy, the issue of peace must be addressed and resolved for the entire globe. In a world in which mutual interdependence appears to be a constant, the serious problems of some require the attention of all.

An ethic of solidarity is an essential element of internal democracy, and it must also be incorporated into the dialogue between nations. With the commitment of all, we will create a world in peace, with greater liberty and well-being for all people.

Democracy
in the
Americas

Part I

DEMOCRACY: ITS FATE AND MEANING

1

Introduction
The Swing of the Pendulum

ROBERT A. PASTOR

"The long age of dictators in Latin America is finally in its twilight."[1] That was the first sentence of a book written by Tad Szulc, an American journalist who has reported on Latin America for over thirty years. After six Latin American dictators fell from power over a four-year period, Szulc described the optimism that swept over Latin America. "Democracy," he wrote, "so late in coming and still taking its first shaky and tentative steps forward, is here to stay in Latin America." That was in 1959; four years later, democracy left as abruptly as it had arrived. The pendulum had swung back to dictatorship.

In the 1980s, the pendulum made its most majestic swing toward democracy. Will it last? Can the pendulum be kept from swinging back? That is the subject of this book. In this chapter, let me review the different paths of political development taken by the United States and Latin America, describe the three swings of the democratic pendulum in Latin America in the period since World War II, analyze the evolution of thinking on the possibilities and problems of democracy in the Americas, and finally offer some thoughts on the final resting place of the pendulum.

Founding Fathers

Even before Columbus sailed west looking for the East Indies, the people of southern America had advanced along a very different path of social and political development than had the people in northern America. The Incas in Peru and the Mayas and Aztecs in Central America and Mexico had developed civilizations as rich and advanced as those in Europe at the time. Temples in Macchu Picchu, Tikal, and Monte Alban rival the Coliseum of Rome or the great cathedrals of France. In contrast, the tribes in North America were mainly nomadic. Instead of building monuments to immortalize men or to glorify gods, the natives of the north roamed the great expanses and hunted for game.

The Europeans who explored the New World were similarly divided in

3

heritage and culture, and winds, ocean currents, and perhaps fate led them to the place where their backgrounds meshed best with the natives. The southern Europeans—the Spanish and Portuguese—were the product of the Counter-reformation, the Inquisition, and a centralized monarchy, and they sailed to the south where they encountered the mineral-rich, hierarchical civilizations of South America and Mexico. The Spanish viewed the Americas as a place to conquer—to extract mineral wealth and convert souls. They replaced the leadership of the Indian civilizations and ruled much as the Indian emperors had, punishing mercilessly those who did not obey. Orders and governors came from Spain.

The English who settled North America were children of the Reformation and the Enlightenment. Generally, they practiced self-government and farmed relatively small plots of land. Some worked with the Indians, but many displayed the same intolerance toward the natives that the Church had shown to their Protestant sects. Some Indians fought; others went west, anticipating Horace Greeley's advice. By a convoluted irony, the North American settlers created a more equal and democratic society by killing the Indians or pushing them west, whereas the settlers in Mexico and South America developed a more stratified, authoritarian system by replacing the leaders of a stationary civilization.

The differences between the regions' two backgrounds are perhaps symbolized most sharply by the two giants—George Washington and Simón Bolívar—who led the United States and part of Latin America to independence. Both were generals, but their differences were more significant than their similarities. George Washington, while frustrated with the Continental Congress, never contemplated either ignoring or suppressing it. He had to be cajoled into seeking the presidency and then did so as a civilian with a fixed term. After two terms, he voluntarily stepped down, despite popular calls that he run again.

While Washington was a practical man, an engineer, Simón Bolívar was a philosopher, a dreamer. Whereas Washington became known as *one* of the "founding fathers," Bolívar was "the great liberator." A writer of constitutions in an age of constitutions, Bolívar conceived of a hereditary Senate and a presidency-for-life. He was skeptical of elections: "Let us be clear on one thing: the majority of men do not know what is in their own best interest and they constantly go against it. . . . Popular elections, with primitive country people and cynical town-dwellers, are yet another obstacle to unity amongst us, for the former are so ignorant that they vote mechanically, while the latter are so ambitious that they turn everything into a contest."[2] Washington left his country a tradition of a two-term presidency and the supremacy of law over military force. Bolívar brought independence to his country but could not bring stability or democracy. In the end, disillusioned, Bolivar wrote to a friend that the region was "ungovernable."[3]

In Latin America, inequalities between classes became wider and the state became stronger than in the United States. Though scarred by slavery and bitterly divided by a civil war, the United States maintained its democracy. Latin America's path was more tragic. "Endemic civil war," writes Octavio Paz, "produced militarism, and militarism produced dictatorships."[4] A few countries like Chile and Uruguay escaped this pattern until the 1970s, but for most of Latin America, this was the past that shaped its future.

Three Swings

Since independence, Latin Americans have often experienced the swing between democracy and despotism, but the contemporary consciousness has been shaped by three swings of the pendulum since the Second World War. Each of these swings went further toward democracy than the previous one. The first swing—beginning in 1944—was the most modest, but it still left an important psychological imprint on the youth of the region and probably made the second swing toward democracy in the late 1950s more profound. Similarly, the lessons learned from the failure of that second swing made the next generation more cautious and shrewd when they had their chance in the 1970s.

The words marshalled by Franklin Roosevelt and Winston Churchill to fight Nazism had a decided, if unintended, effect in Latin America. The region was emerging from more than a decade of depression and dictatorship, and Latin Americans were aroused and energized by the Four Freedoms declared by Roosevelt and Churchill. The first democratic uprising in Latin America that borrowed rhetoric from these two democratic leaders occurred in Guatemala in 1944; the next year, the Venezuelan military dictator was overthrown, and soon after, elections were held. In 1948, after a fraudulent election, Costa Ricans lent their support to a young social democrat, José Figueres, who overthrew the government and, within a year, gave the presidency back to its rightful holder.

Democrats were winning power in Europe and also in Latin America; there was a feeling for a moment that a corner had been turned, but before the feeling could take hold, the pendulum began to swing back. In 1948, the year of Figueres' victory, Venezuela's young democracy was crushed. Six years later, the military in Guatemala stopped following the orders of President Jacobo Arbenz and instead lent their support to an insurgency financed by the United States. Only Costa Rica remained democratic when the pendulum swung back.

In 1959 Tad Szulc heralded the second, much more exuberant swing of Latin America's political pendulum. Beginning in 1955 with the fall of Juan Domingo Perón in Argentina, dictatorships fell like dominoes—Gustavo Rojas Pinilla in Colombia, Marcos Pérez Jiménez in Venezuela, Manuel Odría in Peru, Getúlio Vargas in Brazil, and Fulgencio Batista in Cuba. In September 1956, after twenty years of ruling Nicaragua, General Anastasio Somoza was shot and killed at a dance. His oldest son, Luis Somoza, succeeded him but introduced a measure of freedom not previously known in Nicaragua. Then, in May 1961, the most savage of all the Caribbean dictators, Rafael Leonidas Trujillo, was assassinated by several military officers.

Again Latin Americans felt they had passed an historical watershed. John F.

Kennedy captured this change in his speeches announcing an Alliance for Progress. Scholars and journalists identified the longer-term social and economic trends that had transformed the region since the Second World War. "The fundamental factor in bringing the dictatorial era toward an end in Latin America was the rapid growth of political consciousness on all class and educational levels," wrote Szulc. "It [democracy] accompanied the powerful economic and social ferment of the postwar period."[5] These underlying factors seemed to have made democracy as inevitable as the region's political culture had seemed to have made it impossible. But people then were mistaken in equating the fall of tyrants with the rise of democracy. They were separate events, and the second did not always follow from the first. In some cases, such as Cuba, the new democratic words were never translated into elections. In other cases, the old dictators were soon replaced by new, more modern dictatorships.

Before Dominican democracy could even rise from Trujillo's ashes, the Argentine military struck the first blow against democracy in March 1962. The military then intervened in Peru to prevent the inauguration of Victor Haya de la Torre, who had won the election in June. United States diplomatic pressure prompted the military to hold a second election in June of 1963, and this time Fernando Belaúnde, representing a more moderate coalition, defeated Haya and was permitted by the military to take office. (He was overthrown in 1968.) In September 1963, the newly elected government of Juan Bosch was toppled by the military in the Dominican Republic. A coup followed in Honduras, and finally, the military intervened in Brazil in 1964. By the end of the decade of the Alliance for Progress, the military had taken power in fifteen of twenty-one Latin American nations.

The swing in the 1960s toward dictatorship was different from previous ones that had left in power *caudillos*—charismatic leaders who concentrated power and wielded it ruthlessly and often for private gain. The coups in the 1960s did not produce memorable leaders, other than Fidel Castro. Rather, generals took power in the name of their institution, not as individuals, and said they acted in response to a national emergency and on a temporary basis. In several countries, the military developed a system for rotating power at regular periods, much like the Mexican political system.

Thus the pendulum swung back at an angle, almost as if it had hit a wall of modernization. The new dictatorships were not a simple repetition of those in the past; they were the fruits of the increasing education and communication that some had previously thought would lead inevitably toward democracy. The military itself was no longer a *caudillo*'s vehicle but an institution composed often of the talented children of the lower middle class.

The journey back toward democracy—the third swing—started slowly, but it proceeded more steadily than the two previous swings. The decision in 1974 by General and President Ernesto Geisel gradually to open the Brazilian political system—the *abertura*—was a model adopted by other military governments. The process was controlled by the military, but it led step-by-step toward wider elections for more positions until January 1985 when an opposition leader was elected president in an electoral college vote.

In 1978, power was transferred peacefully from the president to the leader of the opposition party in the Dominican Republic for the first time in a century. In April 1979, a social democratic leader was elected president in Ecuador, and despite reservations by the military, he was inaugurated in August. In May 1980, Fernando Belaúnde, who had been overthrown by the Peruvian military twelve years before, won the presidential election and took power.

Other military governments in Honduras, Panama, El Salvador, and Bolivia had pledged to open up their political systems, but in these smaller, poorer, more divided countries, the transition toward democracy did not follow a straight line. The prospects for democracy in these countries and in others were affected by the economic downturn that began in the oil-consuming countries in 1980 and then struck the oil-producing countries, especially Mexico and Venezuela, in 1982. The conventional wisdom was that it was more difficult to sustain democracy during a depression, but the experience of the 1980s suggested that illegitimate incumbent governments had more difficulty coping with the economic crisis than democracies.

The failed invasion of the Malvinas/Falkland Islands and the subsequent collapse of the Argentine military regime gave added momentum to the democratic swing. The Reagan administration, which had embraced the military regimes when it came into office, had changed its policy by 1984 and it offered sturdy support for democratization. The administration's efforts were probably as important as any other factor in explaining why the military did not overthrow civilian governments in Central America. In 1976 in Central and South America, only Costa Rica, Venezuela, Colombia, and Suriname were democratic. By 1988, all of South America was democratic except Chile and Paraguay, and Guyana and Suriname were taking steps toward democracy. Central America, however, illustrated better both the uneven progress and the continuing problems that existed in assessing the nature of democracy in this region. Presidential elections had been held in every country, but the military continued to govern everywhere except Costa Rica. Nonetheless, the third swing of the pendulum has been the most impressive. It has lasted the longest with the fewest regressions and the most successes. Indeed, some have even begun to question whether the pendulum is the appropriate metaphor. Perhaps democracy in Latin America is like a motor car. It can slow down or stop, but for the time being, it is chugging along on its freedom ride.

Thinking About Democracy: The Theoretical Pendulum

Ideas guide actors, but they are also shaped by actions. In the case of democracy, theories have been more effective in explaining the previous swing of the pendulum than in predicting the next swing. The first swing toward democracy was viewed as evidence of a universal movement toward democracy that accompanied the defeat of Germany, Italy, and Japan. The reversal was interpreted in terms of the region's chronic instability.

The second swing in the 1960s captured more public and scholarly attention. On the upswing, scholars saw the movement toward democracy in terms of an expanding middle class challenging the agrarian oligarchy. The implicit model of political development was that of Western Europe, just as it was the model for economic development for Walt Rostow's *Stages of Economic Growth*. Democracy was perceived as both a positive and an inevitable result of the breakdown of a feudal political and economic system.[6]

On the downswing, the decline of democracy in the mid-1960s forced social scientists to question their assumptions about the inevitability of democracy. Fred Riggs wrote that political development in the Third World was unlikely to lead to democracy or even to lead in any coherent direction. The pendulum was the wrong metaphor. He used the word "prismatic" to suggest that instability was a permanent feature of political development.[7]

A second theory developed by Samuel P. Huntington explained why democracy had failed in those countries like Argentina and Brazil where the population had made great strides in education and health. Huntington wrote that increased social mobilization would follow from economic development and social progress, but that it would not lead to democracy unless political institutions were developed at the same pace. Since this had not occurred, social mobilization was more likely to lead to instability and to military or "praetorian" takeovers.[8]

Guillermo O'Donnell offered an alternative theory to Rostow's to explain why Latin America's economic and political development was different from Europe's. Since the Second World War, Latin America had used an import-substitution strategy, and this had produced an inefficient industrial sector that could only be maintained by a "bureaucratic-authoritarian" government. A decentralized, democratic government would be overwhelmed by the social pressures that were building because of an exhausted development strategy and depressed wages.[9]

A fourth explanation for democracy's failure to take root in Latin America in the 1960s and early 1970s focused on political attitudes and culture. Peter Smith wrote that "the prevalence of nondemocratic, authoritarian ideals in Spanish America . . . [is] a logical expression of the political culture."[10] Howard Wiarda also argued that democracy stems from the U.S. tradition; Latin America's is "hierarchical, authoritarian, and nondemocratic, and its roots predate the liberal tradition."[11]

These theories so convincingly showed why democracy was unlikely or impossible in Latin America that scholars were unprepared to explain democracy's return in the late 1970s. The Latin American authoritarian political culture had not changed. With the region suffering from an economic depression, there was, if anything, a greater need for bureaucratic-authoritarian governments to implement austerity policies. Yet these governments were replaced by new democracies that opened their economies rather than protected them. Even harder to explain was why the pendulum went still further toward democracy in the 1980s, a period of economic crisis, than it had during periods of economic growth.

Both politicians and scholars were sobered. By the third swing, they were less inclined to think that democracy was permanent or that a single theory could explain its fluctuations. Latin American politicians had learned from the previous cycle that they had to share some responsibility for coups, and secondly, they had learned that preserving the democratic system was more important than their contest for power. Scholars shifted their attention away from the questions of whether and why governments become democratic to how they change. Myron Weiner reviewed numerous empirical studies on democratization throughout the Third World and advised scholars to change their subject of inquiry: "The characteristics of societies that have become democratic are sufficiently diverse to suggest that less attention should be paid to conditions and prerequisites [and] more to the strategies available to those who seek a democratic revolution."[12]

That is the point of departure of this book. The contributors assume that there are serious economic, political, and cultural constraints that make it hard for Latin America to be democratic, but that there are also reasons why Latin America with an increasingly educated population should be democratic. The lesson that scholars learned was that theories that used social and economic variables to predict democracy should not be applied mechanically. In this regard, Samuel Huntington offered a crucial insight: developing countries that attain a certain threshold in levels of income and education enter a "zone of transition" where the probabilities increase that they *can* become democratic, but there are no guarantees. In this zone, leaders have considerable room to maneuver and guide their nations toward democracy; strategies, in brief, matter.[13]

After examining the meaning of democracy and the perspectives that different Latin American groups bring to the problem of democratization, the contributors will search through history and theory and from nation to nation to find the strategies that succeeded and those that failed.

Fragility

The playing field of politics has shifted from the barracks to the ballot box, but the rules of the game are still being negotiated. In name, the new civilian presidents govern, but in fact, they negotiate almost daily their authority with the generals, the bankers, opposition politicians and, in some cases, revolutionary terrorists and drug lords. While this goes on, the basis of their legitimacy is being eroded by a shrinking economy. The period of the 1980s may well be remembered not as a period of transition toward democracy but as a complicated, sometimes coercive negotiation in which newly elected leaders struggled for the political space to govern in fact as well as in name. One should therefore proceed with caution in predicting where and when the pendulum will finally come to rest.

In 1948, after the pendulum completed its first swing, only Costa Rica was added to the list of democracies. After the pendulum completed its second cycle, Venezuela and Colombia joined Costa Rica and other longer-standing democracies like Chile and Uruguay. If and when the pendulum completes its current swing, the probability is that more states will be added to the list. The number and identity of states depend on the people and leaders from the region.

The fate of Latin America's democracies is in the hands of the people of the region. This book offers some strategies and proposals for stopping the pendulum from swinging backwards.

Notes

1. Tad Szulc, *Twilight of the Tyrants* (New York: Henry Holt and Company, 1959), p. 3.

2. J. L. Salcedo-Bastardo, *Bolivar: A Continent and Its Destiny* (Richmond, Surrey: The Richmond Publishing Company, 1977), p. 63.

3. Ibid., p. 132.

4. Octavio Paz, "Latin America and Democracy," in *Democracy and Dictatorship in Latin America* (New York: The Foundation for the Study of Independent Social Ideas, 1983), p. 9.

5. Szulc, *Twilight of the Tyrants*, p. 6.

6. See, for example, Charles O. Porter and Robert J. Alexander, *The Struggle for Democracy in Latin America* (New York: The Macmillan Company, 1961), pp. 21–43.

7. Fred W. Riggs, *Administration in Developing Countries* (New York: Houghton Mifflin, 1964).

8. Samuel P. Huntington, *Political Order in Changing Societies* (New Haven: Yale University Press, 1968).

9. Guillermo O'Donnell, *Modernization and Bureaucratic-Authoritarianism: Studies in South American Politics* (Berkeley: Institute of International Studies of the University of California, 1973).

10. Peter Smith, "Political Legitimacy in Spanish America," in *New Approaches to Latin American History*, ed. Richard Graham and Peter Smith (Austin: University of Texas Press, 1974), p. 241.

11. Howard Wiarda, "Can Democracy Be Exported?" in *The United States and Latin America in the 1980s*, ed. Kevin J. Middlebrook and Carlos Rico (Pittsburgh: University of Pittsburgh Press, 1986), p. 329.

12. Myron Weiner, "Empirical Democratic Theory and the Transition from Authoritarianism to Democracy," *PS* 20 (Fall 1987): 863.

13. Samuel P. Huntington, "Will More Countries Become Democratic?" *Political Science Quarterly* 99 (Summer 1984): 193–218.

2

The Modest Meaning
of Democracy

SAMUEL P. HUNTINGTON

Introduction

The meaning of meaning is twofold. At one level, meaning can refer to the definition of something, that is, to its meaning in an essentialist or denotative sense, as in "What is the meaning of this word?" At another level, meaning can refer to the broader implications or consequences of something, to its meaning in an explanative or connotative sense, as in "What is the meaning of all this?" This chapter discusses the meanings of democracy in both these senses and argues that in both senses the meaning of democracy is modest. At the denotative level, democracy can best be understood as a type of institutional arrangement for choosing rulers. At the connotative level, the significant implications of democracy are largely limited to the political sphere, but in that sphere they are of crucial importance.

Denotation: The Institutional Definition of Democracy

The concept of democracy as a form of government goes back, of course, to the Greek philosophers. Its modern usage, however, dates from the revolutionary upheavals in western society at the end of the eighteenth century.[1] Then and for a good part of the nineteenth century, democracy was contrasted with aristocracy, an opposition dramatically set forth in Tocqueville's political thought. During much of this period the term had unfavorable connotations and was, indeed, often used as a term of opprobrium. As popular participation in government increased in the latter part of the nineteenth century and as its consequences turned out to be less calamitous than predicted, the concept of democracy came to be viewed more favorably. It became chic to be a democrat. As James Bryce noted in 1920, "Seventy years ago . . . the word Democracy awakened dislike and fear. Now it is a word of praise. Popular power is welcomed, extolled, worshipped. The few whom it repels or alarms rarely avow

11

their sentiments."[2] Even as he wrote, however, new movements that totally rejected democracy were gathering force. The Bolsheviks had already snuffed out the fragile democratic tendencies that existed in Russia; Mussolini was about to dispose of Italian democracy; and the Nazis were beginning their long march to power. During the 1920s and 1930s opposition to democracy again became respectable among right-wing and upper-class groups in Europe and Latin America.

All this changed with the defeat of the Axis. Articulated opposition to democracy virtually disappeared not only in the western world but in the entire world. Everyone insisted on being identified as a democrat. "For the first time in the history of the world," a UNESCO report noted in 1951, "no doctrines are advanced as antidemocratic. The accusation of antidemocratic action or attitude is frequently directed against others, but practical politicians and political theorists agree in stressing the democratic element in the institutions they defend and the theories they advocate."[3]

Democracy thus became a "hurrah" word. Universal support for democracy, however, came at the price of universal disagreement over its meaning. Everyone defined democracy to suit his own purpose. Everyone had his own favorite variety. A short list would include: direct democracy, representative democracy, liberal (and/or bourgeois) democracy, proletarian democracy, social democracy, totalitarian democracy, industrial democracy, plebiscitarian democracy, constitutional democracy, consociational democracy, pluralist democracy, economic democracy, people's democracy, participatory democracy. Seemingly almost any other political term could gain enhanced legitimacy by being associated with democracy. As meanings of the term proliferated, the meaning of the term evaporated. "When a term has become so universally sanctified, as 'democracy' now is," T. S. Eliot had noted even before World War II, "I begin to wonder whether it means anything, in meaning too many things."[4]

All this created major problems for serious thinking and intelligent discourse, and in the late 1950s and 1960s political theorists made noble efforts to reduce the terminological and conceptual confusion. Their debates crystalized three general approaches to the problem of defining democracy. As a form of government, democracy can be defined in terms of who rules, for what ends, and by what means. Stated otherwise, democracy can be defined in terms of sources, purposes, or institutions.

Sources of Authority

How is the source of authority or of the ruling body defined in a democracy? In the original Greek, of course, democracy was rule by the people and hence distinguishable from monarchy and oligarchy. Rule by the people, taken to mean rule by the entire body of citizens, was in some measure practical in the Greek *polis* and direct democracy is still possible in small communities. The argument that democracy is "government of the people, by the people, and for the people" has, as we know, also been made in other contexts, where it serves useful rhetorical purposes but is analytically and empirically meaningless. Yet the tendency to identify democracy with rule by the people has continued. In the late eighteenth and early nineteenth centuries, democracy was opposed to aristocracy. American theorists in the Progressive tradition have continued to employ this formulation, for all its empirical irrelevance, down to the present. "The people versus the interests" is a recurring slogan in political debate.

The ruling body in a democracy is not always, however, defined so broadly. It may also be defined in terms of attributes rather than numbers. Aristotle grappled with the issue: Was it numbers or class that counted? Was democracy rule by the many or by the poor? He concluded that number was an "accidental attribute" and that "the real ground of the difference between oligarchy and democracy is poverty and riches."[5] Government by a small number of poor people over a large number of rich people was highly unlikely, but if it occurred it would properly be labeled democracy. The key question, in effect, was which social class had power. Subsequent theorists carried forward this approach. Jefferson thought that yeoman farmers should rule; others identified democracy with rule by the middle class; still others have in effect identified democracy with rule by the working class.

A third definition of the ruling body in a democracy departs from Aristotle and identifies democracy not with a particular class but with a particular number, almost always a majority, that may be composed of people from any combination of social groups and that may change over time. Democracy exists, as Bryce put it, when the "will of the majority of qualified citizens rules."[6] In practice, of course, "rule by the people" is only approximated by rule by the majority. Again, however, such rule can only occur in its pure form where all the members of the body politic can be assembled together and can vote issues up or down or in those circumstances where it is possible can conduct referenda on issues. The implicit premise with the majority-rule definition of democracy is that through persuasion and mobilization of support, minorities can become majorities. If, for one reason or another, this is impractical, then majority rule becomes in effect class rule, and people are more or less permanently assigned to majority or minority status. This is the case with Catholics in Northern Ireland, who are generally poorer than the Protestant majority, and it is the case with the English-speaking whites in South Africa, who have been generally wealthier than the Afrikaaner white majority. In instances such as these with permanent majorities and minorities, a case must be made to achieve at least one of Dahl's two criteria of democracy by adopting the mechanisms of consociational democracy.[7]

Serious problems thus exist for the "governing body" approach to democracy, no matter how that body is defined. The "people" can be the governing body only in a small community where they can collectively assemble. Where this is impossible, resort must be had to a process for selecting the governing body. Rulers will often claim that they are acting in the interests of the people. That claim, however, can be validated only by arguing either that they know the interests of the people better than the people do, which may be true but is not democratic, or by resorting to some electoral process to select those rulers. Those who identify democracy with rule by a particular class of people— whether yeoman farmers, middle class, bourgeoisie, proletariat, white South Africans, or Protestant Ulstermen—are legitimizing the division of society into two exclusive bodies, rulers and ruled, with no mobility between them. The processes used within the governing body may well be democratic, but the permanent exclusion of one part of society from access to that governing body clearly violates common sense ideas as to what democracy is all about.

Purposes of Rule

A second way of defining democratic government is in terms of the purposes or goals it serves. A government is democratic to the extent that it is publicly committed to and actually pursues democratic goals. But what are democratic goals? They may be defined either by the leaders of the government (in which case any government whose leaders say it is pursuing democratic goals is a democracy) or by some external source. Theorists have not hesitated to undertake this responsibility. Democratic governments, it has been argued, are those which promote human welfare, equality, personal rights, justice, the "maximization of the self-development of every individual," human dignity, personal realization, "freedom from starvation, ignorance, and early diseased death," and movement toward an "equal society in which everybody can be fully human."[8]

Many problems exist with the definition of democracy in terms of purposes. First, every author has his own set of purposes and hence the debate over the meaning of democracy is transformed into an even more wide-ranging debate over what the morally justifiable goals of the state are. The proponents of this view, as Jeane Kirkpatrick points out, present "a vision of what a more moral society would be like," but "tend to write as though their goals—self-realization, equality, or welfare—were universally shared, for self-evident reasons."[9] Second, the goals set forth are almost always of such an ideal character, so broad and vague, as to be virtually useless in terms of classifying governments. Third, if political leaders' self-definition of goals is accepted, then virtually all states are democratic. Macpherson, for example, explicitly argues that liberal states, Marxist-Leninist states, and Third World one-party states are all democratic. If, as he argues, only the goal counts, and if one accepts at face value Lenin's proclamations of creating a more equal society, "then the vanguard state, so long as it remains true to its purpose, may be called democratic."[10] In Macpherson's sense Pol Pot also had a democratic goal. Finally, if democracy is defined in terms of other major social goals, such as social justice, equality, or individual fulfillment, it becomes impossible to analyze the relation between democracy and these other goals. Yet history shows that simultaneous progress toward all these good things, democracy included, often is not possible and that advance toward one may mean retreat from others.

Institutions

The ambiguity and imprecision that followed the emergence of democracy as a "hurrah" word and the difficulties of defining it in terms of the source of its authority or purposes have led in the past two decades to an increased emphasis on an institutional definition of democracy. One theorist after another has drawn distinctions between rationalistic, utopian, idealistic definitions of democracy, on the one hand, and empirical, descriptive, institutional definitions on the other, with the conclusion invariably being drawn that only the latter type of definition provides the analytical precision and empirical referents that make the concept a useful one.[11] Sweeping discussions of democracy in terms of normative theory have thus sharply declined, at least in American scholarly discussions, and have been replaced by efforts to understand the nature of democratic institutions, how they function, and the reasons why they develop and collapse. The prevailing effort has been to make democracy less of a hurrah word and more of a common sense word. Democracy has a useful meaning only when it is defined in institutional terms.

The key institution in a democracy is the selection of leaders through competitive elections. In other governmental systems people become leaders by reason of birth, lot, wealth, violence, cooptation, learning, appointment, examination. In a democracy people become leaders through election by the people they govern. The most important modern formulation of this concept of democracy was made by Joseph Schumpeter in 1942. In his pathbreaking study, *Capitalism, Socialism, and Democracy,* Schumpeter spelled out the deficiencies of what he termed the "classical theory of democracy," which defined democracy in terms of "the will of the people" (source) and "the common good" (goal). Effectively demolishing these approaches to the subject, Schumpeter advanced what he labeled "another theory of democracy." The "democratic method," he said, "is that institutional arrangement for arriving at political decisions in which individuals acquire the power to decide by means of a competitive struggle for the people's vote."[12] Schumpeter went on to explain at some length the reasons why this definition of democracy is far superior to the classical definition. For some while after World War II a debate went on between those who were determined in the classical vein to define democracy in terms of source or purpose, and the growing number of theorists who adhered to an institutional concept of democracy in the Schumpeterian mode. That debate is now over. Schumpeter has won. His concept of democracy is the established and the Establishment concept of democracy. Consider, for example, just a few recent essays in this direction:

(1) democracy is "made up of at least two dimensions: public contestation in elections and the right to participate" (Robert A. Dahl, 1971);

(2) democracies are "governments whose leaders are selected in periodic, competitive, inclusive elections" (Jeane J. Kirkpatrick, 1981);

(3) democracy is "characterized by competitive elections in which most citizens are eligible to participate" (G. Bingham Powell, 1982);

(4) a political system is "democratic to the extent that its most powerful collective decision-makers are selected through periodic elections in which candidates freely compete for votes and in which virtually all the adult population is eligible to vote" (Samuel P. Huntington, 1984);

(5) freedom "requires that a people has a proven right to change their government through their politically equal votes, and that they are free to organize and propagandize for the purpose of achieving these changes." (Raymond Gastil, 1985).[13]

The institutional approach makes it possible to distinguish democracy from other contemporary systems of government, most notably authoritarianism and totalitarianism. Each of these other systems also has a well-defined institutional identity. A totalitarian system involves a single party usually led by one man, a highly developed secret police, a highly developed ideology setting forth the ideal society that the totalitarian movement is committed to realizing, and government control of mass communications, of all means of coercion, and of all social and economic organizations. An authoritarian system is characterized by a single leader, no party or a weak party, no mass mobilization, no ideology but rather a "mentality" in Linz's term, limited government, "limited, not responsible, political pluralism," and no effort to remake society and human nature.[14]

Three key dimensions along which these political systems can be compared are: (1) the degree to which leaders are selected through competitive elections or by other means; (2) the scope and nature of citizen participation in government; and (3) the scope and nature of government's control of society and particularly of the economy. In these terms, democracy is competitive, and authoritarian and totalitarian systems are noncompetitive; democratic and totalitarian systems are participative (the former with autonomous participation, the latter with mobilized participation), while authoritarian systems are nonparticipative; and totalitarian systems exert extensive to total control over the society and economy, while democratic and authoritarian systems exert only limited to moderate control.

The institutional definition of democracy provides a number of benchpoints—grouped largely along Dahl's dimensions of contestation and participation—that make it possible to judge to what extent political systems are democratic, to compare systems, and to analyze whether systems are becoming more or less democratic. To the extent, for instance, that a political system denies voting participation to any one group in its society—as the South African system does to the 70 percent of its population that is black, as Switzerland did to the 50 percent of its population that was female, or as the United States did to the 10 percent of its population that were southern

TABLE 2.1
Types of Political Systems

Characteristic	Democratic	Totalitarian	Authoritarian
Role of ideology	Limited	Central	Nonexistent
Type of Change	Incremental	Revolutionary	Nonincremental
Participation	Broad autonomous	Broad mobilized	None or very limited
Elections	Effective, competitive, frequent	Ritualistic, noncompetitive, frequent	Nonexistent or noncompetitive
Parties	Two or more	One strong	None or one weak
Freedom of speech, press, assembly	Extensive	Nonexistent	Severely restricted
Government control of economy	Limited to moderate	Extensive to total	Limited

blacks—it is undemocratic. Similarly, a system is undemocratic to the extent that no opposition is permitted in elections, or that the opposition is curbed or harassed in what it can do, or that opposition newspapers are censored or closed down, or that votes are manipulated or miscounted. In any society, the sustained failure of the major opposition political party or parties to win office necessarily raises questions concerning the degree of competition permitted by the system.[15] Most importantly, the institutional approach to democracy accords with the commonsense uses of the term. We all know that military coups, censorship, rigged elections, the coercion and harassment of the opposition, jailing of political opponents, and the prohibition of political meetings are incompatible with democracy. We also all know that informed political observers can apply the institutional conditions of democracy to existing world political systems and rather easily come up with a list of those countries that are clearly democratic, those that are clearly not, and those that fall somewhere in between, and that with minor exceptions those lists will be identical. We also all know that we can make and do make judgments as to how governments change over time and that no one would dispute the proposition that Argentina, Brazil, and Uruguay were more democratic in 1986 than they were in 1976. Political regimes will never fit perfectly into intellectually defined boxes, and any system of classification has to accept the existence of ambiguous borderline and mixed cases. The PRI system in Mexico, for instance, combines elements of all three types. Yet the classification of regimes in terms of their degrees of institutional democracy remains a relatively simple task.

The institutional concept of democracy has clearly won broad acceptance in the United States. Evidence also exists that it is becoming more widely accepted in Latin America, where in the past it has been under sustained attack by ideologues of both left and right. More recently, "Most of the political left and sectors of the right," Guillermo O'Donnell has argued, " . . . have engaged in a positive, authentic revaluation of democracy. Political democracy in the strict [i.e., institutional] sense of the word—linked to the liberal-constitutional model, with its guarantees of individual rights, the right of association, and truly competitive elections—is no longer disdained as being purely 'formal.' "[16]

Connotations: The Consequences of Democracy

What implications follow from having a government by people selected in regular, competitive, honest, inclusive elections rather than in other ways? What, in this sense, is the broader meaning of democracy? What, if any, are the economic, military, and political consequences of democracy?

Economic Consequences

The exit from power of rulers who lose elections means that limits must exist on what is at stake in controlling government. If winning or losing was an all-or-nothing affair, those in power would have overpowering incentives to suppress opposition, to rig elections, and to resort to coercion to remain in power if it appeared they had lost an election. Hence government cannot be the only or even the principal source of status, prestige, wealth, and power. Some dispersion of control over these goods—what Dahl calls "dispersed inequalities"—is necessary. The most important issue here concerns economic power. Democracy is impossible if the government exercises complete control over the economy.

Obviously democratic governments often play major roles in the economies of their societies through regulatory mechanisms, through ownership and control of some productive facilities, and through the provision of welfare benefits (social security, medical insurance, unemployment benefits). In some cases, as in Brazil and other newly industrializing countries, state-owned corporations are major actors in the economy; in other cases, as in Sweden, an elaborate welfare system may push governmental expenditures up to half of the GNP. In all democracies, however, private ownership of property remains the basic norm in theory and in fact, and the basic mechanism for economic allocation is the market rather than governmental command. As Charles Lindblom has pointed out, this is a striking phenomenon, given the extent to which private concentrations of economic power in business corporations appear to be contrary to many prevailing assumptions about democracy.[17] The existence of such private power, however, is essential to the existence of democracy in order both to reduce the incentives of political leaders to maintain themselves in power through undemocratic means and to limit their ability to do so. Democracy, in short, is incompatible with a sustained, centrally controlled command economy.[18]

Defining democracy in terms of goals such as economic well-being, social justice, and overall socioeconomic equity is not, we have argued, very useful. The question remains, however, to what extent are democratic governments more or less likely than other governments to foster progress toward these goals?

Probably the most striking relationship between economics and politics in world affairs is the correlation between political democracy and economic wealth. Apart from the oil states, rich countries are democratic countries and with only a few exceptions democratic countries are rich countries. Why is this? The conventional wisdom is that economic wealth creates the conditions for democracy rather than vice versa, and the conventional wisdom is in this case probably correct. This conclusion is reinforced by the performance of democracies with respect to economic growth. Systematic analysis has been adduced to support the conclusion that "among the poor nations, an authoritarian political system increases the rate of economic development, while a democratic political system does appear to be a luxury which hinders development."[19] In short, a "liberty trade-off" exists between growth and democracy.[20] Yet such sweeping conclusions are dubious because of the wide differences in economic performance among various types of nondemocratic systems. The East Asian authoritarian regimes and some Latin American bureaucratic authoritarian regimes have achieved spectacular growth. Personalistic dictatorships and praetorian regimes have usually performed poorly. Third World Marxist-Leninist regimes have generally been economic disasters. When viewed against a wide spectrum of many different nondemocratic regime types, the democratic regimes have generally compiled a middling record of economic growth. No democratic regime has sustained a spectacular 8–10 percent per annum growth rate for any length of time, as have some authoritarian regimes, and democratic regimes have rarely produced the total economic catastrophes that nondemocratic governments have often generated.[21]

With respect to the relationship between political democracy and social justice or economic equity, the record is equally mixed. The extent to which economic outcomes (e.g., size distribution of income) and economic outputs (e.g., social security programs) tend to be more or less egalitarian is influenced primarily by the level of economic development of the society. The nature of the political system is a secondary influence, although on some issues it can be an important one. A marked distinction exists here in the performance of democratic regimes with respect to the distribution of income and of assets. Historically some alleviation of extreme economic inequalities has generally been a prerequisite to the emergence of democratic political systems. The initial expansion of political participation, however, may well result in government policies producing more inequality in income and material benefits. A little democracy is an unequal thing. In Western Europe, the substantial expansion of democracy in the late nineteenth century was followed by an accelerated trend toward a more equal distribution of income. Other studies have shown that more democratic governments have generally provided earlier and more extensive welfare benefits, such as social security, than have more authoritarian governments, and in Asia, it has been argued, democratic regimes have provided more material equality and welfare than nonauthoritarian ones.[22] Such generalizations have to be qualified, however, by the wide differences among nondemocratic systems. Marxist-Leninist regimes (which are often omitted from these comparative analyses of economic equality) would presumably rank on a par with or ahead of democratic regimes in welfare benefits and income equality. The authoritarian regimes in Taiwan and South Korea, on the other hand, have been generally successful in combining extremely high rates of economic growth and unusually equal patterns of income distribution.

For understandable reasons, political democracies are less apt to promote more equal ownership of economic assets than they are to promote more equal distribution of income. In less developed countries, democratic regimes have with few exceptions experienced great difficulties in bringing about more equal patterns of land ownership.[23] When their leaders make it a high priority, on the other hand, nondemocratic regimes because of their concentrated power can more easily carry out a sweeping redistribution of assets. What is true with respect to land would also be true with respect to other economic assets, although these are usually subjected to collective ownership rather than equitable ownership.

Political democracy is clearly compatible with inequality in both wealth and income, and, in some measure, it may be dependent upon such inequality. High levels of economic equality can only be maintained by extremely high levels of political coercion. As with economic growth, the record of democracy with respect to socioeconomic equality has generally been comfortably between the extremes. Atul Kohli's conclusion with respect to India undoubtedly holds true for poor countries generally: "Simultaneous optimism for India's democracy and for India's poor is not realistic. Either India will have to sacrifice redistribution of wealth for modest improvements over the present conditions of absolute poverty under a democratic regime, or it will have to take the less probable path of revolutionary and authoritarian politics."[24]

Some indication of the performance of a few Third World democracies with respect to these variables and in comparison with other Third World countries for the 1960s and 1970s is provided in Figure 2.1. Six out of eight democracies had annual economic growth rates in the middle zone, between 4 percent and 7 percent, while two, India and Chile, were lower. Two democracies, India and Sri Lanka, had relatively more equitable income distributions, with the poorest 40 percent of the population getting 16 percent or more of the national income; three democracies were in the middle zone between 10 percent and 16 percent; while in three, the poorest 40 percent of the population received less than 10 percent of the national income. In general, on neither measure were democracies either the best or the worst performers, and clearly democratic government did not provide a way out of the growth-equity trade-off, from which only Korea and Taiwan were able to escape.

FIGURE 2.1

Percentage Share of National Income of Lowest 40 Percent of Population, 1975

	6	8	10	12	14	16	18	2022	24
10		Iran				Korea		Taiwan	
9									
8		Brazil	Thailand	Nigeria					
		Kenya	Iv. Coast						
7									
		TURKEY	Tunisia		Tanzania				
		Mexico	MALAYSIA						
			Guatemala						
6	Peru	COLOMBIA	PHILIPPINES			Indonesia	Yugoslavia		
		VENEZUELA				Pakistan			
5				Egypt	Argentina	Ethiopia	SRI LANKA		
				Morocco	Uganda				
					Zaire				
4									
				Zambia	Burma	INDIA			
					Sudan				
3			Ghana	CHILE			Bangladesh		
2		Senegal							
0									

GNP GROWTH RATES, 1960–1975

Countries that were competitive democracies for most of the period from 1960 to 1975 are in CAPITAL LETTERS.

Sources: Economic data—Hollis Chenery, *Structural Change and Development Policy* (Oxford: Oxford University Press, 1979), pp. 472–73.

Political Judgments—Samuel P. Huntington

Military Consequences

The meaning of political democracy is more distinctive in the military than in the economic sphere. The important questions here concern differences between countries in terms of the relative sizes of their military efforts and in their propensities to go to war. Both these factors will be shaped in considerable measure by the countries' international environment. Individual countries that see themselves as having deep security concerns, such as Israel or the Koreas, are likely to have large military forces. Larger military forces and more frequent wars are more likely in regions such as the Middle East where international tensions are extremely high. Given these facts, do types of political regimes themselves also have military consequences?

Despite the obvious importance of international factors, significant differences in military policy exist between countries with different types of political systems. The level of military effort or militarization in a society can be measured by the ratio of governmental expenditures for military purposes to gross national product and the ratio of military manpower to total population (the latter normally expressed in terms of number of soldiers per thousand population). By both indices democratic regimes are considerably less militarized than nondemocratic regimes, particularly Marxist-Leninist regimes. The military manpower ratio in 1982, for instance, was 3.84 for thirty-one democratic countries, 5.21 for twenty-three mixed regimes, 7.3 for fifty-five nondemocratic, non–Marxist-Leninist regimes, and 14.1 for thirty-two Marxist-Leninist countries.[25] Authoritarian regimes, in short, have military manpower ratios roughly twice that of democratic regimes, and Marxist-Leninist regimes have ratios twice that of authoritarian regimes. Comparable differences appear in the ratios of military expenditures to GNP (recognizing that the data in these cases are often not all that reliable). In 1983, for instance, proportions of GNP devoted to military purposes by different types of regimes were as follows:

Democracies (free)	3.35 percent
Mixed regimes (partly free)	3.71 percent
Authoritarian regimes (not free)	5.96 percent
Marxist-Leninist regimes (not free)	7.71 percent

Once again a clear gradation exists, with democracies at one end and Marxist-Leninist regimes at the other.[26]

Countries in the same region or confronting comparable threats but with different political systems often devote different proportions of their resources to military purposes. In 1980, for instance, the military manpower ratios for Western European NATO democracies ran from 0.0 for Iceland up to 9.2 for France; those for Warsaw Pact members varied from 9.7 for Romania up to 18.2 for Bulgaria. More specifically, the adjusted military manpower ratio in 1980 for democratic West Germany was 0.5, for Marxist-Leninist East Germany it was 6.9; in 1983 West German military expenditures were 3.4 percent of the GNP, East Germany's were 6.4 percent. Similarly, for the same years authoritarian South Korea's adjusted military manpower ratio was 11.3, and its military expenditure ratio was 5.8 percent; the comparable figures for Marxist-Leninist North Korea, 33.2 and 16.7 percent, were roughly three times as high.[27] Deviant cases exist, of course, within each category of regime: China is far less militarized than other Marxist-Leninist countries, Israel is far more militarized than other democracies. Yet the overall patterns are clear and dramatic. In terms of proportions of people and resources devoted to military purposes, democracies are less militaristic than other regimes and Marxist-Leninist regimes are more militaristic than other regimes.

With respect to participation in wars, the differences between democracies and other regime types may not be so great. What is perhaps more significant is whether significant differences exist in the propensities of different types of regimes to initiate military action. The difficulty of arriving at objective judgments here is overwhelming. A rough analysis of twenty-seven interstate wars since World War II, however, suggests that seven were initiated by democratic regimes, eight by Marxist-Leninist regimes, and twelve by non–Marxist-Leninist authoritarian regimes.[28] This distribution of war initiations does not differ greatly from the overall distribution of regime types. Only a small number of countries are, however, involved, with regional geopolitical factors central in the decisions of all types of regimes to resort to arms. India and Israel, for instance, figure prominently among the democratic fighters, China and Vietnam among the Marxist-Leninist fighters, and Pakistan and Egypt among the authoritarian fighters.

In none of those twenty-seven interstate wars did a democratic regime fight another democracy. Among democracies, in short, a zone of peace appears to exist with a strong presumption that differences that might lead to conflict will be resolved peacefully.[29] In contrast, authoritarian regimes have obviously fought each other frequently. Marxist-Leninist regimes have been involved in nine wars, two of them with other Marxist-Leninist regimes; of these nine wars, the U.S. invasion of Grenada was the only case where a non–Marxist-Leninist regime initiated war against a Marxist-Leninist regime.

Political Consequences

The most important consequences of democracy are in politics, in its implications for political order and for political liberty. Democratic systems tend to have higher levels of public order than nondemocratic systems. Both the government and its opponents have fewer incentives to resort to disorder and violence. A variety of empirical data support this commonsense proposition. One study ranked seventy-three countries, for instance, according to their levels of instability and degree of coercion or permissiveness (i.e., dictatorship or democracy) between 1945 and 1966.[30] Of twenty-four permissive or democratic countries, all but two ranked above the mean on the stability scale. The twenty-three countries that were rated as highly coercive or authoritarian included nine stable and fourteen unstable societies. In the lowest category were those countries that were moderately coercive: six were stable and twenty unstable. A curvilinear relationship was thus found to exist between stability and regime type, with those that were most democratic also being most stable, those that were least democratic coming next, and those countries that combined elements of democracy and dictatorship suffering the greatest amount of disorder and violence.

Democracy contributes to stability by providing regular opportunities for changing political leaders and hence for changing policies. In democracies, change is almost invariably moderate and incremental. Democracies generally have great trouble making fundamental changes rapidly; when such change is needed, recourse often must be had to nondemocratic mechanisms: constitutional dictatorships, emergency powers, or, in the United States, the Supreme Court.

Democracy and revolution in the sense of major violent social upheaval do not go together. Democratic systems are much more immune to revolutionary overthrow than authoritarian ones. Revolution, as Ché Guevara said, cannot succeed against a government "which has come into power through some form of popular vote, fraudulent or not, and maintains at least an appearance of constitutional legality."[31] Conversely, major violent revolutions that overthrow authoritarian regimes do not generate democratic regimes. The English revolution produced Cromwell and the restoration of the Stuarts, the French Revolution produced Napoleon and the restoration of the Bourbons, the Russian Revolution produced Lenin and Stalin, the Chinese Revolution produced first Nationalist and then Communist dictatorship, the Mexican Revolution produced rule by generals and then by a single party, the Bolivian Revolution the same in reverse order, the Cuban Revolution Castro's one-man dictatorship, and the Nicaraguan Revolution the rapidly developing Sandinista dictatorship. The American Revolution, which might appear to be the exception to the rule, was not because it was not a social revolution but primarily a war of independence and because it led to the recreation after that war of basically the same semidemocratic institutions that existed before the war.

Revolutions thus replace weak nondemocratic governments with strong nondemocratic governments. Their "true historical function," as de Jouvenel said, "is to renovate and strengthen Power."[32] The maintenance of democratic politics and the reconstruction of the social order are fundamentally incompatible. Revolution does not produce democracy and democracy does not produce revolution. At its best, democracy means conservatism without stagnation and reform without revolution.

The great difficulty in framing governments, Madison warned in *The Federalist,* is that "you must first enable the government to control the governed; and in the next place oblige it to control itself." The extreme coercion of which nondemocratic governments may be capable often enables them effectively to control the governed and to impose stability and order. Democracies,

however, can achieve even higher levels of order without resorting to comparable coercion. More importantly, they also provide the mechanism for moving
toward Madison's second goal, obliging government to control itself. The
essence of democracy is the possibility that current rulers may be displaced
from power in the next election a few years hence. This is, in a sense, the
ultimate freedom for a government to allow, and if this is possible within the
system, most other commonly acknowledged rights and freedoms will be safe
also. Free competition for votes requires the freedom to assemble, to organize,
to speak, and to publish. The exercise of these freedoms in a society leads to the
demand for and the establishment of other freedoms, including religious freedom, economic freedom, and civil rights against the arbitrary application of
governmental power.[33] Electoral competition thus provides the incentive and
the mechanism for exposing violations of freedom and for securing their
correction, and elections are the umbrella under which many other freedoms
not necessarily related to politics find protection. The safeguard of liberty is the
most distinctive consequence of democratic government and what distinguishes
it most sharply from all other systems.

Democracies do not provide for the most rapid expansion of economic
wealth and do not necessarily insure an equitable distribution of material
resources among their citizens. Political democracy seems to be incompatible
with high levels of either economic equality or economic inequality. Democracies do impose fewer military burdens on their people than do other systems,
but the price for this may be greater insecurity in the face of foreign danger.
Democratic governments do not seem to be more or less warlike than other
governments, although they also do not fight each other. Political democracy
does not necessarily bring efficient government, honest politics, or social
justice. It does, however, promote political order, permit moderate but not
sweeping changes, and provide an almost sure-fire guarantee against major
revolutionary upheaval. Most distinctly and importantly, democracies alone
among political regimes have the institutional mechanisms necessary to guarantee the basic rights and liberties of their citizens. Apart from politics, the
meaning of democracy is modest. Politically its meaning for liberty is mo-
mentous.

Notes

1. R. R. Palmer, *The Age of the Democratic Revolution*, 2 vols. (Princeton: Princeton
University Press, 1959), 1:13–20.

2. James Bryce, *Modern Democracies*, 2 vols. (New York: Macmillan, 1921), 1:4.

3. Richard McKeon, ed., *Democracy in a World of Tensions* (Chicago: University of
Chicago Press, 1951), p. 522, quoted in Giovanni Sartori, *Democratic Theory* (Detroit:
Wayne State University Press, 1962), pp. 8–9.

4. T. S. Eliot, *The Idea of a Christian Society* (New York: Harcourt, Brace, and
Company, 1940), pp. 11–12.

5. Aristotle, *The Politics,* Book III, Chapter viii.

6. Bryce, *Modern Democracies,* 1:22.

7. See Arend Lijphart, *Democracy in Plural Societies: A Comparative Exploration* (New Haven: Yale University Press, 1978).

8. See Peter Bachrach, *The Theory of Democratic Elitism: A Critique* (Boston: Little, Brown, 1967), pp. 24, 98ff.; C. B. Macpherson, *The Real World of Democracy* (Oxford: Clarendon Press, 1966), p. 33; David Braybrooke, *Three Tests for Democracy* (New York: Random House, 1968).

9. Jeane J. Kirkpatrick, "Democratic Elections, Democratic Government, and Democratic Theory," in *Democracy at the Polls,* ed. David Butler, Howard R. Penniman, and Austin Ranney (Washington: American Enterprise Institute, 1981), pp. 335–36.

10. Macpherson, *Real World,* p. 22.

11. See Robert A. Dahl, *Polyarchy: Participation and Opposition* (New Haven: Yale University Press, 1971), pp. 1–10; Sartori, *Democratic Theory,* pp. 228ff.; Kirkpatrick, "Democratic Elections," pp. 325ff.; Raymond English, *Constitutional Democracy vs. Utopian Democracy* (Washington: Ethics and Public Policy Center, 1983).

12. Joseph A. Schumpeter, *Capitalism, Socialism, and Democracy,* 2d ed. (New York: Harper, 1947), chap. 21 and p. 269.

13. Dahl, *Polyarchy,* p. 7; Kirkpatrick, "Democratic Elections," p. 326; G. Bingham Powell, Jr., *Contemporary Democracies* (Cambridge: Harvard University Press, 1982), p. 3; Samuel P. Huntington, "Will More Countries Become Democratic?" *Political Science Quarterly* 99 (Summer 1984): 195; Raymond D. Gastil, *Freedom in the World: Political Rights and Civil Liberties, 1984–1985* (Westport, Conn.: Greenwood Press, 1985), p. 4.

14. See Carl J. Friedrich and Zbigniew Brzezinski, *Totalitarian Dictatorship and Autocracy* (New York: Praeger, 1965), and Juan J. Linz, "Totalitarian and Authoritarian Regimes," in *Macropolitical Theory,* vol. 3 of the *Handbook of Political Science,* ed. Fred I. Greenstein and Nelson W. Polsby (Reading, Mass.: Addison-Wesley, 1975), pp. 175ff.

15. This is not to say that the sustained failure of the principal opposition party to win office at the national level necessarily proves that the system is undemocratic. It does suggest the need to investigate the conditions under which competition is conducted, an investigation that could lead, as in the cases of Japan and Mexico, to quite different conclusions as to how competitive the systems are.

16. Guillermo O'Donnell, "The United States, Latin America, Democracy: Variations on a Very Old Theme," in *The United States and Latin America in the 1980s,* ed. Kevin J. Middlebrook and Carlos Rico (Pittsburgh: University of Pittsburgh Press, 1986), p. 358.

17. Charles E. Lindblom, *Politics and Markets* (New York: Basic Books, 1977), chaps. 12, 13.

18. The argument here is a functional one: a market economy is functionally necessary for a political democracy. Clearly the functional requirements do not operate in the other direction, however, and as many instances testify political democracy is not necessary for a market economy.

19. Robert M. Marsh, "Does Democracy Hinder Economic Development in the Latecomer Developing Nations?" *Comparative Social Research* 2 (1979): 244.

20. Jack Donnelly, "Human Rights and Development: Complementary or Competing Concerns?" *World Politics* 36 (January 1984): 257ff.

21. For a parallel argument with supporting evidence, see Dirk Berg-Schlosser,

"Third World Political Systems: Classification and Evaluation," paper prepared for the Annual Meeting, American Political Science Association, September 1984, Washington, D.C.

22. See Sidney Verba, Norman Nie, Jae-On Kim, *Participation and Political Equality* (Cambridge: Cambridge University Press, 1978), pp. 2–6; Samuel P. Huntington and Joan M. Nelson, *No Easy Choice* (Cambridge: Harvard University Press, 1976), pp. 72–78; Phillips Cutright, "Political Structure, Economic Development, and National Social Security Programs," *American Journal of Sociology* 70 (March 1965): 536–50 and "Inequality: A Cross-National Analysis," *American Sociological Review* 32 (August 1967): 562–78; Jonathan Sunshine, "Economic Causes and Consequences of Democracy," (Ph.D. dissertation, Columbia University, 1972); Dwight Y. King, "Regime Type and Performance," *Comparative Political Studies* 13 (January 1981): 477–504, and *contra,* Scott D. Grosse, "'Regime Type and Performance': A Blind Alley?" *Comparative Political Studies* 14 (January 1982): 543–48.

23. I set forth the evidence to support this proposition almost two decades ago, in *Political Order in Changing Societies* (New Haven: Yale University Press, 1968), pp. 380–96. Experience since has not disproved this judgment.

24. Atul Kohli, "Democracy, Economic Growth, and Inequality in India's Development," *World Politics* 32 (July 1980): 636.

25. James L. Payne, "Marxism, Militarism, and Freedom," unpublished paper, Texas A&M University, Table 2. These figures are for adjusted force ratios that take into account differences in wealth among countries and thus correct for the ability of wealthier countries to maintain larger military establishments. For a more complete presentation by Payne of his data and his analysis of it, see *Why Nations Arm,* to be published by Basil Blackwell.

26. These figures are calculated from data for individual countries in U.S. Arms Control and Disarmament Agency, *World Military Expenditures and Arms Transfers 1985* (Washington, 1985), pp. 52–88. Countries are classified as free, partly free, or not free according to Raymond Gastil, ed., *Freedom in the World: Political Rights and Civil Liberties 1982* (Westport, Conn.: Greenwood Press, 1982), pp. 10–13. Classification of Third World countries as Marxist-Leninist is based on that classification by the Soviets, as reported in Francis Fukuyama, *Moscow's Post-Brezhnev Reassessment of the Third World* (Santa Monica: Rand Corporation, 1986), p. 84.

27. James L. Payne, "Marxism and Militarism," *Polity* 19 (Winter 1986), Tables 2 and 4; Arms Control and Disarmament Agency, *Military Expenditures 1985,* pp. 63, 69.

28. These wars are drawn from data in Ruth Leger Sivard, *World Military and Social Expenditures 1985* (Washington: World Priorities, 1985), pp. 9–11. The list does not include what Sivard classifies as "interventions," that is, the involvement of a foreign government in a civil war in another society.

29. This apparently has historically been the case. A study of 116 major wars between 1789 and 1941 involving 438 participating countries showed that no wars had been fought between democratically elected governments. Dean V. Babst, "A Force for Peace," *Industrial Research,* vol. A, no. 114 (April 1972): 55–58. (I am indebted to Dr. Amron Katz for calling this source to my attention.) In addition, liberal societies have never fought each other. See Michael W. Doyle, "Kant, Liberal Legacies, and Foreign Affairs, Part I," *Philosophy and Public Affairs* 12 (1983): 213ff.

30. Ivo K. Feierabend with Rosalind L. Feierabend and Betty A. Nesvold, "The

Comparative Study of Revolution and Violence," *Comparative Politics* 5 (April 1973): 414–19.

31. Ché Guevara, *Guerilla Warfare* (New York: Vintage Books, 1961), p. 2.

32. Bertrand de Jouvenel, *On Power* (Boston: Beacon Press, 1962), p. 218.

33. See Samuel P. Huntington, "The Meaning of Democracy," *Geopolitique* 11 (Fall 1985): 83–87.

3

Democracy from Three Latin American Perspectives

LORENZO MEYER

Political democracy is still more a pilot project than a reality in Latin America. For this reason, the term democracy means different things to different people. The objective of this chapter is to present three different Latin American perspectives to the same set of propositions about democracy that are offered by several of the authors in this book.

The perspectives correspond to three views of the world that are prevalent among Latin American political elites: the conservative, authoritarian, and anticommunist point of view, that is associated with the military establishments in the region; the view of those who are as willing to be authoritarian as democratic depending on how the wind blows (the opportunists mentioned by Guillermo O'Donnell); and finally, the view of the bona fide democrats, whether conservatives, centrists, or leftists, who are united in their opposition both to the past and to the present authoritarian regimes of the region.

It is obvious that other perspectives—the two extremes—are missing. However, because the radical right and the radical left reject the philosophical and practical values associated with political democracy, there is no common ground with either of these groups for debating the ideas of those who are trying to understand and reinforce democracy south of the Rio Grande.

It should be understood that there exists no unified view of democracy among the military, the "fair weather" democrats, or the real democrats. Nevertheless, for the purposes of this essay, it is necessary to use some sort of an ideal model in the Weberian sense in order to focus on the important differences existing among the three views.

What is Democracy in and for Latin America?

As Latin America entered the twentieth century, democracy became in principle the only legitimate way to claim and exert the political power of the state. At the same time, the social, economic, and cultural bases for democracy in the region were weak or nonexistent. For this reason, political reality and theory marched down very different paths in almost all cases of Latin American polities. Until the Second World War, democracy in the area was very much an idea without empirical content. After that, democracy became an experiment that failed in almost all countries.

Today we are looking at the resurgence of democracy and at brave attempts to make it a viable way of life in Latin America. At the same time we are becoming aware of the fact that there is no theory that can explain or guide those who are trying to understand or institutionalize political democracy in the region. Latin American political theory is rich in the analysis and explanation of dictatorship and authoritarianism but not in the theory of democracy. In more than one sense, democracy is still a *terra incognita* for the great majority of Latin American societies, and theory reflects this obvious and tragic fact. Masses as well as elites, social scientists as well as political practitioners are only now beginning to learn about democracy. The building of an adequate theory of Latin American democracy is a necessary step for advancing it in the region.

Huntington's proposition about the nature of modern democracy is basically the product of the historical experiences of the industrial western societies. Two centuries after the French Revolution, the political practices of the United States, Canada, and Western Europe have tended to give the concept of democracy an institutional definition. This is the "modest meaning" of democracy that Huntington stresses. From his vantage point, the essence of democracy is an "institutional arrangement for choosing rulers," and the core of such an arrangement is competitive elections.

Historical experience, says Huntington, shows that modern political democracies tend to behave in a way that may be called Aristotelian—always between the extremes. Their economies are mixed (with ample opportunities for private enterprise), their material growth tends to be moderate, and their income distribution is not too inequitable. Though they are not militaristic, they are also not well known for their pacifism. According to Huntington, there is one area in which mature democracies are closer to one of the extremes and that is the area of political stability. Democracies are extremely stable politically and they are also extreme in their respect for individual rights and liberties. But according to this view, these are virtues, not vices.

If democracy in Latin America ends up having the meaning that Huntington suggests—"At its best, democracy means conservatism without stagnation and reform without revolution"—there is nothing in that system that would make it unacceptable either to the military establishment or to opportunistic democrats. In fact, this kind of democracy may be a desirable goal for enlightened conservatives—military and civilian—because its institutionalized pluralism inhibits extremism by organized working classes, preserves internal stability, and avoids unnecessary and dangerous military confrontations with neighboring countries. These three elements are cherished by the military establishment and they are entirely compatible with the interests of the propertied classes, civilian administrators, and technocrats who accompanied the military in establishing the bureaucratic-authoritarian regimes of the 1970s. Today these groups tend to have distanced themselves from this form of government.

To committed or real democrats, Huntington's definition of democracy may appear less than satisfactory, especially for those on the left. Because of the state of economic and political backwardness and the social injustice that prevails in Latin America, and in order to fire the imagination and attract the allegiance of the masses to political democracy and away from authoritarianism, the democratic system of government must strive to achieve, at the same time, an institutional arrangement for choosing rulers and the preservation of individual rights, freedoms, and a significant degree of social justice. Latin American democracy, as late democracy, may have to be compatible with a higher degree of state intervention than what has been and remains the case in the industrial democracies of the West.

The dissatisfaction that democrats of Latin America, the Caribbean, and Canada have with the institutional definition of democracy stems from the differences between those who see political democracy as an end in itself (the institutional school) and those who consider it an instrument to transform society and achieve justice—not only in the formal but also in the substantive sense of the word. Within the wide spectrum of democrats in today's Latin America, those located to the left are more willing to emphasize the view of political democracy as an instrument to achieve economic and social democracy, and those to the right are more inclined to put the accent on democracy as an end in itself.

In any case, what is important is that a great number of those political activists who are committed to economic development and social justice as the ultimate goals of political action in Latin America are now more willing than they have been in the past to achieve these goals through political democracy and not through such dangerous shortcuts as the one-party system or other authoritarian and nonpluralistic solutions. With the passing of time, Cuba has lost some of its appeal as the best model for Latin America to achieve economic growth, development, social equality, and freedom. In short, political democracy is now a nonnegotiable item on the agenda of many progressive groups and movements in Latin America and the Caribbean.

There may be profound differences among key political actors in Latin America and the Caribbean regarding the ultimate ends of politics, but there is an amazing consensus—be it permanent or transitory—about the necessity to accept and defend formal democracy as the basis for the political game.

Mistakes to Be Avoided and How

Democracy needs a memory to learn from the past what to avoid and what to acquire. Historical and comparative analysis is necessary as an aid to new democracies as they confront the current danger, i.e., the economic crisis, through political crafting and institutional building.

In chapter 4, Juan Linz and Alfred Stepan suggest that democratic legitimacy can be insulated from perceptions of socioeconomic efficacy. Given the lack of real legitimacy, both historical and ethical, of the authoritarian regimes of the present and recent past in Latin America, leaders tried to base their right to govern on their ability to produce economic growth, to maintain social discipline, and to defend national sovereignty. These justifications have been undermined by the current economic crisis in the region, by the Argentine army's failure to regain control of the Malvinas islands, and by the exposure of systematic violations of human rights in authoritarian regimes. It seems that there is no easy way out of the current economic crisis of Latin America and the Caribbean. It is a structural and not a temporary problem. Therefore, from the perspective of the military and of opportunistic democrats, the best exit is to let the new democratic regimes face the very difficult task of substituting nonmaterial rewards for economic growth while restructuring these economies. If democracy fails, authoritarianism can recover some legitimacy. If democracy succeeds, the military, business, and bureaucratic establishments will ensure that their long-term interests will be preserved at a modest cost by remaining in the wings.

While regime legitimacy may not be explicitly connected to socioeconomic efficacy, democrats would be mistaken to ignore the latter. Rather, they should, as Linz and Stepan suggest in the next chapter, educate the population to some of the reasons for the current crisis: the mistakes and the abuses of the recent authoritarian past, the unjust and exploitative nature of some central aspects of the international economic system, and the contradictions and shortcomings of the economic model of development adopted by Latin America after the Second World War.

It is especially important that democratic ruling elites be perceived as frugal, honest, and efficient in their administration of public resources in the midst of economic crisis. In contrast with the previous regimes, they should live without ostentation. This external symbol of austerity and sympathy for the average citizen can help direct the anger and frustration of the masses away from leaders and the new democracy. This task is difficult, but it is not impossible. For democratic leadership, the observance of the rule of law above all expediency is paramount. Democracy can maintain the loyalty of the great majority of people in society in difficult times if leaders can capture the imagination of the people by words and actions.

One of the key propositions of Linz and Stepan as well as Laurence Whitehead in chapter 6 is the necessity to introduce into the new democracies of Latin America permanent and effective mechanisms of civilian control over the military. Like similar mechanisms in the industrial democracies, such controls should include the appointment of a civilian minister of defense, the development of academic expertise in military matters, the separation of internal intelligence activities from military responsibilities, and the establishment of legislative committees to oversee the armed forces.

These recommendations will be resented and resisted by present military establishments in Latin America. From their point of view, the less the government and the civilian elite know about their professional, social, and ideological structures the better. The more the military remains unpredictable to the civilians, the greater their importance as a political factor. On the other hand, democrats of all types need to know about the military in order to control it by introducing some or all of these changes.

However, it is possible and even convenient to wait a little longer to initiate some of these reforms because the democratic regimes cannot wage war on all fronts at the same time. Priority should go to the consolidation of power and to the resolution of the current economic crisis. The delicate problem of containing the military—a problem in existence since Latin America's independence—has to be accomplished one step at a time. It is a vital but long-term objective of the new democratic regimes.

Linz and Stepan have presented another idea to make Latin American democracy more resistant to political crisis: to replace presidential systems with parliamentarian ones. In times of crisis, it is easier to change the administration without damaging the government in a parliamentarian system than in a presidential one. The strong presidential tradition in the region combined with the weakness of political parties in some countries makes this idea problematic. In particular, the military, the semidemocratic and the democratic political elites are unlikely to accept this change. (One possible exception would be Chile, where the fragmentation of the democratic opposition could permit a parliamentary system to be set up in the post-Pinochet era.) However, in general, at this initial stage of the rebirth of democracy in Latin America there are more urgent matters—at least they seem more urgent—than initiating a debate and gaining a consensus in favor of parliamentarianism. The public has first to be educated and convinced of the virtues of democracy before addressing rationally a more refined and sophisticated issue like presidentialism versus parliamentarianism.

Guillermo O'Donnell in chapter 5 explores the critical period between the breakdown of authoritarianism and the establishment of a working democratic system. He describes the most common transitions: by collapse and by negotiation. In the latter case, such as has occurred in Brazil, there is a complex web of negotiations and accommodations between the leadership of the ending authoritarian regime and the opposition that is about to take power. Negotiation is much less common when the transition occurs by collapse (as in the Argentine case).

The main interest of the military is to persuade the new civilian rulers to respect its corporatist interest. This can be done for example by avoiding or reducing to a minimum all investigations of its past brutalities and by preventing any interference with its internal structure. Opportunistic democrats— often former collaborators of the military in the previous regime—and the military will try to reduce to the minimum the social and economic changes that the incoming democratic government may try to implement. However, opportunistic democrats will be more concerned with avoiding changes in rules regarding property, taxation, tariffs, and similar matters than with preserving the privileges or reputation of the military.

After the breakdown of authoritarianism, civil society must be resurrected if democracy is to take root. The democratic leadership has to give this step highest priority or risk a return to the status quo ante. Unavoidably, this resurrection reopens class, regional and group differences and contradictions. It is the task of the democratic leadership to direct the social energies liberated by the disappearance of authoritarianism into a process of negotiation by means of the recreation of the party system.

More attention should be paid to the role of parties. In many cases, such parties will have few or no roots in the past. The task of creating and organizing such parties has to have a high priority on the agenda of the democratic leadership in the transition period. Parties have to be the institutions created to channel the energies of social movements, labor unions, and other anti-authoritarian forces present at the beginning of the reemergence of civil society. Without parties it would be very difficult to negotiate the necessary compromises among the main political actors and to neutralize the understandable but dangerous tendencies let loose by the "maximalists" (mentioned by Guillermo O'Donnell) who can undermine the transition to a stable democracy.

Whatever their ideological preference, Latin American democrats should take O'Donnell's point seriously: for democracy to succeed, it is necessary to abandon maximalist positions and learn how to negotiate with political adversaries. This is more easily said than done. Historically, Latin American political culture has placed a low value on moderation, as illustrated by the names, e.g., "intransigent" or "radical," of some prestigious political parties. It is time to change this deeply rooted conception of politics and to start by digging up those seeds of the next round of authoritarian politics.

In chapter 6 Lawrence Whitehead is concerned with the current problem of the great majority of the countries in Latin America and the Caribbean. Whitehead poses the question: what is the best way to keep democracy alive until it develops roots and can shape in an adequate way its internal and external environments? Whitehead explains the fragility of democracy from the Rio Grande to Patagonia "in contemporary regional history and geopolitics, rather than in any supposedly inherent cultural or psychological attributes." This idea can easily be accepted by the democratic leadership, but not necessarily by the military or the neodemocrats. The authoritarian mind has tried to justify the repression it has exerted in the present or recent past with some variant of asserting the cultural (or even radical) impossibility of the Latin American masses acquiring the habits of self-discipline and self-restraint that are prerequisites of democracy. Only time and success can erase this deeply rooted mistrust of the traditional ruling elites toward the masses.

Whitehead also emphasizes the importance of imposing some limits on social reforms in order to make democracy tolerable to the propertied classes. If confronted with expropriations, radical tax reforms, or similar measures, vested propertied interests may react by subverting the new regime or by sabotaging the economy. In any case, it will be a real test for the democratic leadership to demand and introduce enough social reforms so as to give the lower classes a stake in the new regime without triggering a reaction by the military and the bourgeoisie. As Whitehead correctly points out, "the business sector has . . . served as a key constitutive element of virtually all the authoritarian regimes of the sixties and seventies [in Latin America]."

Whitehead's position on the neodemocrats is troubling. He is very clear that crimes committed by the military during the authoritarian period must be investigated and punished; no law of *punto final* should give the military impunity. On the other hand and to avoid unnecessary polarization, he advocates treating those civilians from the center to the right that collaborated with the military dictatorships as democrats if they claim to be converted. This proposition may be difficult to accept by those democrats who were persecuted by these new converts. However, ethical considerations apart, for democracy to survive in such an inhospitable environment as the one in Latin America, a marriage of convenience between true and opportunistic democrats may be indispensable. However, to forgive is not to forget. For the time being, opportunistic democrats have to be considered by bona fide democrats as partners today but as potential enemies tomorrow.

Another troublesome proposition in Whitehead's analysis is the one concerning radical and violent movements such as *Sendero Luminoso* in Peru. "This [type] of revolutionary leadership must be destroyed, or at least isolated from all social support, if their followers are to be 'reabsorbed' into the democratic mainstream. On this point, democrats must be clear and united, even sectarian." True, but this "destruction" must be accomplished within the law, while recognizing that some if not all the reasons motivating the radical and the violent left may be legitimate, even if their methods are not.

At the end, Whitehead returns to one of the central issues of this book: what can be done from the outside to foster and reinforce political democracy in the region? It has been almost a unanimous conclusion that democracy, like revolutions, cannot be exported, nor can it be imposed from without if it is going to endure. At the same time, a clear recognition emerges that external actors can make it easier or more difficult for democracy to establish roots in the region.

The most important external actor in the Latin American and Caribbean region is without any doubt the United States. Since the United States displaced the Europeans as the dominant power at the beginning of this century, a power with more strength and less sophistication than its predecessors, the policymakers of North America have tried to legitimize indirect or direct intervention in Latin America and the Caribbean by claiming to support democracy. At the beginning of the century, Woodrow Wilson intervened in the Mexican Revolution in the name of democracy, and in the name of the same democracy the administration of Ronald Reagan promoted a counterrevolutionary army on the borders of Nicaragua. In between, there have been other both direct and indirect interventions of the United States in Latin America, but their efficacy as instruments of democratization has been rather poor.

One of the cardinal elements in the relationship between the dominant power in the Western Hemisphere, the United States, and the countries of Latin America has been the principle of nonintervention. This principle was accepted by the inter-American community in the 1930s, after Europe ceased to represent a threat to the Monroe Doctrine and U.S. hegemony. No great power can abstain from interfering in the internal affairs of countries that it considers within its natural sphere of influence, especially when it is engaged in a global struggle, as has been the case of the United States vis-à-vis the Soviet Union since the end of the Second World War. Nevertheless, principles such as the juridical equality of states and the nonintervention of one state in the internal affairs of others are important ideological and legal instruments by which Latin America and the Caribbean can try to redress the imbalances in the economic and political exchange between the societies north and south of the Rio Grande. For these reasons, such principles have to be defended very strongly by the new democratic regimes and even by the not-so-democratic ones.

Nationalism is always the byproduct of bitter confrontations. In this century, the main international conflicts of Latin America and the Caribbean countries have been among themselves or with the United States. The lines that divide nationalists from nonnationalists in Latin America and the Caribbean do not correspond exactly to the lines that divide democratic elements from nondemocratic ones. However, in spite of the nationalist attitudes adopted occasionally by some Latin American military establishments regarding the United States, the general pattern since the 1950s has been one of close collaboration based on a shared anticommunist view of the world. Exceptions have been few. The same can be said about conservatives and right-of-center politicians. The nationalist credentials of some of the neodemocrats are tainted by their alliances with the United States when they were part of the authoritarian systems of the recent past.

The new democracies in Latin America and the Caribbean do not have to define their nationalism as openly anti-American, but their leadership will be weakened if they are perceived by the public as being too close to Washington. Nationalism is still a potent political force in the region, and one way to gain and maintain legitimacy for democracy is to contrast the independence and nonaligned foreign policy of present leaders with the willingness of many past and present authoritarian systems to take the side of the United States in the struggle of the two superpowers.

Whitehead's proposition that "there are compelling reasons why the promotion of democracy in Latin America can only be, at best, a secondary objective for the U.S. policymakers" is considered as self-evident by the majority of the leaders of the region, regardless of their political preferences. This does not mean that the United States and other governments should not reinforce democracy. Quite the contrary.

To repeat, the main responsibility for establishing democracy in the region lies with the internal actors. The external environment can (except in extraordinary circumstances) weaken or reinforce democracy, but it cannot be the main force that creates or destroys it. Whatever their value, external efforts to reinforce democracy should be compatible with the nonintervention principle. For this reason, reinforcement will be more effective when it is positive, i.e., providing economic assistance, opening up markets, or softening the conditions of new and old loans to help new democracies, rather than when it is negative, i.e., punishing with boycotts or trade embargoes those regimes declared undemocratic. In any event, sanctions against nondemocratic regimes may work better if they are pursued collectively rather than unilaterally. Multilateral actions that are not contradictory with the principles of the United Nations and the Organization of American States have to be the result of open negotiations and consultation among the partners, lest they be viewed as part of an imperial policy.

Governments should not be the sole source of positive and negative external efforts in favor of democracy. In some cases, governmental actions may be counterproductive. Nongovernmental actors are not bound by the nonintervention principle, and they can be open in their partnership with democratic forces abroad. They can use a moral language that loses credibility when it comes from governments. Actors such as political parties, human rights groups, and ad hoc organizations are some of the political forces already acting as watchdogs of democracy. Actors outside the hemisphere, especially Europeans, are helpful. In summary, the political costs of deviance from what today is considered the democratic standard can be increased in Latin America and the Caribbean if international public opinion is mobilized against actual or potential enemies of democracy.

It is unfortunate that the new and the few old democracies in Latin America and the Caribbean that are trying to establish themselves as viable alternatives to the authoritarian tradition have to act in a very difficult international environment. The war in Central America is undermining the basis of the oldest democracy in the region, Costa Rica, and is making very difficult, if not impossible, the establishment and advance of democracy and pluralism among the other countries involved in the struggle. The generalized economic crisis—high foreign debt, inflation, unemployment, a depressed raw materials market—is making democratic regimes the managers of a disastrous economic situation. Under these conditions, it is going to be almost impossible to give an adequate response to the demands of the people for social justice. However, if Linz and Stepan are correct about the relative insulation of democratic legitimacy from economic performance, the economic crisis is going to make life even more difficult for existing authoritarian regimes. It is only in this limited and negative sense that economic hardships may produce something positive, because they will be helping—by eroding legitimacy—to create some of the conditions that are necessary for a transition to democracy in the hardest or oldest authoritarian systems in the region. Of course democracy remains fragile in the region, and one hopes that the oldest and richest democracies in and outside the Western Hemisphere will take positive actions—political as well as economic actions—to facilitate the resurrection of civil society in the new Latin American and Caribbean democracies.

The idea of demanding from the great powers, especially from the United States, respect for autonomy and support for the economic development of Latin American democracies may sound like wishful thinking, particularly in Central America. Nevertheless, if stability in the Western Hemisphere is an important element in the definition of national security of the industrial democracies, then the support of democracies in Latin America and the Caribbean is an act of self-interest on the part of the western powers. Unfortunately, past experiences show that there are no strong constituencies within the United States, Western Europe, or Japan willing to sponsor acts of national enlightened self-interest if there is nothing immediate to be gained, and this is precisely the case of democracy in backward regions: few concrete groups or interests in the industrial nations will be better off if democracy succeeds in its struggle in Latin America. For this reason, democratic leaders in Latin America and the Caribbean should plan for the future without expecting any significant amount of external support from the great powers. In fact, they can count themselves lucky if they get no opposition in this difficult endeavour.

Part II

THE DECLINE AND RISE
OF DEMOCRACY

4

Political Crafting of Democratic Consolidation or Destruction: European and South American Comparisons

JUAN LINZ and ALFRED STEPAN

Introduction

To what extent can our knowledge about the breakdown of democratic regimes in Europe and Latin America contribute to a better understanding of the conditions under which reborn democracies in Latin America can acquire stability and avoid renewed breakdown? Does our knowledge about past crises in democracies tell us something about the future of democracies? Our answer is a qualified yes. We think that a reading of the work of the many social scientists and historians who have addressed the great theme of democratic stability could help avoid some of the mistakes that in the past have led to the demise of democracy.[1] However, we feel obliged to caution against facile extrapolations from the study of the past. Polities and political actors have to face crises and conflicts as new challenges. As an ancient philosopher said, "We never bathe in the same river twice." We should be conscious that our knowledge of the past is limited, and that it is sometimes selective, particularly when so much of it is derived from the intensive study of a limited number of historically important cases of breakdown and often on an insufficient analysis of those that avoided the drama of democratic breakdown.

More than is commonly deemed to be the case, we think that the difference between political survival or breakdown is a question, as our title implies, of "political crafting." Thus in this essay we will attempt to identify some of the most important dimensions of "crafting" that have contributed to European democratic breakdowns or consolidations.

We believe our conclusions can be of reasonably general theoretical interest to those concerned with the question of democratic breakdown and consolidation. However, the Latin American countries that we have most in mind are those relatively developed countries that have recently had a traumatic experience with bureaucratic-authoritarian regimes and now have fledgling democracies. We refer to Brazil, Argentina, and Uruguay. These are the countries we know best and that we think would benefit most directly from a close comparison with European cases. If democracy were consolidated in these countries this would have a beneficial impact on the even more difficult, more problematic tasks facing many other Latin American countries.[2]

Three sets of questions that emerged from the European struggle for democracy seem to us of particular importance for the current democratizing efforts in Latin America. First, what is the relationship between socioeconomic efficacy and regime legitimacy? Did those democratic regimes that survived major hardships craft their responses to adversity in very different ways from those countries where democracy broke down? How important for democratic survival or breakdown were intervening variables that were primarily political in nature?

Second, how have democracies that have survived or broken down crafted their reactions to nonstate violence and to control of what Max Weber referred to as the state's legitimate monopoly of force? For the purposes of this essay, we think it is especially important to explore how democratic forces might attempt to empower themselves in the major arenas of the polity so as to be able to increase their capacity to control the means of force in society, especially the military.

Third, do some institutional arrangements put greater pressure on democratic governments than others? Could any changes be crafted, such as a shift from presidentialism to parliamentarianism, that might increase the flexibility and crisis-surviving capacity of many Latin American democracies?

Collectively, three sets of problems—worries about the efficacy of the new democracies in the context of the debt crisis, worries about military reentry into power in the context of still heavily militarized polities, and worries about whether Latin American presidents will be overwhelmed by demands on their resources—contribute to a significant portion of the anxiety about the future of the current redemocratization efforts in Latin America. The tasks facing the new Latin American democracies are undeniably multiple and difficult. Nonetheless, we think that a correct appreciation of these three sets of problems we have chosen to explore can point to areas of choice and possibility that may be of some value to those who would attempt to craft democratic consolidation.

Socioeconomic Efficacy and Regime Legitimacy: The Political "Processing of Adversity"

What is the relationship between citizens' perceptions of the socioeconomic efficacy of a democratic regime and their perceptions of the legitimacy of that regime? There is a certain pessimism about this point in the new democracies of Latin America because the region is living through a severe economic crisis and many of the intellectual leaders believe that socioeconomic efficacy and democratic legitimacy are very tightly coupled. While we do believe that in the long run it erodes the accrued political capital of the regime if it is seen as completely incapable of solving major socioeconomic problems—and thus we are very supportive of efforts to solve the debt crises with growth—we believe that perceptions of a regime's socioeconomic efficacy are less tightly coupled to perceptions of a regime's democratic legitimacy than is commonly supposed.

There are a number of theory-based reasons why we would expect democratic legitimacy to be somewhat insulated from perceptions of socioeconomic efficacy. Claims to ruling authority based on democratic procedural origins rather than on governmental performance per se are one insulating factor. The possibility of the democratic alternation of government—the promise of new policies to solve socioeconomic problems—provides another. Another major insulating factor is citizens' perceptions about the past and their worries about the future. Citizens, the high bourgeoisie as well as the working class, care about being protected from personal human rights abuses. A regime in which state behavior is constrained by a rule of law is a vital asset in a new democracy. As long as a democratic regime completely respects the rule of law, this respect can act as an important insulating factor for the regime and one to which citizens can attach an independent value, just as socioeconomic reforms also constitute values in themselves. Indeed the more there is a strongly negative cross-class collective memory about a particularly abusive regime (e.g., Nazi Germany), the more the question of procedural guarantees for personal safety will be a significant value among all classes. In such circumstances, the more that alternative, nondemocratic legitimacy options are not able to dispel serious doubts about their potential respect for personal freedoms, the more the existing democratic regime will be perceived by citizens as the most appropriate (legitimate) political formula for the country. All of the above considerations argue against a tight coupling of a democratic regime's socioeconomic efficacy and its perceived legitimacy. What does the European experience suggest? Let us turn first to post-Franco Spain.

There is absolutely no doubt that the economic situation of Spain deteriorated under democracy. Spanish unemployment in the early 1970s under Franco was one of the lowest in Europe and hovered around 3 percent. With democracy, unemployment rose dramatically. Spain's 20 percent unemployment rate in the mid-1980s was the highest in Western Europe.[3] Economic growth rates, which averaged over 7 percent from 1960 to 1974 and were among the highest in the world, averaged only 1.7 percent between 1975 and 1985.[4]

The "tightly coupled" hypothesis would lead us to predict a corresponding decline in the legitimacy of democracy. What do Spanish public opinion polls indicate? From 1978 through 1983, a poll asked Spaniards whether democracy would enable the problems that have been identified as important by Spaniards to be resolved. (See Table 4.1.) Six years after the death of Franco and the beginning of the Spanish transition and four years after the first democratic

TABLE 4.1
"Does Democracy Allow the Resolution of the Problems That We As Spaniards Face?"

	1978	1980	1981	1982–83	1983
Yes	68	45	43	55	61
No	22	46	45	16	30
Depends			12	21	9
Other, n.a.	10	9	12	8	9
100%	(5898)	N.A.	(1703)	(5463)	(3952)

TABLE 4.2
"Democracy Is The Best Political System for A Country Like OURS."

	1978	1980	1981	1982–83	1983
Yes	77	69	81	74	85
No	15	20	13	6	10
Depends				12	
Other, n.a.	8	11	6	7	5
100%	(5898)	N.A.	(1703)	(5463)	(3952)

Source: National surveys by Data S.A., Madrid. For 1978 (July) and 1980 see: J. J. Linz, M. Gómez-Reino, D. Vila and F. A. Orizo, *Informe sociológico sobre el cambio político en España, 1975–1981* (IV Informe FOESSA, vol. I, Fundación FOESSA), Madrid: Euramérica, 1981, 656 pp., pp. 627–29. For 1981, March 4 to 21 (after the February 23 attempted coup), *Cambio* 16, no. 488, April 6, 1981, pp. 42–45; for 1982–83, November–January, postelection survey with the support of the Volkswagen-Stiftung, unpublished (for the study see J. J. Linz and J. R. Montero, *Crisis y cambio. Electores y partidos en la España de los años ochenta,* Madrid: Centro de Estudios Constitucionales, 1986; for 1983 (Fall) see J. J. Linz, "La sociedad española: presente, pasado y futuro", in J. J. Linz, ed., *España, un presente para el future,* I: *La sociedad,* Madrid: Instituto de Estudios Económicos, 1984, pp. 57–95; and J. Linz, "Legitimacy of Democracy and the Socioeconomic System," in Mattei Dogan, ed., *Comparing Pluralist Democracies: Strains on Legitimacy,* Boulder, Colo.: Westview Press, 1988, pp. 65–113.

election in 1977, negative responses about the efficacy of democracy for solving problems slightly outnumbered positive responses. Belief in the socioeconomic efficacy of democracy had declined by twenty-five points.

How tightly was this dramatic erosion of the belief in the socioeconomic efficacy of democracy tied to beliefs in democracy as the best political formula for Spain? As Table 4.2 demonstrates, the data indicate that for Spanish citizens there was virtually no coupling. Between 1978 and 1983, there was a decline of 5 percent of respondents who indicated that democracy was not the best political system for Spain. More important, affirmative responses that democracy was the best political system for Spain increased by 8 percent.

Clearly in Spain, at least for the short or medium run, other factors besides belief in economic and social efficacy were powerfully affecting citizens' beliefs about the best political formula for the country.

Earlier in this essay we suggested that citizens' evaluations of the specific alternative political formulas of their recent past, or of their plausible future, are a powerful intervening variable. For the Spanish case, despite the 25 percent decline between 1978 and 1981 in the belief in the efficacy of democracy, the politically relevant question was: What available political formula might people want instead of democracy? Here the phrasing of the Spanish question was to the point: "Is democracy the best political system for a country like ours?" A negative answer implied an affirmative response to a different political formula. In the Spanish context the most likely alternative political formula would have been a regime with a strong nondemocratic military component. Unlike in the 1930s, right-wing fascist mobilization was not a real alternative. Neither, given the antiviolence positions of the Spanish people and the Euro-Communist, non-Leninist positions of the Communist Party at the time, was violent revolution a plausible alternative. In fact, of the thirteen countries polled in the European Values Study of 1981, Spain had the highest percentage of people who supported the "gradual reform" option.[5]

But how much legitimacy did Spanish citizens actually accord to what could have appeared to have been the most available alternative ruling formula,

TABLE 4.3

"At This Time, What do You Think is Best: A Government Only of the UCD (The Unión de Centro Democrático, Then the Ruling Party), A Political Party Coalition, A Civil-Military Government, or a Military Government?"

UCD government	27%
Coalition government	52%
Civil-military government	5%
Military government	2%
Others (no response, don't know, hard to classify)	14%
	100%

(N = 1703)

*"En estos momentos, ¿qué cree usted que es el mejor: un gobierno sólo de UCD, un gobierno de coalición entre partidos políticos, un gobierno cívico-militar, o un gobierno militar?"

Source: Special poll carried out by Data, S.A., Madrid, Spain, between March 4 and 21, 1981 after the putsch attempt of February 23, 1981. Unpublished.

military rule? As Table 4.3 makes starkly clear, in the context of four decades of authoritarian rule and a recent coup attempt, a legitimacy formula that entailed military participation in government was an extremely weak competitor to political democracy, notwithstanding the widespread disenchantment with the efficacy of democracy.

What are the implications of the European experience for Latin America? The post-Franco opinion polls and our analysis of interwar Europe lead us to believe that the *political perception of desired alternatives has a greater impact on the survival of democratic regimes than economic and social problems per se.* The economic crisis of the 1930s was felt throughout Europe. For many of the democracies that survived, it was a period of intense and creative political crafting in which new coalitions and new policies were forged. The Netherlands had the highest rate of unemployment in interwar Europe; indeed, thirty thousand Dutch workers went to Germany for employment. But Prime Minister Colijn enlarged the governing coalition to include the Liberals and forged a national crisis cabinet of great longevity. In Sweden, the Saltsjobaden Agreement of 1938 set the basis for the modern social-democratic welfare state, which won acceptance by business and labor. In Belgium, the Rexist fascist movement was turned back by a coalition that included Catholic, Liberal and Socialist parties. In the United States the "New Deal" was launched. Based on his major study of the impact of the depression on democracies, Ekkart Zimmermann concludes that in the above cases, "the underlying variable of all these outcomes seems to be the ability of group leaders to come together, form new coalitions, sometimes on the basis of reaffirming older ones (such as in Belgium), and then to settle on how to steer the economy."[6] Zimmerman was particularly concerned in his research design to determine the relative weight of political and economic factors in the German and Austrian breakdowns. In the end he assigns greater weight to political factors, especially to what he calls the presence or absence of *system blame.* "In some countries (Germany and Austria) system blame was so widespread that the forces coming to the defense of the democratic polity were already in a minority."[7]

In our judgment, in both Germany and Austria there was more active crafting of democratic destruction than there was crafting of democratic consolidation. The key variable in Germany and Austria was that strong groups on the left and on the right attacked the political regime for political reasons as much as for economic and social reasons.[8] In the German case, the Weimar conservatives saw the alternative to be a nondemocratic monarchy, but they assumed that such a monarchy would be constrained as in the past by the rule of law. However, after Nazi Germany, an entire generation of conservatives and rightists realized that a nondemocratic alternative on the right could be one that entailed absolutely no respect for the rule of law and could possibly put their own lives and personal rights as well as their material interests at stake.

Part of the glue of post–World War II European democracy for the left and right alike is that procedural democracy allowed them to continue to struggle for the advancement of their material interests in a context where there were procedural, constitutional, and legal constraints on government and state behavior. Here we think that Adam Przeworski's widely cited and otherwise insightful discussion of democracy should be refined. Przeworski asserts that "the process of establishing democracy is a process of institutionalizing uncertainty."[9] He is clearly right when he says that democracy presents the permanent opportunity that a party on the right or left could win and implement major changes in laws concerning property and social relations. But democratic governments are constitutional governments and constitutions are not normally changed by simple majorities. Democracy certainly implies long-range "institutionalized uncertainty" about policy alternatives, but it just as strongly implies a system of constitutionally sanctioned procedural guarantees that constrain arbitrary and abusive state behavior.

One of the most interesting and important developments that occurred in Brazil, Uruguay, and Argentina as a result of the massive and unprecedented abuses of state power by the bureaucratic-authoritarian regimes in these states was the increased valorization of democracy as an important end that needed to be protected in and for itself. In the past, a significant part of the left had been ambivalent about democracy and believed that only revolutionary rule could bring about social change. Important parts of the left attached only an instrumental value to democracy. It was a vehicle to be used in pursuit of other goals. The contemporary left, correctly, will not be satisfied with a procedural democracy alone. However, procedural democracy in the 1980s has come to be seen by more and more on the left in Brazil, Uruguay, and Argentina as an indispensible political formula that is a valuable norm in itself and as a political arrangement that offers both protection against state terrorism and some hope of electoral progress toward social and economic democracy.

For Brazil, Argentina, and Uruguay, the contributions by the left in creating a political discourse that validates procedural democracy must be recognized. In this context one of the most destructive things that groups on the right could do to these new prodemocratic values and practices of the left is to encourage forms of force or fraud that do not allow the left the full enjoyment of their rights under the procedural guarantees of democracy.

Much of the bourgeoisie in Brazil, Uruguay, and Argentina emerged from the recent bureaucratic-authoritarian experience with new worries about their ability to control authoritarian regimes. Important sectors of the bourgeoisie had encouraged and strongly supported the overthrow of democratic rule and the advent of military rule. But they learned from personal experience that the state's repressive apparatus was difficult for them to contain. In Argentina many upper-class and middle-class families were drawn into the vortex of indiscriminate and criminal state terrorism against which social contacts and economic influences were powerless.[10]

In Brazil, state terrorism was less salient, but by 1976 many of the most significant Brazilian entrepreneurs were actively struggling to expand their range of influence in the economy and increasingly they began to argue for a political system in which the military's weight was less, and where public policy could be more openly contested and discussed. Notwithstanding the uncertainty of democracy that Adam Przeworski correctly stresses, more and more of the bourgeoisie in Brazil decided that in the long run a context in which they could attempt to advance their personal and material interests within a framework of the rule of law and of periodic elections was the system that was most appropriate (legitimate) for them and for Brazil. They had seen that the "Brumairean moment" where they had momentarily abdicated their claims to rule had become praetorian decades. They were also aware that, given the new social forces in Brazil, a new round of authoritarianism might lead to a more dangerous degree of societal conflict and polarization. A political arena could very well emerge in which it would be no means certain that their resources and interests would prevail. Thus in Robert Dahl's terms, for much of the Brazilian bourgeoisie the costs of the repression of democracy now came to be seen as high, and because of the more democratic values on the left, the costs of toleration are now lower.

From the perspective we have just analyzed we believe that reports such as *Nunca Más* in Argentina and *Nunca Mais* in Brazil (reports that have been best sellers in their respective countries) are useful for the consolidation of democracy. These reports have performed an important political task. Groups in civil society, from radicals to conservatives, are increasing their understanding of the potential for criminal, even anarchic, repression by the state apparatus if it is not constrained and if it prescribes to itself a position of complete nonaccountability either to votes or to the law. One of the tasks of the democratic forces is to deepen the collective memory of the reality of these recent authoritarian political pasts. Another task of the democratic forces is to make citizens acutely aware that attacks on the democratic regime could pave the way for an authoritarian political future in which no personal or institutional guarantees against state abuses are ensured.

We also think that the more extensive carrying out and dissemination of political polls could probably serve as a useful check against those who claim that a military regime might be desired by the majority of the people. In Spain, trials of the military leaders of the failed coup in 1981 in which military disputes and goals were made clearly visible to the population, together with the circulation of respected public opinion polls showing that those who wanted military participation in government represented a tiny minority of the population, strengthened the forces working for democratic consolidation.

Control of the Means of Force in Democratic Polities

How should nonstate political violence be handled by the new democracies? Specifically, if political violence occurs, what reaction will minimize the negative consequences for democratic survival and consolidation? More generally, how can the new democratic polities increase their capacity to control, monitor, and manage their own military establishments?[11]

The Management of Nonstate Violence

A widespread worry in Latin America is that the military have a very low tolerance for insurgent violence in a political system. Some argue that it is so important to avoid insurgency that if it occurs, the state should act by whatever means to end it. This often implies giving the military a free hand in the suppression, so that the military cannot blame the government for having prevented them from solving the crisis.

Clearly, guerrilla violence, like economic recession, creates problems for a new democratic regime. However, we believe that as with economic recession, the most important variable is the way the political system processes the facts of guerrilla and political violence.

Once again the Spanish case is illustrative. Table 4.4 shows deaths due to extremists and Basque separatists in the period from 1968 to 1983. We should also note that not one army officer was killed during the Basque insurgency in the 1968–75 Franco period, or in the 1975–77 transition period. But in the postelectoral period of democratic rule between 1978 and 1983, thirty-seven army officers died.[12]

Despite the sharp increase in deaths due to Basque terrorists in the democratic period, the general belief in the legitimacy of democracy in Spain, as we have seen, stayed at a very high level and in fact grew between 1979 and 1983.

Once again the key question is not the undeniable increase in violence, but whether political leaders choose to manipulate the information to the detriment of democracy. In the Spanish case, a complex series of political actions and attitudes helped to minimize the negative consequences of the growing violence by Basque separatists on the new Spanish democracy.

Probably the most important fact was that not one single national political party chose to use the deaths associated with the Basque issue to attempt to delegitimize the democratic regime. No major political party manipulated the data to "craft" a democratic breakdown. There was of course a discussion about the best way to handle the Basque violence. However, no party persisted in blaming the various governments for creating the problem. No party claimed that the problem could be handled better outside of a democratic regime. No national party urged that democratic government throw all constitutional constraints aside and allow the army to wage unlimited war against the terrorists and their sympathizers.

In fact the democratic government made a concerted effort to ensure that the state security forces acted legally. The government and the police have made a considerable effort to avoid political deaths. The police, not the army, is implementing antiterrorist operations.[13] Significantly, to date the Spanish military has made no claim that the Basque situation would be better handled if the army were given control.[14]

Very importantly, the overall climate of public opinion in Spain is not supportive of violence. In post–Civil War Spain there is little romanticism

TABLE 4.4

Victims of Terrorism in the Period 1968–1983

1. Distribution by Months and Years

Year													Total
1968						1		1					2
1969			1										1
1970													
1971			1										1
1972								1		1			2
1973			3		1			1			3		8
1974					1		1		12	1	2		17
1975			1	1	3	2	3	4	1	10	1		26
1976	1	2	3	4	3	1			1	5	1		21
1977	10	1	2	1	2	3			2	4	2	1	28
1978	9		10	1	5	6	4	5	4	13	15	13	85
1979	15	10	6	15	21	8	14	6	10	4	6	3	118
1980	13	14	6	7	15	7	9	3	13	15	17	5	124
1981	4	1	5	5	9	7	4			1	2		38
1982	1	2	9	2	3	4	2	2	7	6	3	3	44
1983		5	2	2	5	6	4	1	2	8	4	(4)	(43)
Total	53	35	48	40	67	46	40	23	53	67	52	(34)	558

2. Distribution by Historical Stages

1) General Franco (1968–Nov. 1975) 57
2) Period of Transition (Dec. 1975–Jun. 1977)......................... 40
3) Constituent Assembly Period (Jul. 1977–Dec. 1978) 94
4) Democracy (from January 1979) 367
                                                                     558

Major Groups Responsible for Terrorism (%):

ETA... 75.36
GRAPO.. 11.69
Extreme Right.. 7.01
Others (Extreme Left, Anarchist, International)...................... 5.94

Source: Ministry of the Interior

Reproduced from Ricardo García Damborenea, *La Encruicijada Vasca* (Barcelona: Editorial Argos Vargara, 1985), p. 51.

about violence. In a public opinion poll that had an eleven-point scale on attitudes toward the Basque insurgents, with zero indicating the most hostile position and ten the most favorable attitude, 99 percent of the Spanish population polled in 1983 located themselves in one of the six most disapproving positions. Even in the Basque country itself, the average support was a low 1.79 on the eleven-point scale and the largest Basque nationalist party, the PNU, was only 1.4.[15]

Italy is another European country where terrorism has continued at a reasonably high level, but where terrorism has not been politically transformed into an issue or manipulated to craft democratic breakdown.[16]

Interwar Austria is the strongest example of the opposite trend, where deaths due to political violence were persistently manipulated to craft political breakdown. Both extremes of the political spectrum used the existence of a high rate of violence to bolster their argument that democracy contributed to, and could not resolve, the question of violence.[17] In both Austria and Germany in the 1920s a very high percentage of political elites and their associated mass movements legitimized violence. This contrasts with the fundamentally different atmosphere of Western Europe in the 1980s, where there is a very low degree of intellectual or popular defense of the use of violence.

In Argentina in the 1970s (and to a lesser extent Brazil and Uruguay in the 1960s and early 1970s) there was a diffuse intellectual and popular legitimization of the use of political violence. Part of the revalorization of democratic procedures has been the corresponding delegitimization of political violence.[18]

Once again, the recent European effort to avoid political deaths is important to assess. Democratic control of the means of state coercion, rather than abdication to the military, also needs to be studied closely. Democratic control of the military, the police, and the intelligence apparatus, however, requires a major effort by democratic civilians to empower themselves with new knowledge and new institutions so that they can assume effective command of the legitimate use of force by the state. This is not simply a vague injunction. Every part of the polity in the new democracies of Argentina, Uruguay, and Brazil will have to address this task. What could be done by civil society, especially civic groups, and by research institutes? By political society, especially by legislatures? And what could be done at the level of the state by changes in the organization of the executive?[19]

Democratic Management of State Force: The Tasks of Civil Society

Democracy is about an open contest for state power by means of elections and the oversight and control of state power by the representatives of the people. In virtually all polities of the world, and very much so in Latin America, the military are a permanent factor in any calculus of power. Therefore, by definition, civil society must consider how it can make a contribution to the democratic control of military, police, and intelligence systems. It is an obvious point but one that bears repeating that the capacity of the military as a complex institution to develop a consensus for intervention is greatly aided by the extent to which civil society "knocks on the doors" of the barracks. In 1964 in Brazil, and in Chile in 1973, many powerful representatives of civil society—including the church—"knocked on the door" and created the "Brumairean moment." The transitional military governments hoped for by many middle-class and upper-class members of civil society became long-lasting bureaucratic-authoritarian regimes with significant interests of their own. This fundamental point granted, what else is important for civil society to consider?

Turning specifically to the technical capacities of civil society vis-à-vis the military, police, and intelligence systems, what could be done that has not already been done in the past? Latin American social scientists have become the leaders of the world social science community in conceptualizing the realities and implications of the new global political economy. They have also done some of the best work in the world on social movements and popular culture. However, until recently the formal study of military organizations and international relations—especially geopolitics, and most specifically the study of territorial disputes and military strategy—has been neglected. Those civilians who have concerned themselves with these matters have tended to be professors who attended institutions such as the Escola Superior de Guerra in Brazil or Argentina's Escuela de Defensa Nacional, where the intellectual agenda was set by the military and where, sanctioned by national security doctrines, French, U.S., and Latin American military cold war and internal subversion preoccupations are dominant. This situation has often meant that few members of the democratic opposition in civil society have been specialists on military matters and few wrote alternative geopolitical works. In Argentina especially, this privileged the military's perception of the country's geomilitary problems.

Most major democracies have at least one major civilian-led independent research institute that concentrates on international military politics. In the United States, the Brookings Institution has often supplied authoritative and well-researched expert alternative assessments of military strategy. In England, the International Institute for Strategic Studies performs a comparable function. The creation of such prestigious, independent, and civilian-led institutes would seem to be high on the agenda of civil society. Latin American universities also have not to date routinely incorporated military sociology and geopolitics into their curricula. This is a vital task because in most major democratic polities the newspapers, television networks, and weeklies have military specialists on their staffs. Just as important, the constant academic production of a cadre of citizens who are experts on military questions relating to force structure, organizational style, budgetary affairs, doctrine formation, and the specific details of weapons systems are indispensible for the fulfillment of the military and intelligence oversight functions of political society, especially in the legislative branch.

The Tasks of Political Society

Most major stable democracies have crafted over time permanent standing committees in their legislatures or cabinets that devote themselves exclusively to the routine oversight and monitoring of their country's military and intelligence systems. These committees characteristically have professional staffs who are specialists in matters of military strategy, budgeting, or intelligence. Often these staffs pull their talents both from the ranks of the professional civil service and from the political parties. In Latin American legislatures, such permanent committees with large staffs and independent research capacities often either do not exist or are understaffed and have few resources. What is needed therefore is a deliberate strategy for the empowerment of legislatures to carry out their military and intelligence oversight functions in a routine democratic and legislative fashion.

Military and intelligence officials do occasionally appear before the legislatures in Latin America, but most often this occurs under the circumstances of a special commission of inquiry established to examine a particular controversy. From the perspective of comparative civil-military relations in a democracy, this is a dangerous and ineffective review mechanism for three fundamental reasons. First, precisely because it is *ad hoc* and does not involve a standing committee, legislative leaders are not supported by a cadre of professional staff members with expert knowledge of the intricacies of the field. Second, by its very nature, an *ad hoc* special commission of inquiry occurs in a controversial, conflictual setting that tends to increase the latent paranoia most military organizations throughout the world feel about political "interference" in their professional activities. Thus a primary requirement must be to reduce the atmosphere of an exceptional confrontational inquiry by making the military's appearance before legislative leaders a routine occurrence. Third, if political party leaders know that these permanent standing committees are a routine yet important part of legislative life, some members of all parties will attempt to acquire special expertise in these areas and will be able to conduct or chair these committee meetings in a respectful, but deeply authoritative, manner. The routinization of legislative-military transactions can help reduce mutual fears and ignorance on the part of military leaders and party leaders alike. The self-empowerment of legislatures in national security matters is an imperative and a possible goal.

The Tasks of The State

Working together, political leaders in the legislature and democratic government leaders of the state apparatus can also begin the difficult task of restructuring the military, police, and intelligence systems so they are more consistent with the normal checks and balances of democratic regimes. Without attacking, dismantling, or for the most part demoralizing their intelligence systems, England, France and the United States have crafted mechanisms for the democratic management, monitoring, and oversight of their intelligence systems. In Brazil, even using the existing laws drafted by the previous military regime, the New Republic could eventually demilitarize the four top offices in the Serviço Nacional de Informações (SNI)—none of which are required by law to be occupied by military officers. This would remove the army from direct control of the intelligence system, something many professional officers would welcome because they believe that the SNI collects dossiers on them and heavily influences promotion patterns for reasons that may be extraneous to the officers' own professional capacities, but for reasons that are of direct interest to the SNI's own bureaucratic concerns.

The post-Malvinas concern of Latin America militaries, and especially the military in Brazil, to upgrade their professional capacity for joint operations may present a propitious moment for making changes in the military's representation in democratic governments. The democratic government of Brazil's New Republic has twenty-six ministers, six of whom are active-duty military officers. These cabinet ministers are: the minister of the air force; the minister of the navy; the minister of the army; the director of the SNI; the head of the military household; and, the chief of the Joint General Staff of the Armed Forces. All but the last of these positions are quite important in managing a crisis stemming from Brazilian state politics. Thus even in a democracy the military remains deeply involved in the day-to-day political discussions of Brazil's affairs. This pattern in which the three service chiefs and the intelligence director all have cabinet status is often replicated in other Latin American countries, even under democratic regimes. Such representation is of course to a great extent a direct reflection of the power and capacity of the military in Latin American democracies. To our knowledge, in any given year under nonwartime conditions, normally not even one Western European or North American democracy has even one active-duty military officer with full cabinet status.

Three possible changes that can be initiated within the state apparatus by new democratic leaders are worth serious theoretical and political consideration, and while they would be resisted, they might even present some advantages for the military as an institution and could thus possibly gain some military adherents. First, because of the new appreciation by the military of the importance of an effective joint interservice professional operational capacity— and the military's recognition that historic interservice rivalries make interservice cooperation virtually impossible—it is conceivable that a single civilian minister of defense could replace the traditional ministers of the army, navy, and air force. Politically, this would be the easiest change to implement if some new net resources for joint operations were added to the budget, but Brazil is the only former bureaucratic-authoritarian regime where this is presently possible. Argentina under Alfonsín has recreated a minister of defense, but it was under such confrontational circumstances and in the midst of such a financial crisis that no new resources for joint operations were made available to soften the blow. Second, the intelligence chief could be removed from ministerial status, especially if the institutional power of a monolithic organization such as the SNI in Brazil were divided into separate organizations for external and internal intelligence and if the chief presidential advisor for intelligence did not also command a large operational service. Third, Latin American liberal politicians are deeply suspicious of the idea of an important National Security Council with permanent military representatives. However, if the military representatives have an institutional voice but not institutional command within such an organization, it could in fact strengthen democracy. Precisely because the military constitute a permanent factor of power in all polities, it is better to encapsulate them professionally—but not politically—into the state apparatus.

Military ministers are widely understood in the Latin American military to be political, not professional, appointments to the cabinet. Thus, paradoxically, even with five or six military ministers, the military at times perceive that their enduring professional interests are not represented in the democratic government. Within the state, a paradoxical mix of fewer politically appointed military ministers and more systematic professional incorporation into serious standing national security councils might reduce the military's sense of isolation and create a more effective system of mutual exchange of information and grievances, and thus lessen the tendency for the pendulum to swing violently from radical military aspirations for total control of the state apparatus to liberal civilian fantasies about the total isolation of the military from a modern polity.

Thus, in order to increase its effective control of the military and intelligence systems, any contemporary democratic polity must promote an effort by civil society and political society to empower themselves through improvement of their own capacity for control.

Can the Weight of Democratic Rule be Lightened by New Institutional Arrangements?

A common anxiety that we hear expressed in the new Latin American democracies is that the weight of democratic rule is extremely heavy for the presidency and the cabinet as institutions. While this lamentation is often heard, one seldom hears much discussion of alternative institutional arrangements that might lead toward greater burden-sharing among democrats, toward greater sharing of the responsibility for policy failures and successes, and toward greater flexibility in making coalitional shifts without appealing to nonconstitutional mechanisms.

In this section we will raise such themes because we think that this period of redemocratization and of new constituent assemblies is the right moment to begin serious theoretical and political reflection about what if anything can be done to share the burdens of democratic rule.

Sometimes we are tempted to overemphasize the weaknesses of democracy when confronted with serious problems and crises. There is undoubtedly a certain vulnerability of democratic institutions, due in part to the freedoms created by the state of law, civil liberties, the autonomy of institutions, and the unfettered articulation of interests.

We tend, however, to ignore the advantages of democratic regimes, once they have acquired a certain legitimacy, in confronting difficult or even unsolvable problems. A critical advantage of democracy is that it is possible to distinguish the democratic regime itself from the government of the day. The failure of one government, or of the parties in power at a given moment, does not need to imply the questioning of the type of regime, the constitution, or the legal processes for changing governments. In a democracy one government can be substituted for another without the need to overthrow the institutions or to disrupt the legal order. In a democracy, those dissatisfied with the performance of a particular government or with a particular leadership can within the framework of the institutions find others that might be more successful. The expectation that this will be so gives hope to those who are dissatisfied; a change of government in itself can generate considerable support not only among those who are actively dissatisfied, but also among those who only passively supported the previous government. There is no need for revolutions or coups when people believe in the institutions and in the fairness of the political process, particularly in elections as a method for changing governments. Certainly there will always be small minorities who, knowing that they cannot rally a large number of voters to their support, will turn to violence via terrorism or *pronunciamientos*. The important point, however, is that these attempts are not likely to be successful in a democracy unless there is a much broader basis of support for those engaging in the use of violence. That is why in our model of democratic breakdown we put so much emphasis on the semiloyalty of parties, institutions, or groups, rather than limiting our attention to the antisystem forces. It is painful to remember, but it must be stressed, that strong centrist and center-right elements in civil and political society supported the advent of the bureaucratic-authoritarian regimes in Brazil, Chile, Uruguay, and Argentina.

The possibility of changing governments and leaders without a legitimacy crisis is thus one of the greatest advantages of democracy over most forms of authoritarian rule. That possibility depends fundamentally on the trust of the people in democratic institutions, in the guarantees for political freedoms, in the fairness of electoral process, and in the conviction that those in power will give it up, according to the rules, to others who can be expected to do the same in the future. Both incumbents and the opposition can undermine that trust by their actions and by equivocal statements about their intentions.

In practice the possibility of distinguishing particular governments from the regime becomes more difficult when one party becomes hegemonic, especially if that party creates social conditions that make free competition for the support of the people very difficult. The distinction between the state and society should not be obliterated in a democracy.

The distinction between a government and those exercising temporary authority on the one hand, and the regime on the other hand, is facilitated in parliamentary systems. A vote of no confidence, a break-up of a coalition, or internal conflicts within the governing party can easily lead to a change in government or leaders, and sometimes to a timely dissolution. In a deep crisis, rapidly called elections can give the opposition the chance to govern without a crisis of institutions. This is certainly much more difficult in presidential democracies, where the removal of an incumbent easily becomes a constitutional crisis. Impeachment of a president is a much more traumatic process than the fall of a parliamentary government.[20] The fixed term of office is likely to be more frustrating for the opposition in a presidential system than in a parliamentary system. This potential for greater frustration becomes especially strong if many of the circumstances that made the election of the incumbent possible and his exercise of authority acceptable have changed sharply. In such instances we believe that it is structurally predictable that the opposition in a presidential system is more prone to turn to nondemocratic methods to remove the incumbent from office in order to facilitate a policy realignment than it would be in a parliamentary system. Obviously, parliamentarism has been accused of the opposite danger: the constant overthrowing of governments and discontinuity in government action. Modern constitutionalism, however, has found ways of reducing that danger. It could be argued that the principle of barring reelection so sacred in the political tradition of Latin America and so often violated in practice offers a similar guarantee. We feel, however, that it also has the disadvantage of barring from the continuing exercise of power a leader who might have shown considerable leadership qualities, something that would not be problematic in a parliamentary system, where the same leaders continuously or discontinuously occupy the position of premier.

It might not be an accident that with the exception of the United States, a country that is in so many ways exceptional, almost all stable democracies in the world have been parliamentary democracies. Presidential constitutions have in most of the world not assured stable democracy, and they have easily been converted into authoritarian rule. In fact, the only historically stable purely presidential system in the world exists in the United States. Unfortunately, the presidential example of the United States has always had a great attraction for Latin Americans, although in many respects their polities and social structures have had more similarities with Europe. The success of American presidentialism is based on many institutional and social factors whose combination is not found in one Latin American country: the federal and decentralized government that allows the opposition an important share in power, the separation of powers, the powerful role of the Supreme Court, the sacredness attributed to the Constitution, and the absence of disciplined and ideological parties.[21] Latin Americans, who for so many problems look to Europe and who so often reject the American model, might look at European political institutions, especially the classic parliamentary formula or, under exceptional circumstances, a semipresidential formula such as the French Fifth Republic, as alternatives.[22] The Constituent Assembly that was convened in Brazil in 1987, an analogous body that could be convened in Chile after the fall of the dictatorship, and the debate on constitutional reform along French parliamentarian lines presently underway in Argentina could all provide opportunities to explore the comparative advantages of parliamentarianism over presidentialism.[23]

If practitioners and scholars take up this question in greater detail we think it will be particularly useful to attempt to assess how the presidential and parliamentary systems both manage stress. What is the comparative flexibility of these systems to craft solutions to respond to new situations? Unfortunately, we know of no systematic research into comparative political processes under parliamentary and presidential systems.[24]

We think a full-scale research effort could profitably employ four different approaches. The first would be rational choice theory. The second would be comparative historical studies of the political process under a specified number of parliamentary systems and presidential systems. The third approach would be counterfactual analysis of the historical cases presented above in which it would be assumed that the presidential system had been parliamentary and vice versa. The fourth approach would entail extensive use of computer simulations of domestic crisis resolution in parliamentary and presidential systems.

Notes

1. See for example the many studies of democratic breakdown and survival in Juan J. Linz and Alfred Stepan, eds., *The Breakdown of Democratic Regimes* (Baltimore and London: The Johns Hopkins University Press, 1978).

2. For a global review, see Samuel P. Huntington, "Will More Countries Become Democratic?" *Political Science Quarterly* 99 (Summer 1984): 193–218.

3. Banco de Bilbao, Economic Research Department, *Situación: Review of the Spanish Economy,* International Edition, No. 10–11, 1986.

4. Figures are derived from *United Nations Statistical Yearbook,* 1976, 1982, and *Economist* Intelligence Unit, *Quarterly Reports: Spain,* (2nd Quarter 1986).

5. See Francisco Andrés Orizo, *España, Entre la Apatía y el Cambio Social* (Madrid: Editorial Mapfre, 1983). For a general discussion of the relationship between the legitimacy accorded to economic systems and to political systems in contemporary Western Europe, see Juan J. Linz, "Legitimacy of Democracy and the Socioeconomic System," in *Comparing Pluralist Democracies: Strains on Legitimacy,* ed. Mattei Dogan (Boulder and London: Westview Press, 1988), pp. 65–113. The data on comparative support for revolution and reform is found on p. 98.

6. Ekkart Zimmermann, "Economic and Political Reactions to World Economic Crises of the 1930s in Six European Countries," paper prepared for the Midwest Political Science Association Convention, Chicago, 10–12 April 1986, p. 51. Other related studies of Zimmerman on this theme are his "The 1930s World Economic Crisis in Six European Countries: A First Report on Causes of Political Instability and Reactions to Crisis" in Paul M. Johnson and W. R. Thompson, eds., *Rhythms in Politics and Economics* (New York: Praeger, 1985), pp. 84–127, and "Government Stability in Six European Countries during the World Economic Crisis of the 1930s: Some Preliminary Considerations," *European Journal of Political Research* 15, no. 1 (1987): 23–52. Also see P. A. Gourevitch, "Breaking With Orthodoxy: The Politics of Economic Policy Responses to the Depression of the 1930s," *International Organization* 38 (1984): 95–129 and M. Weir and T. Skocpol, "State Structures and Social Keynesianism: Responses to the Great Depression in Sweden and the United States," *International Journal of Comparative Sociology* 24 (1983): 4–29.

7. Ekkart Zimmermann, "The World Economic Crisis of the Thirties in Six European

Countries: Causes of Political Instability and Reaction to Crisis; A First Report," paper prepared for European Consortium for Political Research, Salzburg, Austria, 13–18 April 1984, p. 43.

8. It should be remembered that Germany and Austria were exceptions among the advanced capitalist democracies. The "Great Depression led to political breakdown and fascism" thesis needs to be strongly qualified when the actual historical record is examined. Unemployment in Norway, Denmark, and the Netherlands in the early thirties was higher than in Germany, but in all three countries democratic governments became more stable and broad-based in the 1930s. In the West European country where unemployment was the worst, the Netherlands, fascist parties were never able to gain more than 7.9 percent of the vote. Also, some important cases of breakdown in the less advanced capitalist countries of Europe, such as the rise of fascism in Italy in 1922, the emergence of the Primo de Rivera dictatorship in Spain in 1923, and the Polish, Portuguese, and Lithuanian crises of 1926, all preceded the Great Depression.

9. See Adam Przeworski, "Some Problems in the Study of the Transition to Democracy," in *Transitions from Authoritarian Rule: Comparative Perspectives,* ed. Guillermo O'Donnell, Philippe C. Schmitter, and Laurence Whitehead (Baltimore and London: The Johns Hopkins University Press, 1986), esp. pp. 58–61.

10. The government commission that investigated human rights abuses during the military regime estimated in its report, *Nunca Más,* that over 55 percent of all disappeared persons fell into occupational categories such as white-collar employees, professionals, academics, journalists, and students. See *Nunca Más: Informe de la Comisión Nacional Sobre la Desaparición de Personas,* 10th ed. (Buenos Aires: Editorial Universitaria de Buenos Aires, 1985) pp. 293–99. English translation: *Nunca Más: Report of the Argentine Commission on the Disappeared* (New York: Farrar, Straus and Giroux, 1986). See also Arquidiocese de São Paulo, Brasil, *Nunca Mais,* preface by D. Paulo Evaristo Cardenal Arns (Petrópolis: Editora Vozes, 1985).

11. In our previous studies we have arrived at a number of conclusions that we will simply assert here. State toleration of or ambivalence about paramilitary violence, such as occurred in Weimar Germany or Argentina in the mid-1970s, erodes democratic authority. The responsibility for guaranteeing the peacefulness of the political process is the task of the state, not of uniformed political parties. The police, not the army, is the preferred instrument for the control of domestic violence; the police should have a political not a military chain of command. The temptation for progressive democratic governments to alleviate their anxieties about military loyalty in the face of democratic reforms by encouraging the arming of the government's civilian supporters militarizes the polity and normally destabilizes the chief executive. Democratic governments should consult the military about key decisions concerning law and order, but it is normally a mistake to attempt to generate the military's support by seeking their permission or having them authoritatively share in the decision-making process. It is a mistake because the military often divides over the issues involved and feels co-responsible for the policy. Professional compliance and correct policy distance from inherently controversial tasks becomes difficult.

12. See Ricardo García Damborenea, *La Encruicijada Vasca* (Barcelona: Editorial Argos Vergara, 1984), p. 52.

13. For a more detailed analysis of how the new Spanish democracy handled Basque violence, see Robert P. Clark, *The Basque Insurgents: ETA, 1952–1980* (Madison: The University of Wisconsin Press, 1984) esp. pp. 126–39. Also see Christopher Hewitt, *The Effectiveness of Anti-Terrorist Policies* (New York and London: University Press of

America, 1984), and Damborenea, *La Encruicijada Vasca*. For an extensive discussion of the Basque question, see Juan Linz, *Conflicto en Euskadi* (Madrid: Espasa Calpe, 1986).

14. For a very incisive analysis of how avoiding political deaths and the strong political control of the state coercive apparatus were crucial to the weathering of a political crisis in France during 1968, see Mattei Dogan, "How Civil War was Avoided in France," *International Political Science Review* 5, 3 (1984): 245–77.

15. See Linz, *Conflicto en Euskadi*, p. 615.

16. An important paper discussing this point is Leonardo Morlino, "Crisis Without Breakdown: Italy as a Crucial Case," paper prepared for the International Political Science Association Congress, Rio de Janeiro, 7–11 August 1982.

17. The best study of the question of violence and the deliberate effort to delegitimize the new Austrian democracy is Gerhart Botz, *Krisenzonen einer Demokratie: Gewalt, Streik und Konfliktunterdrückung in Österreich seit 1918* (Frankfurt: Campus Verlag, 1987). See also Gerhart Botz, *Gewalt in der Politik* (München: Wilhem Fink Verlag, 1983).

18. For a discussion of the revalorization of democracy and the delegitimization of violence by a leading theorist of the left, see Francisco Weffort, "Why Democracy?", in *Democratizing Brazil: Problems of Transition and Consolidation*, ed. Alfred Stepan (New York and London: Oxford University Press, 1989), pp. 327–50. Extensive references to the Uruguayan, Argentine, and Brazilian cases are found in Guillermo O'Donnell, Philippe C. Schmitter, and Laurence Whitehead, eds., *Transitions from Authoritarian Rule: Prospects for Democracy*, 4 vols. (Baltimore and London: The Johns Hopkins University Press, 1986).

19. The following section draws heavily upon analysis and documentation contained in Alfred Stepan, *Rethinking Military Politics: Brazil and the Southern Cone* (Princeton: Princeton University Press, 1988). We thank Princeton University Press for permission to reuse this material.

20. For a discussion of how the political process operates under parliamentary as opposed to presidential systems, see Juan J. Linz, "Democracy: Presidential or Parliamentary; Does it Make a Difference?" Paper prepared for the project "The Role of Political Parties in the Return to Democracy in the Southern Cone," sponsored by the Latin American Program of the Woodrow Wilson International Center for Scholars, the Smithsonian Institution, and the World Peace Foundation, July 1985.

21. The very special conditions that have facilitated presidentialism in the United States are the subject of an important work by Fred W. Riggs, "The Survival of Presidentialism in America: Para-constitutional Practices," *International Political Science Review* 9, 4 (October 1988), pp. 247–78.

22. Post–World War II Europe has experimented with a variety of formulas that build a presidential component into parliamentary rule. Three studies of this experience are Maurice Duverger, *Echec Au Roi* (Paris: Albin Michel, 1978), his "A New Political System Model: Semi-Presidential Government," *European Journal of Political Research* 8 (1980): 165–87, and Stefano Bartolini, "Sistema Partitico ed Elezzione Diretta del Capo dello Stato in Europa," *Revista Italiana di Scienza Politica* 14, 2, (Agosto 1984): 223–44. However, the actual functioning of this institution has not been well studied, except for the important book by Werner Kaltefleiter, *Die Funktionen des Staatsoberhauptes in der parlamentarischen Demokratie* (Köln: Westdeutscher Verlag, 1970).

23. For an extensive discussion of a parliamentary proposal for Chile, see Arturo Valenzuela, "Origins and Characteristics of the Chilean Party System: A Proposal for a Parliamentary Form of Government," paper prepared for the project "The Role of

Political Parties in the Return to Democracy in the Southern Cone," sponsored by the Latin America Program of the Woodrow Wilson International Center for Scholars, the Smithsonian Institution, and the World Peace Foundation, May 1985, Working Papers, 164. In Brazil, Bolivar Lamounier, who has participated in a preparatory commission for the Constituent Assembly, has extensively discussed parliamentary formulas. In Argentina, President Raúl Alfonsín's proposal for territorial and administrative reform suggests combining "elements of our traditional presidential regime with elements of parliamentary systems." See "Argentina: Next, Government by Prime Minister," *Latin American Weekly Report,* 25 April 1986.

24. This is not the appropriate place for a full discussion of semipresidentialism but we would like to register a strong caveat. Among politicians and theorists in Latin America who discuss parliamentarianism, there is frequently an almost automatic preference for semipresidential varieties as opposed to classical parliamentarianism. We do not share this preference. Semipresidentialism works best if a majoritarian party or coalition controls both the presidency and the parliament. Failing this, the tasks of governing in a semipresidential system require higher levels of political skill and greater willingness to compromise than are required in a classic parliamentary system. Semipresidentialism, to a degree impossible in classic parliamentarianism, can produce two democratically legitimated centers of power, a "dual executive" that leaves an ambiguity about who controls the military. The consequences of a "dual executive" in the Weimar Republic during the second presidency of Hindenburg were extremely unfortunate. For an analysis of the exceptional conditions under which a semipresidential system can work well and the unique historical conditions under which it was introduced, see the book by Kaltefleiter.

5

Transitions to Democracy: Some Navigation Instruments

GUILLERMO O'DONNELL

This chapter looks at the processes that begin with the breakdown of authoritarian rule and lead, hopefully, to the inauguration of political democracy. The first part of the assignment is difficult because the subject is so complex. The second part—the one that deals with practical criteria aimed at achieving democracy—is not the kind of work that has built (except perhaps negatively) the reputation of university professors.[1]

Transitions (and Transitions)

Both before and after nonrevolutionary transitions from authoritarian rule, the countries involved have been capitalist and the armed forces have had overwhelming superiority in the control of the means of coercion over territory. Revolutionary transitions, those in which one or both of those conditions do not hold, raise important issues but these are not the theme of this chapter (nor are they a likely event in South America).

Transitions do not have inevitable outcomes. After some liberalizing steps, an authoritarian regime may decide to close all the emerging arenas of participation and contest. In another possibility, an authoritarian regime may end, only to be succeeded by another often more repressive authoritarian regime. Finally, as in Argentina from 1973 to 1976, an authoritarian regime may end and a democracy emerge but the very conditions under which the transition occurred as well as the predominance of authoritarian actors of various ideological colors may have already heavily weighted the dice in favor of another, harsher authoritarian regression.

The last possibility mentioned will be discussed in Laurence Whitehead's chapter in this volume so it will not be discussed here, but the other scenarios highlight one of the distinguishing features of these transitions: they are extremely uncertain. They entail navigating in poorly mapped seas that are full of dangerous reefs. Skillful use of some navigational instruments surely helps, but it does not guarantee a safe end to the journey.

The sources of uncertainty are many and they often reinforce each other, but let us first draw the main features of the overall scene. A first important feature pertains to the types of transitions. The most important distinction is between transitions that occur by collapse and transitions that occur by transaction.[2] In the former case, a series of crises and failures of the authoritarian regime does not lead to a venting of the situation through liberalization. Instead, pressure accumulates until the rather sudden emergence of massive and active opposition or defeat in an external war (the surest mechanism for collapse, as illustrated by the misadventures of the colonial Portuguese army, the Cyprus fiasco of the colonels' regime in Greece, and the Malvinas/Falklands war), leads the armed forces to a hasty retreat to the barracks. It also leads some social sectors that had earlier supported the authoritarian regime (typically, entrepreneurs and various middle-class sectors) to initiate a no-less-hasty search for political solutions that will prevent a (more or less realistically feared) revolutionary transformation. Transitions by collapse are short. The authoritarian incumbents have comparatively little control over who will become the main actors in this process and over who will govern in the near future. Authoritarian incumbents desperately try to reach agreement with (or impose upon) the opposition some "pact of guarantees" that basically consists of a commitment by the future democratic government not to investigate the uglier features of the authoritarian past, but despite extensive negotiations with the opposition, the transitional rulers often wind up having to hand over government without any such pact.

Transitions by transaction occur when a decisive set of incumbents of the authoritarian regime decides to open or "depressurize" the situation. This is not a hasty retreat. Even if some crises and policy failures have pushed them to initiate depressurization, these incumbents and their political and social allies are very much in control of the situation. They feel they can dictate the rules of the game to the opposition, that they can perpetuate themselves as an elected, more or less democratic, government (or at least that the eventual winners of the future elections will be the more friendly sectors of the opposition), that the bargain they will force the latter to accept will guarantee that the armed forces will play a powerful institutionalized role in the future regime, and that the interests of their social allies will be generously considered.

Transitions by transaction are typical of authoritarian regimes that consider themselves (and have been at least for some time considered by important parts of the population) successful in achieving economic growth and "enhancing the international status of the country." Spain and Brazil are the paramount examples, but less successful authoritarian regimes such as the ones in Uruguay and Turkey have also managed to channel a transition through this path. Typically, these are pact-transitions. More precisely, a series of agreements is made and renegotiated between the authoritarian incumbents and the opposition during what is usually a significantly longer process than occurs in the case of transitions by collapse. Initially, the incumbents envisage as the end point of the process some sort of liberalization that would stop short of submitting the top governmental positions to competitive elections (what Schmitter and I have called a *dictablanda* in *Transitions to Democracy*) or, at most, that general elections being held would be subject to strong restrictions concerning who is allowed to compete electorally and who is allowed to organize politically in the society *(democradura)*. But in most cases the dynamics of the transition—the changing relation of forces between authoritarian incumbents and the opposition—lead as in the cases of Brazil and Uruguay, although by more convoluted paths than those of transitions by collapse, to regimes that also meet the criteria of political democracy (or polyarchy, according to Robert Dahl's influential concept).[3] But even though what is finally incorporated into the pact at the end of the transition often goes beyond the *dictablanda* or *democradura* that the authoritarian incumbents hoped for when they launched the process, these democracies are born with a series of embedded guarantees of an extensive presence of the armed forces in the new institutional system. Another crucial guarantee is that the democratic government will not investigate the darker sides of the authoritarian past.

As a consequence, democratic governments resulting from a transition by collapse have fewer constraints on the policies they can undertake than those that result from a transacted transition. The other side of the coin is that transitions by collapse tend to be more seriously threatened in their survival by powerful, disaffected actors who, in contrast with the transacted cases, have not had some of their crucial interests adequately accommodated in the new situation.

Main Actors in the Transition

Close to the beginning of the transition, there are at least two main groups within the authoritarian regime. The hardliners *(duros)* believe that the perpetuation of authoritarian rule is possible and desirable, if not by rejecting outright all democratic forms, then by erecting some façade (à la Pinochet) behind which they can maintain the hierarchical and authoritarian nature of their rule. These hardliners are usually composed of several factions. Some adopt this position out of an opportunistic calculus; they are indifferent to longer-term political projects, but they are preoccupied with their own survival in office and with retaining their share of the spoils. But the main core of the hardliners is formed by ideologues who reject viscerally the "disorders" of democracy.

The other main actors in the authoritarian regime are the softliners. They may be indistinguishable from the *duros* in the first, reactive phase of the regime, when they may be equally disposed to use severe repression.[4] But they become increasingly aware that the regime they helped to implant and in which they have usually occupied important positions will in the foreseeable future have to make use of some form of electoral mechanism. They also recognize that if such a mechanism is going to generate some legitimacy for their rule, the regime cannot wait too long before reintroducing certain freedoms, at least to an extent that will be acceptable to moderate segments of the opposition and to international opinion.

The opposition is also composed of several sectors. There is an opportunistic opposition (or pseudo-opposition) ready to accept any offer made by the softliners. This sector is actually an obstacle to democratization because if it manages to win supremacy within the opposition camp, the transition will tend to stop at a few liberalizing measures—well short of political democracy. There is also a maximalist opposition that abhors negotiating with any incumbents of the regime, which attacks as traitors those who are willing to enter into some understanding with the softliners, and which condemns the transition as just a wise trick performed by the authoritarian rulers to perpetuate their rule. Often the maximalists also advocate a revolutionary route aimed at ending both capitalism and the existing armed forces; anything less than that is just "consolidating the system" under the trappings of "formal democracy." As already noted, opportunists play too passively into the hands of the softliners of the regime. In their turn, hardliners of the regime and maximalists of the opposition in fact support each other: the latter validate the fears of the former about the dangers entailed by even limited liberalization measures and help them in their efforts to convince the undecided sectors in the regime, including the armed forces and its supporters. On the other hand, the maximalists see the repressive policies advocated by the hardliners as a demonstration of the impossibility and the inappropriateness of attempting to navigate the uncertain waters of the transition. These two actors are in effect allies in promoting a polarization that threatens to eliminate the softliners from important positions in the authoritarian regime and to liquidate politically the only actor that can bring about a successful transition: the democratic opposition.

The democratic opposition is a genuine, valid opposition. Its goal is not only the end of the authoritarian regime or the achievement of some liberalization, but the installation of political democracy. It is composed of sectors more or less committed to advances in social and economic equity, but all view the achievement of political democracy as the most crucial goal. This goal differentiates this opposition from the softliners and from the opportunists, since both would stop the transition before actual political democracy has been achieved. Although it often contains parties of the left (some of them proclaiming very radical goals), this is nevertheless a moderate opposition: it is aware that democracy is unlikely (or if it comes about, will be too fragile) if solid guarantees are not given that a relatively free economy will govern and that the vertical structure of command and the domestic monopoly on force of the armed forces will be maintained in the future. Some in the democratic opposition may not be particularly happy with these outcomes, but this group is aware that without such guarantees the achievement of democracy is unlikely. As a result, it is willing to accept them. This opens another area of conflict for the democratic opposition: conflict with the maximalists, who angrily reject such guarantees and may even conclude that the democratic opposition is their principal "enemy."

Notice that the categories used here are analytical, not concrete or institutional; for example, one cannot assume that the armed forces are always, homogeneously hardliners. The uncertainties of the transition lead to some flexibility in the positions taken by numerous actors: some nondogmatic hardliners may come to accept, however grudgingly, the softliners' positions; some parties may abandon their maximalist stance; some opportunists, whether by calculus or because they are impressed by exemplary attitudes of leaders of the democratic opposition, may move into the latter's camp. The purpose of the categories chosen here is to allow one to map such changes and through them to map the various processes of the transition.

These actors are the main domestic political forces involved in the transition; however, there are some junctures when democratically oriented international influences seem to be particularly important:[5] (1) before and during the transition, international forces can impinge on the process by raising the perceived costs of maintaining a closed and repressive authoritarian regime. This strengthens the softliners and encourages undecided members of the ruling coalition to join them; (2) before and during the transition, such forces can help the democratic opposition create "feasible political spaces," both by symbolic (but crucial) signals of support to the transition and by raising the perceived costs to the regime of suppressing that opposition; and (3) during the transition, they can help by mobilizing contacts for persuading the hardliners (especially diehard military and business elements) that if the coup they might try during the transition were to succeed, serious sanctions would be forthcoming from a hostile international environment. Given the influence of the United States in the region, there is no doubt that consistent and clear action by the U.S. government in this period is of particular importance;[6] but other governments as well as the international press and various kinds of private organizations are crucial as well. None of these actions seem to be a sufficient condition either for launching the transition or for guaranteeing its successful completion, but in some cases they may be necessary conditions for achieving those goals, and in all instances they help significantly.

One additional domestic element should be mentioned. It is a process that is multifaceted, often explosive, and always profoundly unsettling to the authoritarian rulers, both *duros* and *blandos*. It is "the resurrection of civil society."[7] At some point, what used to be a silent, depoliticized society, ridden by fears of governmental repression and a return to the convulsive periods that have usually preceded the inauguration of these authoritarian regimes, begins to show unmistakable signs of massive opposition. The heroic, exemplary actions of human rights organizations and of some churches, though they have been present for some time, are of little political significance until the first signals of opposition are made by other actors. The first of these signals usually comes, obliquely but eloquently, from journalists, from other intellectuals, and from some leaders in the popular arts. Signals also come, often at very high cost, from isolated worker protests. They come, too—and very importantly, because this deeply corrodes the internal cohesion of the regime—from business leaders and groups who initially supported the authoritarian regime, but who now reject its most repressive features or find it unresponsive or unpredictable regarding their policy demands. Other crucial components are the various middle-class associations. They have authority when speaking to society at large and like business organizations they are very costly to repress. *Colegios* of lawyers, journalists, natural and social scientists and the like begin to criticize the regime in terms of the matters in which they can claim special expertise. At some moment—when liberalization begins or when the divisions within the authoritarian regime attenuate its repressive capacities—these voices converge with the first massive strikes and street demonstrations and with demonstrations at the local level of popular social movements. Long-repressed political and economic demands are voiced by a reactivated, increasingly bold society.

Old opponents, many previously depoliticized groups and persons, and not a few of the original supporters of the authoritarian regime converge around two basic themes in a broad, multiclass movement. The first theme involves no less than the unalterable demand for democracy. This call represents the most basic, widely shared negation of the authoritarian period and, to many, the somewhat mythical hope that once democracy is implanted, practically all of the nation's problems will be solved at once. This is a useful myth because it further motivates what soon becomes an intense and widespread oppositional mobilization of society. Yet later, when democracy is achieved and the realities and the intractability of many of those problems becomes evident, these mythical hopes about democracy often give way to widespread *desencanto* (disenchantment) and political apathy that weakens those new and still fragile democracies.

The second theme is intensely ethical. It is the demand for an end to arbitrary decision making and abuse of power, and for the application of harsh justice to those who have committed these abuses. The intense moral rejection of the authoritarian past transforms itself into exceptional courage and dedication. Later, however, when pacts adopted during transacted transitions make it impossible to apply such justice (or when, as in Argentina, trials take place, but not all those responsible could possibly be judged if democracy were to survive), the more intransigent of the militants bitterly add to the dangerous pool of *desencanto*.

The importance of civil society's resurrection cannot be exaggerated. This mobilization and the intense demands it places upon all political actors greatly strengthen the position of the democratic opposition. It forces softliners constantly to renegotiate whatever agreements they may have forced upon the democratic opposition, and it cautions opportunists against making premature agreements with the softliners. Mobilization greatly increases both the fears of the hardliners and their commitment to a coup that would abort the transition. At the same time, however, the anticipated costs of such a coup increase dramatically, and the perceived likelihood that the coup would succeed in its regressive goal decreases correspondingly. This perception often has a crucial impact within the armed forces, the public bureaucracy, and the social sectors that support the authoritarian regime and were undecided (between supporting the hardliners or the softliners) during the first stages of the transition. Their support is indispensable for a successful coup, and because they perceive higher costs and less potential for success, they tend to continue to be undecided. This is sufficient for the transition process to continue advancing.

Playing the Transition Game

The preceding section takes us back to the theme of uncertainty. The main factor of uncertainty is obvious: during the transition, as the democratic opposition becomes more assertive and civil society unfolds, the reasons that both induce and deter a regressive coup grow together. One of the archetypal dramas of these transitions is the possibility of a coup—a coup that all actors (except, of course, the hardliners and often the maximalists) have as their paramount goal to avoid, which in certain dramatic circumstances seems imminent . . . and which does not happen. Bolivia has been the only exception to this rule. In all the other cases, acute and recurrent concern about a coup existed. This anxiety helps explain what is otherwise the surprising moderation of the democratic opposition in successful transitions. Despite increasingly angry (often violent) protests from the hardliners, the perceived high costs of a coup and shrewd maneuvering by the democratic opposition and the softliners tend to lead the transition to a successful conclusion—one that goes far beyond what the softliners initially intended.

These interesting and from a democratic point of view positive paradoxes merit further exploration. At the beginning of the transition, it is the softliners who play the coup card in this complex game. If the opposition does not "behave reasonably" (i.e., if it does not accept the limited liberalization or the *democradura* that by then the softliners typically envisage), the softliners argue that they will have to conclude that "the conditions are not ripe" and they "will be forced" to regress to a fully closed authoritarian situation. The other ace that the softliners hold is the argument that even if they should agree to make "further concessions" to the democratic opposition, the hardliners would be so enraged that they would ensure that such a regression occurs. This is a powerful bargaining card, because it is plausible and the costs of a mistaken assessment would be terribly high for the opposition.

This is the main reason why the opportunistic opposition tries immediately to draw the opposition camp into a final agreement with the softliners. It also produces serious doubts and vacillation in the democratic opposition and seems to confirm the worst fears of the maximalists concerning what the transition is really about. On the other hand, the resurrection of civil society pushes political actors toward no less than political democracy proper. In situations when crucial information is scarce and unreliable (in this context, especially in relation to who and under what circumstances and which alliances would really join a coup), and consequently reasonably safe predictions about the impacts of many decisions are practically impossible, the nerve, clearmindedness, and commitment to democracy of the opposition's leadership is put to a most stringent test.

The dangerous path those leaders must traverse allows us to understand the nonlinear rhythm of these transitions. Partial authoritarian regressions, periods during which the democratic opposition must accept the fact that the softliners monopolize the initiative, and agreements with the latter that are renegotiated in the next round of the game punctuate the uncertain routes by means of which these countries may arrive at democracy.

That the emergence of democracy may occur at all is greatly helped when the democratic opposition and the softliners discover that the trump card of the latter's own regressive coup is a bluff (*autogolpe,* in the rich jargon that, like eskimos for naming varieties of ice, Latin Americans have developed for varieties of coups). The launching and even more the numerous unexpected events of the transition enrage the hardliners. They rapidly come to see the softliners as leading the process—and with it most of their cherished achievements—to a suicidal ending: chaos, disorder, "loss of authority," "subversion," and eventually revolution. This is why the risk of a coup is very real. But the coup, if it occurs, will not be the *autogolpe* of the softliners; it will be one executed by the hardliners, and among the surest victims will be not only the opposition but also the softliners. When this crucial fact is recognized, the softliners become the most effective allies of the nonmaximalist opposition in the very specific, but all-important, goal of preventing any coup. As long as a coup does not occur, the softliners retain their positions in government. Yet they lose the leverage with which they had hoped to force the opposition to give up any further extension of the transition beyond the point preferred by the softliners. Great caution is still required, because the "other coup," the real one—led by the hardliners—is a serious possibility. But now the nonmaximalist opposition knows that it shares a crucial interest with the softliners, and the latter for this very reason are deeply weakened in their bargaining position vis-à-vis the democratic opposition. This is the subtle channel through which the democratizing demands of a resurrected society as well as the goals of the democratic opposition powerfully filter into the often apparently byzantine political process of the transition.

Elections

If the softliners remain in decisive political and military positions in government, it is likely that national elections will be announced for a specific date. If it becomes credible that voters will be free to choose, i.e., that parties will be free to compete by putting forth candidates and that incumbents will not be free to count votes or eliminate candidates as they see fit—in short, if the outcome of the election appears reasonably uncertain,[8] then relations between contending actors, inside and outside the regime, change rapidly. The main reason for this change is that the prospect of elections brings parties and the main currency they deal with—votes—to center stage.

In the earliest stages of the transition—including the palace negotiations and conflicts between hardliners and softliners, and the resurrection of civil society—the role of organized parties is relatively small. This resurrection is usually led by social movements, unions, professional associations, churches, human rights associations, intellectuals, and artists. Parties are often in too great a state of disarray, too divided, or too busy choosing their own leadership to accomplish such a task. Indeed one of the goals of the softliners in convoking elections may well be to get off their backs that multitude of disparate and remonstrative groups, diverting most of that energy into more orderly, party channels. The softliners typically hope that their magnanimous gesture of convoking reasonably free elections will be so appreciated by the population that the electoral chances of their preferred party or candidate will be greatly enhanced. However, transitional incumbents have consistently (sometimes grossly) overestimated their electoral support. This is a welcome exercise in self-deception by those incumbents, similar to that of the many who believe that the future democracy will magically solve all the problems of the country. This self-deception reinforces their commitment to hold elections and to defeat the hardliners' attempts to stage a coup.

Parties are the main modern institution for structuring and aggregating preferences along territorial, noncorporatist lines. They generate symbols of political identity that bridge many of the gaps that otherwise divide major sectors of society: class, status, family, gender, religion, region, ethnicity, language. The sheer logic of putting together symbols capable of attracting sufficient votes and crossing the numerical threshold for gaining representation tends to deemphasize the various idiosyncrasies that emerge during the anti-authoritarian mobilization of society.

Furthermore, convoking elections generates another peculiar convergence. Regime opponents—especially if they believe they will perform satisfactorily in the elections—now have further incentive to cooperate with the softliners to guarantee that the elections will not be aborted by a coup. This cooperation frequently involves demobilizing radical or militant groups who provide opposition parties with efficient support, but whose actions—particularly those involving violence and "excessive" activism in streets and workplaces—might discredit them in the eyes of more moderate voters or jeopardize the holding of elections at all. Thus, in this period, electorally viable parties act not so much as agents of mobilization but as agents of social and political control of their own constituencies.

Finally, the prospect of elections shifts attention to a new issue: the definition of the rules under which the contest will take place. The complicated problems this issue generates are too obvious and lengthy to be elaborated here; the point is that parties have a crucial interest in influencing such rules, and that this interest further pushes them into converging with the softliners in detailed negotiations. The price the parties pay for this achievement often involves compromises or explicit pacts with the softliners. The basis of opposition tends to shift from expressions of principle to the discussion of rules.

The first indications of *desencanto* appear at this moment. The maximalists find that their worst fears have been confirmed, and the hardliners reach a similar conclusion. Yet the moderation and "responsibility" that most parties of the democratic opposition are showing as well as the obvious intense desire of the population that elections be held (shown, among other indicators, by the unusually high voter participation in this "founding election"), deprives the hardliners of the allies needed for a successful coup.

A Brief Recapitulation

This is a sketch of some of the main topics in the transition and only implicitly alludes to some of the practical corollaries of those topics. Among those corollaries, the following are central:

(1) If the softliners in the regime have not gained decisive control over the top political positions in government and over the armed forces' high command, then transitions are extremely unlikely to begin, and if begun, they are extremely unlikely to continue after some very limited and reversible liberalizing steps.

(2) If the democratic opposition does not gain the upper hand in the opposition's camp, then transitions are unlikely to continue, and if continued, they are unlikely to arrive at political democracy; or, if democracy is achieved, the emergent regime is likely to be too weak and too threatened by powerful hostile forces to endure.

(3) Putting the preceding proposition in a more specific form with regard to the maximalist opposition, the negative consequences of (2) are likely to occur even if the maximalists do not win the upper hand in the opposition camp. Even when they do not, if there is an intense and active maximalist opposition, especially if it is ready to use violence, then the same consequences are likely to occur unless the democratic opposition sharply and unequivocally differentiates itself from the maximalists and from violence. This decision often entails agonizing doubts and high short-term political costs for the democratic opposition, because both they and the maximalists have been victimized by the authoritarian regime and their militants often work together in many social organizations and movements. Yet if the democratic opposition remains ambiguous on this issue, the hardliners' position is likely to be decisively reinforced.

(4) The softliners and the democratic opposition may sharply disagree on many issues (beginning with no less a matter than their views about the authoritarian regime), but they share decisive interests: that the transition be launched, and that it not be interrupted by a coup. Mutual awareness of these decisive converging interests is enhanced by the very unfolding of the transition, especially by the at times high costs both have to pay for preventing the coup.

(5) The softliners and the democratic opposition usually disagree, however, on the preferred endpoint of the transition. By definition, the latter aim at political democracy; the former usually would like to stop the process at some kind of *democradura* or even *dictablanda*. But the mobilization of society strongly pushes toward a more fully democratic outcome. Thus at least during the initial stages of the transition—until it has advanced to the point when competitive elections for decisive governmental positions are announced— mobilization is strongly in the interest of the democratic opposition.

(6) The mobilization of society strengthens the hardliners' motivation for inciting a coup. But at the same time, especially for the undecided actors who must be persuaded to support a successful coup, such mobilization also raises the perceived uncertainties and costs of an attempted coup. Thus provided that the mobilization of society does not involve increasing violence or does not explicitly aim at destroying the capitalist organization of society (in which case propositions (2) and (3) would hold), the danger of a coup should not deter the democratic opposition from effecting and supporting such mobilization. On the other hand, when the announcement of elections begins to channel the main processes of the transition toward parties as the main interlocutors of the government, the mobilization of society tends to decrease in scope and intensity. This is regrettable in many ways, but it helps the successful completion of the transition.

(7) Signals of international support for the transition are useful, especially if they are clearly and consistently aimed at raising the perceived costs of a coup. Those signals will not convince the hardliners, but they can be effective in discouraging those who are still undecided, particularly in the armed forces.

(8) If the transition is successful, the outcome will be a new and fragile democracy whose initial workings will disappoint many of those who more effectively and courageously fought for it. The new democracy will be constrained by agreements that had to be made with the softliners and their supporters in society. Alternatively, in the case of transitions by collapse, the new democracies are likely to be threatened by powerful disgruntled actors. Furthermore, in the transitions of the 1980s, these new democracies have been cursed by economic and social difficulties that reflect the impact of the international crisis, and they have been crippled by mismanagement and widespread corruption that typically accompany the last stages of authoritarian rule. But the arrival of democracy is a great achievement that opens the possibility and the challenge of its consolidation and expansion.

This analysis has omitted one important variety of authoritarian regime. It is the kind that is led by a *caudillo*, not by a military *junta*, where the president is a *primus inter pares* in relation to the senior command of the armed forces. The *caudillo*-centered type of rule has a dimension that cuts across various types of authoritarian regimes. It is of contemporary interest in South America because of Chile and Paraguay. That these regimes are the two surviving authoritarian forms suggests the particular difficulties they present for a democratic transition.

The Caudillo-Centered Authoritarian Regimes and the Transition

Caudillos-Führers cannot imagine that their countries could do without their enlightened services. They know much better than anyone else what is to be done. They do not willingly accept constraints on their rule, not even from their senior colleagues in the armed forces or in the party. When they are forced to accept constraints, they do everything within their reach to get rid of them. They are extremely unreliable participants in any pact or agreement. *Caudillos* are profoundly paranoid; they do not want any source of power independent of their whims. In no case has there been a transition initiated by a *caudillo*. The only way out is to depend on the supreme leader's death in bed (Franco and Salazar and, although in a different overall system, Lenin and Stalin) or violent death (Trujillo, Hitler, Mussolini), or on the leader's overthrow (Ongania, Galtieri, Somoza, Batista, Papadoupolos, Duvalier).

The first scenario is not too encouraging and the second one is too unpredictable. In the third scenario involving the regime's overthrow, leaders of the armed forces reach the conclusion that to remain in power (i.e., to preserve their capacity to intervene decisively in matters that they deem important), they will have to remove themselves from direct responsibility for governing. This may trigger a successful *putsch* aimed at transferring office to civilians. The positive side of this scenario is that the more personalistic and concentrated power is in the authoritarian regime, the easier it is for the *putschists* to make the ousted despot and his clique uniquely responsible for the failures and "excesses" of the regime, and the less the armed forces are likely to feel institutionally threatened by the transition.

But the situation becomes more complicated when the armed forces have participated extensively in the errors, abuses, and spoils of the authoritarian regime. In this case no easy corporate retreat is feasible. Furthermore, astute *caudillos* will follow to the limit their compulsion to eliminate all sources of independent power in their regimes. Specifically, they will try to eliminate the softliners. As *caudillo* rule continues and the risks of its perpetuation become more and more apparent, softliners will continue to appear. But because they do not control the most decisive nucleus of power within the regime, they cannot move too far toward liberalization without being removed by the *caudillo*. Furthermore, in *junta*-based regimes, the opposition can reasonably trust that their interlocutors in the regime will continue in the future in their leadership positions in government or the armed forces; in the *caudillo*-centered type of regime no such assumption can be made. Thus, even if the softliners in this case are ready to make significant moves toward the transition, it is doubtful that it makes sense for the opposition to incur the costs of beginning serious bargaining.

As long as the *caudillo* manages to prevent a military *putsch,* even though all other factors push toward the transition, it will be aborted. With the engine running at high speed but the bus firmly braked, the situation plays strongly into the hands of the maximalists, particularly those who advocate—quite persuasively, given the context—armed struggle. This in turn "demonstrates" to the *caudillo* and his clique the need to continue in power and often to increase repression. Concomitantly, the absence of softliners or their precarious hold on positions in the regime further contributes to the undermining of the political space of the democratic opposition. A process of sharp polarization is likely to ensue between the *caudillo* and his clique on one side and a violent maximalist opposition on the other. The *caudillo* is happy to further undermine the softliners, and the maximalists are no less happy to further undermine the democratic opposition. If this process proceeds, war—with its distinctive actors and logic—progressively asphyxiates politics. Change can indeed occur, but the probabilities will not be tilted toward a democratic outcome.

Notes

1. I am grateful to David Collier for his extremely helpful comments on the first draft of this paper. What follows draws extensively on a collective endeavor, generously supported by the Latin American Program of the Woodrow Wilson Center for International Scholars and its former director, Abraham Lowenthal. The result of this endeavor is the collective volume *Transitions to Democracy: Latin American and Southern Europe,* edited by Philippe Schmitter, Laurence Whitehead, and myself (Baltimore: The Johns Hopkins University Press, 1986).

2. These distinctions are elaborated in *Transitions to Democracy.* For further useful analysis of this matter, Scott Mainwaring and Donald Share, "Transitions through Transaction: Democratization in Spain and Brazil," in *Political Liberalization in Brazil: Dynamics, Dilemmas, and Future Prospects,* ed. Wayne Selcher (Boulder: Westview Press, 1986).

3. Robert Dahl, *Polyarchy: Participation and Opposition* (New Haven: Yale University Press, 1971).

4. On the first, reactive phase of bureaucratic-authoritarian regimes, see Manuel Antonio Garreton, "En Torno a la Discusión de los Nuevos Regímenes Autoritarios en América Latina," Woodrow Wilson Center for International Scholars, Latin American Program Working Paper 52 (Washington D.C.: 1979).

5. For a more detailed discussion of the role of international actors, see the chapters by Tom Farer and Robert Pastor in this volume.

6. I have discussed this matter in more detail in "The United States, Latin America, and Democracy: Variations on an Old Theme," in *The United States and Latin America: Contending Perspectives on a Decade of Crisis,* ed. Carlos Rico and Kevin Middlebrook (Pittsburgh: Pittsburgh University Press, 1986).

7. I have analyzed this theme in relation to the recent Argentine transition in "On the Fruitful Convergences of Hirschman's 'Exit, Voice and Loyalty' and 'Shifting Involvements': Reflections from the Recent Argentine Experience," in *Development, Democracy and the Art of Trespassing. Essays in Honor of Albert O. Hirschman,* ed.

Alejandro Foxley, Michael McPherson and Guillermo O'Donnell (Notre Dame: The University of Notre Dame Press, 1986).

8. On uncertain outcomes as a defining characteristic of democracy, see Adam Przeworski, "Some Problems in the Study of the Transition to Democracy," in *Transition to Democracy*.

6

The Consolidation of Fragile Democracies: A Discussion with Illustrations

LAURENCE WHITEHEAD

This chapter discusses the notion of democratic "consolidation" and illustrates what it would imply for five key groups of political actors. The illustrations are drawn mainly, but not exclusively, from the fragile democracies of contemporary Latin America and the actors are identified by reference to the recent history of that region. There are at present few fully consolidated democratic regimes in Latin America, but the past decade has witnessed a strong drive toward democratization almost throughout the subcontinent. By considering the requirements of consolidation it should be possible to identify some critical choices confronting the key actors. If the consolidation process is to stay "on track," there are some apparently "unnatural" alliances that must be negotiated and reinforced. In many countries, the eventual success of current attempts at democratization remains uncertain, leaving the way open to creative (or destructive) choices by specific strategic actors.

A Clarification of Terms

To begin, there must be some clarification of terms and assumptions in order to select and interpret specific cases and to make sense of the decisions taken at critical conjunctures. First, consider the term "democracy." This chapter is concerned with contemporary Latin America, a region notorious for its extremes of social inequality and for its uneven and incomplete provision of citizenship rights. In such a setting democratic forms of government cannot just be taken at face value. For example, the Salvadoran constitution of 1962 was an admirable charter (all persons were entitled to due process of law before they could be deprived of life, liberty or property, and so forth). Until 1979 competitive elections were held under this constitution at regular intervals using a sophisticated system of proportional representation. But to label El Salvador a "democracy" in the 1960s and 1970s would have been a highly partisan act;

and one showing little respect either for democratic values or for the political aspirations of the Salvadoran people. On the other hand, defenders of national sovereignty might consider it partisan and disrespectful to withold the designation of "democracy" until the highest standards of proof had been met. Fortunately, it is not necessary that we identify precise borderline conditions according to which the term might or might not properly be applied (probably a misguided enterprise in any case). Robert Dahl's observations apply with special force to Latin America: "it seems impossible to find terms already in use that do not carry with them a large freight of ambiguity and surplus meaning," and "no large system in the real world is fully democratized," but what we are referring to are "regimes that have been substantially popularized and liberalized, that is, highly inclusive and extensively open to public contestation."[1]

The absence of a clear, objectively determinable definitional boundary does not mean that we can be casual about our use of this label, as has sometimes been the case in foreign policy discussions of democratization. This chapter will propose two litmus tests of sincerity. How does a purportedly democratic regime treat those held in its prisons? Would we describe the regime as sufficiently democratic to qualify as a leading western democracy? Opinions may differ about the precise application of these inherently qualitative criteria, but they differ within a limited range. It would be a grave disservice to the cause of democratic consolidation to misapply the term to regimes that fall short of a well-anchored standard. At best (if the evidence permits) most of the current postauthoritarian regimes of Latin America might be described as aspiring, incipient, or "fragile" democracies.

Wherein lies this fragility? In contemporary Latin America two elements require special emphasis: sectarianism and the lack of regime continuity. One particular form of sectarianism will be emphasized in the second half of this chapter—the tendency to deny or undermine the democratic credentials of political rivals in a context in which few political actors have impeccably pure records. For democratic consolidation to occur, a variety of "potential" democrats must be given the benefit of the doubt. This is no easy matter in countries where democratic regimes have few traditions of durability, such that both the recent past and the foreseeable future evoke vivid images of what price might have to be paid by those who were too trusting. This insecurity and its associated sectarianism tend to be self-fulfilling, and this goes far toward explaining the fragility of most Latin American democracies. Some illustrations will be provided later in this chapter, for example, how a lack of regime continuity may hamper the imposition of constitutional restraints on the military; how "potential" democrats may fall out because of inauthenticity; and how ideological sectarianism may affect the willingness to participate of the radical left.

In any serious political conflict, disagreement is likely to extend to the question of which sectors are to blame for putting a fragile democracy at risk. In practice there will probably be many potential sources of fragility, perhaps making it a partisan act to emphasize one source of danger and to downplay others. True defenders of democracy shall not rely on a priori assumptions about some supposedly inevitable source of danger. *How Democracies Perish* is an example of this fallacy from the right; *The Illusion of Democracy in Dependent Nations* is another from the left.[2]

Consider the assumption that Marxism is the major threat to democracy in contemporary Latin America. This could be a carefully considered judgement made reluctantly and in a nonsectarian spirit, of course. But it is a charge more commonly made with ideological animus; and indeed it may frequently be an axiom adopted unthinkingly, as a consequence of the social group to which one belongs or even as a purely definitional deduction from the concept of democracy one espouses. For example, a military officer may sincerely believe that his institution is the indispensable guarantor of any true democratic order because it is a bulwark against Marxism. This partisan and incomplete concept of democracy would probably receive easy acceptance and reinforcement from his fellow officers. An extension of press freedom and a widening of the boundaries of political participation that brought criticisms of the military to public attention could easily from this viewpoint be regarded as a subversive threat to "democracy."

On the left, Latin America has no shortage of radical groups propagating analogous definitions of democracy, definitions that more or less exempt radicals from any responsibility for antidemocratic provocations while questioning the democratic credentials of their political rivals. Of course, if this sort of ideological blindness was only a practice of the extreme right and the extreme left, democracy in Latin America would not be all that fragile. In practice, there are many supposedly "centrist" political forces in the region who consciously or inadvertently play this kind of game. Neither U.S. embassies nor Christian Democrats nor Social Democrats can be regarded as immune to the temptation of adopting sectarian definitions of what constitutes a true democracy and thus of undermining the democratic credentials of rival centrist or potentially centrist groupings.

The generalized nature of political sectarianism in Latin America is hardly surprising, given the highly fragmented character of most Latin American societies, not to mention the social inequalities, the political insecurities, and the international vulnerabilities to which the region is prone. But if democracies are currently more fragile in Latin America than in southern Europe, the main explanation must be sought in contemporary regional history and geopolitics rather than in any supposedly inherent cultural or psychological attributes.

Besides "democracy" and "transition," the third term requiring clarification is "consolidation." This idea can only be elucidated in contrast to the notion of the "transition" that precedes it. Guillermo O'Donnell's chapter on democratic transitions demonstrates the high degree of uncertainty that characteristically accompanies the transition phase. After any transition from authoritarian rule, the emergent democracy will be a regime in which not all significant political actors have impeccable democratic credentials and where democratic rules of procedure have yet to be "internalized" by the society at large. Many established institutions must be restructured, some demoted, some virtually created anew, to make them conform to democratic rather than authoritarian modes of governance. New and inexperienced political actors enter the stage, while long-established parties and interests find themselves required to compete on a quite different basis than before. The rules of competition are up for negotiation, the outcomes are uncertain and often quite unexpected, no one is quite sure which elements of continuity will remain in place. Improbable coalitions must be formed and tested, and the partners and rivals in the process have little guidance as to their various specific weights. Public opinion may well be in flux, as the media fills with formerly forbidden messages, whilst the old verities are cast into oblivion. In short, the transition phase is often one of acute uncertainty and high anxiety for many social actors. Such uncertainty may be exciting and creative—spurring increased political participation and the invention of new political forms—but if it becomes too generally threatening or if it lasts too long without any fruitful outcome, then the chances of an authoritarian relapse become very great.

If the transition phase is not aborted, it may pave the way for a process of democratic consolidation. The hallmark of this process will be that the many uncertainties of the transition period are progressively diminished as the new assumptions and procedures become better known and understood and more widely accepted. The new regime becomes institutionalized, its framework of open and competitive political expression becomes internalized, and thus in large measure the preceding uncertainties and insecurities are overcome. It is unlikely that such a process can ever by fully accomplished in less than a generation. Thus what should concern us in this analysis is not so much the factors assuring a full consolidation of democracy, but the conditions necessary to keep the process on track.

When a democratization process advances from the end of transition to full consolidation there is a widening of the range of political actors who come to assume democratic conduct on the part of their adversaries; there is a deepening of the commitment of most actors to the mutually negotiated democratic framework (that is, they increasingly take a "principled" rather than an "instrumental" approach to the observances of this framework); and there seems an interactive sequence of moves, akin to a round of tariff cuts or arms reduction in international relations, whereby all participants in the democratic game withdraw some of their barriers to enhance trust and cooperation with their rivals. By these means political actors learn to change their perceptions of themselves, their significant others, and the system as a whole. All this is likely to be accompanied by either a conscious and coordinated, or at least a tacitly agreed upon, campaign to "socialize" the population at large into the acceptance of democratic forms. I have in mind here more than just appeals to rational self-interest or campaigns of education. Socialization may well involve the revision, selective repression, or even the outright suppression of previous history, as the two Colombian parties had to do after the *violencia*. A democratic mythology might have to be introduced that must be carefully defended against scrutiny—consider the legend of Figueres in Costa Rica. (Perhaps the best single test of when the process of consolidation has reached its conclusion is when the real history of the transition can be debated without fear of the consequences.)

This perspective on democratic consolidation directs attention toward *processes* of political interaction but away from the substantive *policies* that need to be adopted. The evidence suggests that a surprisingly wide range of policy choices may be compatible with democratic consolidation, provided that agreed-upon procedures are observed in making such choices. It could also be argued that a variety of possible institutional forms may also be compatible with democratization. Parliamentarism may have significant advantages, as Linz and Stepan insist, but presidentialism is not necessarily a fatal impediment. If it were, then the chances of democratic consolidation in Latin America would be bleak indeed. (There must, however, be some genuine division of powers, as in Costa Rica and Venezuela.) There is no single voting system uniquely well-suited to the requirements of democratization. Some form of neocorporatism may be almost inescapable, but this term can embrace many variants of interest articulation.

Nevertheless, there are some limits to the range of policy choices and of institutional arrangements that are compatible with democratization.

On the policy front, there are limits to the speed and scale of social redistribution compatible with democratic consolidation. Those who wish to stabilize a fragile democracy will at least be obliged initially to offer some guarantees to the privileged classes inherited from the authoritarian period. To put this more crudely, it will be necessary to "purchase the loyalty of the bourgeoisie." How high a price it is necessary to pay may be a question of fine judgement, but the principle is clear. Those who insist on using the transition to press for unrestrained redistribution are not promoting stable democratization. Consciously or not, they are a destabilizing factor. Is there also a limit on the other side? That is to say is there some minimum degree of social reform without which the incipient democracy will suffer, having failed to distance itself in any way from the inequities of the authoritarian period? In principle, there should be, but in practice it may take very little in material rewards to "purchase the loyalty" of the lower classes. Liberals would say this is because political freedom is as much an aspiration of the poor as of the rich. Radicals might explain the asymmetry by pointing to the high expectations and strong capacity for organization of the bourgeoisie compared to those of the masses. Latin American societies are far from uniform in this respect, however. Moreover, the distribution of social power may shift quite markedly in the course of democratization.

In institutional terms, there is also some limit to the variety of arrangements compatible with growing democratization. One crude minimum requirement would be that there must be more than one "democratic actor" on the political stage. It is, for instance, an illusion to suppose that democracy can be implanted by a Napoleonic president, acting without opposition or constraint, to bestow the system on a grateful populace (as some in Mexico and Peru seem to imagine). A consolidated democracy is one in which rival forces have a shared sense of authorship and make a common investment in the future. This sense can only be implanted through negotiation between antagonists, and only in that way will it endure after the prime mover has lost his power. At the other extreme, there are some institutional arrangements that disperse power too widely (the radical federalism that so often led to anarchy in nineteenth-century Spanish America, for example), and which therefore obstruct democratic consolidation. But in contemporary Latin America, overcentralization and excessive personalization of power is by far the greater danger.

Another institutional provision, closely related to the requirements for impersonal and generally accessible administration, is a reasonably effective rule of law, applicable to all. Without being too purist about the quality of the legal order it is possible to establish, a consolidated democracy cannot be said to exist where there are groups or sectors that systematically enjoy immunity from the requirements of the law. (Thus, for example, unconstrained drug trafficking has become a major source of institutional fragility in several of the new democracies of Latin America.)

The rest of this chapter provides some illustrations of this general approach. It discusses some critical choices and conjunctures that have periodically confronted various of the key actors to be found in almost any attempted democratic consolidation, that is, the military; the business sector; the centrist politicians; the radical left; and U.S. policymakers.

Some Key Actors, Some Critical Choices—The Military

A thoroughly consolidated democracy is one in which the military establishment fully accepts its subordination to legally constituted civil power. One of the most critical issues in a fragile democracy is how to move toward this highly desirable but apparently almost unattainable condition. In principle there are three possible models of civil-military relations that might be chosen: the abolition of a permanent military establishment; the integration of the military into a ruling party; or a reliance on constitutionalism. All three approaches have been attempted by Latin American governments aspiring to democracy and all three have encountered significant difficulties.

The oldest established democracy in Latin America made the following "critical choice" in 1949:

> The army as a permanent institution is abolished. For security and the maintenance of public order appropriate police forces will be maintained. Military forces may only be organised as part of a continental agreement, or for the defense of the nation. Any such force will always be subordinate to civilian power and may not enter into deliberations, nor demonstrate nor issue declarations either as individuals or collectively.

(Article 12 of the Costa Rican Constitution of 1949).

This case is by no means unique. Other democracies have also attempted to dispense with a permanent standing army, including the United States after 1787. (In James Madison's words: "With respect to a standing army, I believe there was not a member of the Federal Convention who did not feel indignation at such an institution.") Perhaps the most striking contemporary example is postwar Japan, in Article 9 of the 1947 Japanese constitution. Needless to say, this approach is only adopted in relatively unusual circumstances. In addition there is usually a considerable discrepancy between the rhetoric and the reality, and with the passage of time or the erosion of initial favorable conditions, the rhetoric tends to lose its bite. Nevertheless it is an approach to the consolidation of democracy in Latin America that has a considerable logic on its side. The region contains all too many countries in which the political and economic costs of maintaining a permanent military establishment may be thought to have outweighed the benefits.

In several other Latin American countries, civilian politicians made a quite different "critical choice" about the armed forces. This was to integrate the military within a dominant party and thereby to establish firm political control. In this case overt political opposition to the governing party readily becomes a quarrel with the armed forces as well, and vice versa. Both Cuba and Nicaragua currently rely on this approach, of course. It is, however, important to realize that this route has been followed not only by Marxist revolutionaries but also by Washington-backed centrist politicians, who were regarded as attempting to democratize their countries. This applies to Ávila Camacho and Alemán in Mexico in the forties, and also to Paz Estenssoro and Siles Suazo in Bolivia in the fifties. If the aim is just to establish civilian ascendancy in political life, this approach may succeed, but it has proved to be unpromising as a way of creating a broadly based and stable democracy. In Mexico, for example, although the electoral calendar is meticulously observed and there is considerable political pluralism and interparty competition, the close identification of the armed forces (and the rest of the state apparatus) with the governing party makes it most unlikely that an electorally successful opposition candidate could secure recognition of his victory against the wishes of the incumbents.

Neither of these approaches to civil-military relations has been adopted by any of the eight democracies of contemporary South America. Instead, they have all chosen to maintain significant military establishments, formally subordinated to civilian control through nonpartisan constitutional restraints. The principles behind this choice are easy to explain, but the practical experiences of it give few grounds for complacency. Colombia and Venezuela have the longest track records (thirty years each, as compared with less than a decade since the military directly arrogated to themselves the right to rule in the other six countries) but, even in those countries, democratic control over the military may not be fully consolidated. In the more recently democratized nations, such as Argentina, Brazil, Peru, and Uruguay, not to mention those elected governments facing continuing insurgencies, such as Guatemala and El Salvador, constitutional restraints on the arbitrary power of the armed forces are transparently incomplete.

In Colombia, for example, guerrilla warfare has ebbed and flowed but never entirely ceased over the whole thirty-year period. As a result, critics of Colombian democracy have long asserted that in large portions of the national territory, liberal guarantees have always been a sham—that Colombia presents an appearance of democracy to the outside world and to the middle classes of the big cities, but it involves the reality of military authoritarianism in strife-torn areas of the countryside. Such charges were dramatized and magnified by the events of November 1985, when the army responded to a guerrilla seizure of the Supreme Court building with an assault that left ninety-five people dead, including eleven of the justices. In June 1986 the attorney general issued a remarkably bold and thorough report in which he flatly concluded that the Colombian "political class" had failed in a prime responsibility, namely to elaborate a policy of leadership and collaboration with the armed forces in defense of the rule of law.[3] Unfortunately, events in the ensuing three years showed that Colombian constitutionalism and the judicial system are still caught in a downward spiral of violence and decline, leaving the armed forces with very little effective guidance or constraint.

If constitutionalism remains so ineffective in Colombia, after thirty years of competitive elections, what are the chances of establishing a clear civilian supremacy over the armed forces by purely constitutional means in the newer democracies of South and Central America? During the transition phase of democratization, it is not uncommon for the new authorities to enter into some tacit (or even formal) arrangement with the military, assuring them some institutional continuity and perhaps even permitting them a certain reserve domain, sheltered from civilian interference. In such cases consolidation will require the constitutional authorities to claw back ultimate authority over any reserve domain and to gradually establish full civilian ascendancy. Such efforts may well involve a protracted trial of strength, as President Alfonsín has found in Argentina. Consolidation need not be simply a matter of demoting the military; it can involve the allocation of rewards and new responsibilities as well. (For example, the Spanish armed forces were reshaped to play a more active role in European defense, the Greeks faced a serious conflict with Turkey, and the Venezuelan military helped Betancourt defeat a guerrilla challenge.) But a deliberate and sustained strategy will be required from the civilian authorities, and it will be necessary for them to build a broad base of political support for this enterprise. The mere proclamation of a constitution asserting civilian supremacy will not secure the far-reaching changes in attitudes that are required for democratic consolidation. Civilian politicians must have the will and the unity for a sustained assertion of their authority and the military leadership must also choose to play a cooperative role.

Depending on the circumstances it may be possible to advance by stealth (gradually training and promoting more nonpolitical officers, slowly encroaching on the reserve domain); or it may be necessary to risk a showdown over some test issue, such as the willingness of officers (when duly charged) to submit themselves to the judgement of civilian courts. Unfortunately many of Latin America's new civilian governments are overshadowed by the grave human rights abuses committed under preceding military regimes. President Alfonsín has faced exceptional difficulties in his efforts to establish civilian authority over the military and to define a generally acceptable boundary between punishment and forgetfulness for the crimes committed during the "dirty war." The Argentine experience suggests that in some circumstances there may be no "right answer" that assures the consolidation of civilian supremacy. The Uruguayan strategy of amnesty also faces a severe challenge. After President Sanguinetti backed away from a confrontation with the military and conceded a blanket amnesty, the Uruguayan administration found itself facing a strong demand for a plebiscite on whether to reverse his action. The issue was resolved democratically in Uruguay when the April 1989 plebiscite upheld Sanguinetti's decision, but the problem still festers in Argentina.

Elsewhere the question of military accountability for human rights abuses is hardly even on the political agenda, and democracy is correspondingly in doubt. If the military withdraws to barracks "in good order" (undefeated) as in Brazil, Uruguay, and Guatemala, it might be considered unrealistic to expect that antidemocratic elements would still be purged in the same way as, say, occurred in Argentina. But unless major crimes are investigated and punished there can be no real growth of trust, no "implanting" of democratic norms in the society at large; and therefore no genuine "consolidation" of democracy as defined in this chapter.

The Business Sector

In a fully consolidated democracy, business interests and the propertied classes in general will react to economic insecurity or to what they consider to be bad policies by backing the campaigns of the legitimate right. If they dislike the results they obtain, they may redouble their campaigning, but (either for reasons of prudence or out of conviction) they will have to confine their resistance within constitutional limits. In a fragile democracy the choice of strategy is more uncertain. A vital element in the process of democratic consolidation is therefore to induce such dominant groups (which may have benefited considerably from previous authoritarian rule) to confine their lobbying within legitimate bounds and to relinquish their ties with the undemocratic right. External reassurance (and if possible guarantees) may provide a critical inducement at the beginning of a consolidation process, although the need for this should diminish as democratization advances.

Elsewhere[4] it has been argued that membership in the European Economic Community offered critical external guarantees to the business and propertied classes of Greece, Portugal, and Spain. Whatever parties the newly empowered electorate might favor, the EEC would insist on prompt and adequate compensation for all private property acquired by the state, it would create very strong momentum for tax and welfare harmonization with the rest of (capitalist) Western Europe, and it would ensure relatively free movement of capital. With all these provisions assured, democracy would lose much of its sting for the rich. (There would have been far less need for them to support Franco against the Spanish Republic if such external guarantees had been available in the 1930s). Moreover, for reasons elaborated in the *Transitions* volume, the European Community was bound to refuse membership (and therefore to withold these highly prized guarantees) to all undemocratic regimes. Between the mid-fifties and the mid-seventies this situation set up most powerful, immutable, and long-run incentives for democratic transitions and consolidation in southern Europe. Particular importance may be attached to the nondiscretionary character of these incentives and to the permanence of their effects. These two features may have limited the flexibility with which the EEC could respond to the uncertainties of the democratic transition phase, but they greatly added to the community's effectiveness as a long-term external guarantor of democratic consolidation. The same pattern could be repeated for Turkey, if the European Community responds favorably to her application for membership.[5]

The propertied classes of Latin America have a mixed record on the question of political democracy. On the one hand, historically, before the advent of mass democracy there was often a close relationship between the "emergence of the bourgeoisie" and the strengthening of representative government and the authority of impersonal legal institutions. This mutually reinforcing relationship can be observed at work even now in the better-established "bourgeois democracies" of the subcontinent. On the other hand, for reasons quite similar to those that rallied most property owners against the Spanish Republic in the 1930s, the business sector has also served as a key constitutive element of virtually all the authoritarian regimes of the sixties and seventies. (In some cases, there was also the hope that authoritarian rule would facilitate a rapid growth of profits; also the Cuban Revolution surely pushed business interests to the right, but neither of these explanations should be pushed too far).

Fernando Henrique Cardoso[6] has shed much light on the role played by the São Paulo industrialists in promoting the recent gradual transition toward democracy in Brazil, and there are also thoughtful analyses of the part played by business organizations in the Colombian, Dominican, and Venezuelan transitions. But even in these countries, where the business sector initially played a facilitating role, private enterprise support was likely to waver as the democratic consolidation process proceeded. In any democratic system, the business community will find itself required to share the stage with a wide range of other political interests, including trade union organizations and leftist activists. Such sharing is liable to come as an abrupt shock to many property owners accustomed to the comfort and shelter of authoritarian rule. Often businessmen will have to come to terms with newly constituted and inexperienced political movements, some of which will be principled opponents of private enterprise, while many more will be practitioners of populist rhetoric. In addition, the new constitutional framework may itself contain provisions that are unpopular with business interests (those concerning the social nature of property, restrictions on foreign investment, and so forth). In consequence, the business sector may become equivocal and halfhearted in its commitment to the emerging democratic order.

Since Latin American countries are not eligible for membership in the EEC, are there any functional equivalents of membership that can be devised to "lock in" the business sector as a reliable source of support for the democratic order? External guarantees might in principle be created by the United States or by an association of Latin American democracies. For various reasons, elaborated in the *Transitions* volume, it may be doubted that either of these approaches would work as reliably as in Europe, but it should be noted that both the Caribbean Basin Initiative and the Kissinger Commission Report contain some suggestions along these lines (also see the final section of this chapter).

Turning to internal guarantees, it is a commonplace to suggest that one important source of stability for Venezuelan democracy has been that property owners received assurances about their rights to full compensation (this greatly eased the tensions associated with land reform, for example), and about the freedom of capital movements and the burden of taxation. It presumably required a considerable shift of emphasis for the leaders of *Acción Democrática* to underwrite such guarantees, but it seems that one lesson they learned from the abortive democratization of the *trienio* (1945–48) was that their original policies toward the bourgeoisie had been too destabilizing. The "critical choice" to offer reassurance was only made possible, of course, because of the abundant state revenues generated by the petroleum industry. Following this analysis, the question naturally arises whether such loyalty to the democratic system has now become "internalized" by the Venezuelan bourgeoisie to the extent that such assurances can now safely be withdrawn or revised as oil rents dwindle.

More generally, such implicit bargains between the democratic regime and key social sectors must be constantly renewed and renegotiated in order to keep the consolidation process on track. It is misguided to think in terms of any mechanical relationship between the loss of economic privileges and political disloyalty. The essential task of the democratic politician is to smooth over painful adjustments of this kind by elaborating the reasons for any policy change, and by patiently and respectfully consulting with those affected.

The Centrist Politicians

It follows from this chapter's definition of consolidation that a very wide range of political actors and organizations must be regarded as *potentially* democratic. Service in the preceding authoritarian administration would not constitute an automatic disqualification (except where political crimes were proven in a court of law); nor would a record of armed subversion. Even those who publicly opposed or denounced the process of democratization should have the chance to change their minds and to participate in democratic politics as the new system takes hold. (There may be a political price for them to pay for past misdeeds, but there should be no exclusion from the process). Thus the category of "centrist politicians" must embrace a very broad spectrum. All who claim to be democrats and who are not proven to be otherwise should be formally treated as converts to democracy. But so long as the consolidation process is underway, the final verdict on all participants must remain open. Democratic credentials only become impeccable *post mortem*.

In the interim many centrist politicians can be expected to sail close to the wind and to practice a fair amount of sectarianism. As one among many objectives they have to pursue in an unstable setting, the consolidation of democracy is not invariably their overriding priority. Even for those who do put this goal above all others, they will not all prove skillful and effective in its pursuit. According to the framework adopted in this chapter, the three main Venezuelan parties of the *trienio* period were all centrist and potentially demo-cratic—but they were unskillful (and inexperienced) in pursuing democratic goals. Similarly, both the Liberal and the Conservative Parties of Colombia may be regarded as potentially democratic, but as the *violencia* of the late forties gathered momentum, the centrist elements of the political leadership lost the authority to impose restraint on their *ultras*. Turning to a more recent example, in Jamaica it would be appropriate to classify both Seaga and Manley as potential democrats, although the interaction between them has not always served to consolidate democracy on the island.

It may be objected that too all-embracing a view of "the center" will leave insufficient common ground for collective action designed to entrench demo-cratic norms in society. In my view, the correct approach is to welcome all those who claim devotion to democratic norms, but then to direct their attention to the practical consequences that must follow from any serious application of such principles. Whatever their *arrière-pensées* or hidden agendas, centrist politicians will almost all agree on at least the principles of upholding the rule of law and of extending basic rights to all citizens.

Granting these premises, it would be difficult to escape the conclusion that the public administration must set an example. At the very least it must maintain some minimum standard of behavior. This is all very well at the level of rhetoric, but how can we verify that it is not just rhetoric? One excellent litmus test of the truth value of such claims is to evaluate the treatment of those who are imprisoned. No matter what crimes they may have commited, or what actions they might wish to commit in the future, in any democratic regime those who are legally deprived of their freedom still have some residual rights. Moreover, since they are directly held by the power of the state, it is clear where responsibility lies for the preservation of those rights. Finally, thanks to the disinterested efforts of Amnesty International, we have a reasonably accurate and unpartisan method of checking on whether this crucial aspect of societal democratisation is receiving adequate attention.

Sadly, the recent evidence from South American prisons shows that a great deal needs to be done to turn centrist rhetoric into any kind of democratic reality. On 19 June 1986 the Peruvian army launched a military assault on three prisons in Lima where jailed guerrillas had staged coordinated revolts. The outcome was several hundred deaths (of whom only three were soldiers). The international secretary of the Italian Socialist Party (present for a Congress of the Socialist International), passed the following verdict: "We came here to show solidarity with a new democracy, and found ourselves here at a time when several hundred people were slaughtered—there is no other way to describe people being killed in prison but slaughter." One Peruvian newspaper had the temerity to criticize official tactics, for which it was temporarily closed. President García has subsequently taken the lead in promoting a full investigation of the attack and the punishment of those responsible, but the fact remains that a large number of prisoners were evidently killed after surrendering. In order to consolidate Peruvian democracy, it will be necessary to establish the strongest possible assurances that such episodes will never be allowed to recur. More recently there have been prison revolts in São Paulo, Brasilia, and Bahia in Brazil, also with tragic outcomes.

These are not conditions that favor the consolidation of fragile democracies. Centrist politicians of all colorations need to unite around the principle of constitutional justice for all prisoners. This applies both to common criminals and to those affiliated with my next category of strategic actor:

The Revolutionary Left

The existence of a large well-organized Communist Party need not mean that a democracy is unconsolidated, as France and Italy have demonstrated. In Latin America both Chile and Uruguay stood out as relatively well-consolidated democracies in the 1960s, despite the existence of similar parties; and contemporary Peru and Venezuela both have significant parties professing allegiance to Marxism that nevertheless try to play by the rules of democracy. But even in the most durable Latin American democracies, and certainly in the more fragile ones, democrats on the radical left may periodically come under strong pressure from their revolutionary rivals, who will argue on both political and ideological grounds that there is no alternative to breaking the rules. The more consolidated the democracy, the easier it should be for leftist parties to resist such pressures, but it will never be very easy. In fragile democracies such as contemporary Peru, the sacrifices required may be very serious. (Similarly in Colombia, the democratic left has found itself paying a terrible price for its nonviolent opposition to the drugs mafia.)

The *Senderista* movement, which organized the prison revolts in Peru, constitutes an exceptionally hard case, because the insurgents are unambiguous enemies of what has here been called democracy, enemies who are determined to seize any opportunity provided by official self-restraint to "sharpen the contradictions" that they see in the prevailing social order. Whatever system they might implant if they were victorious, they make no pretense of espousing liberal values. Their leaders offer no possibility of détente, amnesty, or reconciliation. This revolutionary leadership will have to be destroyed, or at least isolated from all social support, if their followers are ever to be "reabsorbed" into a consolidated democratic regime. On this point democrats must be clear and united (even sectarian). In fact, Peruvian politicians from the legal (Marxist) left to strong conservatives on the democratic right seem fairly solid on this basic question, although they differ greatly over the best strategy to be used for defeating or isolating the *Senderista* apparatus. (Underlying these differences are widely divergent views about the basic requirements for establishing a durable democracy in Peru).

In general, the western press often has difficulty distinguishing between "Marxist" politicians and subversive terrorists, but this is no better than automatically equating the military as a whole with the "death squads." The military and death squads may, in principle, act in unity; or they may potentially overlap; or they may even be bitter enemies. The same holds on the left. The Italian Communist Party (PCI), for example, has staunchly defended the constitutional order against the Red Brigades; the Spanish Socialist Party has resolutely opposed ETA violence; and Venezuela's Movement toward Socialism (MAS) has clearly broken with its guerrilla past.

Unfortunately for the process of democratic consolidation, there are many elements on the radical-revolutionary left whose strategy is more opaque than that of either the *Senderistas* or of the PCI and MAS. Some are equivocal and halfhearted converts to democracy (the very same words used above to categorize the business sector). There are also some (not as many as the CIA would have us believe, but nevertheless a significant element) deliberately engaged in a "Stalinist strategy of deception." During a democratic transition all these different left-wing elements are likely to gain in support, and they may well join together in a tacit or even an explicit alliance. Once the consolidation phase begins, however, the "potential democrats" of the radical left will have to decide whether to dissociate themselves from the antidemocratic methods of their former allies. Their scope for equivocation will rapidly diminish in the same way as it diminishes for the right.

If democratic consolidation is to be kept on track, the revolutionary left must be either reabsorbed into democratic life or isolated and defeated. All democrats, including those on the radical left, will therefore be required to opt for defense of the regime against a continuing revolutionary challenge. But on the other hand, the prosecution of the left for anything other than unlawful actions (which require a fair trial) would also undermine democracy, forcing an important current of "potential democrats" into clandestine opposition. Both lack of vigilance and unjustified persecution have to be avoided. A Stalinist "strategy of deception" will have less chance of success after a democratic transition than before. Thus Batista, Somoza, and Marcos were ideal targets for such a strategy, whereas Betancourt and Soares created a very different dynamic for the revolutionary left. "Reabsorption" of the Portuguese and Venezuelan left required firmness, but also moderation. The temptations of an anti-left witchhunt were resisted. By contrast El Salvador after 1979 offers a tragic demonstration of what can happen to "potential democrats" on the radical left when an incipient democratization elicits punitive violence from the right.

The example of El Salvador raises a more general point about "reabsorption." A fledgling democracy that has failed to confront the authoritarian right, which has left parts of the state apparatus in the hands of those who enforced the old order, and which has turned a blind eye to the political crimes of the powerful, will be poorly placed to conduct a campaign against left-wingers who either sincerely or manipulatively claim to be defending genuine democratization. If firm measures are required to expose the pretenses of the revolutionary left and to force the leadership to choose between violent and democratic and PCI alternatives, then a regime that has displayed firmness toward the still powerful and privileged hangovers from the ancien regime will have some political capital it can invest in the enterprise. But weakness toward the unregenerate right would cripple the new democracy's chances of rechanneling the energies of the left.

The credibility of such a democratic undertaking will also depend upon its authenticity as a national project. Consolidation requires that democratic forces are seen to be doing their own bidding, rather than acting at the behest of their external backers.

U.S. Policymakers

The United States promoted polarization and sectarianism rather than the consolidation of such fragile democracies as Venezuela (1945–48), Guatemala (1944–54), Brazil (between 1961 and 1964), the Dominican Republic (1963–65) and Chile (before 1973). The case of Haiti (since 1986) remains uncertain. On the other hand, Washington probably mildly assisted the consolidation of democracy in Costa Rica after 1948, and in Venezuela after 1958, and in particular the Carter administration played a positive role in supporting an incipient democracy in the Dominican Republic in 1978. President Reagan's "rescue mission" successfully imposed a democratic regime in Grenada. But contemporary Central America provides much the most critical test of U.S. claims to be providing support for democratization. In this region the initial task would be to establish a clear transition to democracy, and thereafter to provide the steady but unobtrusive support required for its consolidation. At a minimum, this external support would require two ingredients that have been noticeably lacking from recent American policies: (1) strict adherence to honest and impartial criteria for evaluating democratic performance, and (2) sufficient disengagement from domestic power struggles to enable all the local "potential democrats" to establish their national authenticity and to prove their independence from outside sponsorship. No external power that disregards these two basic conditions can be said to be contributing to the consolidation of democracy. The Esquipulas summit of the five Central American presidents in August 1987 posed this issue with exceptional clarity.

How serious is the difficulty of arriving at honest and impartial criteria for evaluating democratic performance? If the political will exists, the technical problems are manageable. But U.S. policymakers have often shown reluctance to offend undemocratic allies by applying rigorous criteria of democratic performance; and Washington has also developed a reputation in Latin America for using double standards when denouncing unfriendly governments as undemocratic. Thus for example Resolution 32 of the 1948 Act of Bogotá "in Defense of Democracy" was drafted among others by representatives of the Somoza regime, thus delegitimizing the OAS from its foundation. In 1954 this provision was invoked against a Guatemalan government that, whatever its other failings, was certainly no more undemocratic than the government of Nicaragua (or of Cuba, the Dominican Republic, Peru, or Venezuela).

Conscious of such antecedents, recent advisers to Washington have stressed the need for great objectivity. Thus, for example, the second report of the "Inter-American Dialogue" (published in May 1984) opted for precision of language in its ten recommendations on supporting democracy in the Western Hemisphere. Recommendation number seven was extremely clear. It read, in part, "elections that are rigged or manipulated, whether by stuffing ballot boxes, intimidating candidates, preventing assemblies, or censoring mass media, encourage cynicism. Support by foreign governments for unfair elections undermines the idea of democracy and reinforces the view that political change must result from bullets rather than ballots."

The Kissinger Commission Report on Central America recommended the creation of a Central American development organization composed of the seven isthmian nations (including Nicaragua) and the United States. Associate membership status was to be offered to any democracy willing to contribute significant resources to promote regional development. (The Contadora nations, Europe, Canada, and Japan were specifically mentioned.) Central American participation would depend upon acceptance of, and continued progress toward "the protection of personal and economic liberties, freedom of expression, respect for human rights, and an independent system of equal justice and criminal law enforcement" (together with some form of periodic and open electoral competition for office).

Such an organization could be asked to monitor the progress toward democracy that would be required in order for a government to secure economic or military assistance from the democracies. For example,

> With respect to El Salvador, military aid should, through legislation requiring periodic reports, be made contingent upon demonstrated progress toward free elections; freedom of association; the establishment of the rule of law and an effective judicial system; and the termination of the activities of the so-called death squads, as well as *vigorous action against those guilty of crimes and the prosecution to the extent possible of past offenders.* These conditions should be *seriously enforced.*"[7]

But in a personal reservation expressed at the end of this report, Henry Kissinger (and others) qualified their support for this recommendation to the extent that it might conflict with what they viewed as U.S. security interests. In practice, of course, no such organization has been created, U.S. military aid continues flowing to El Salvador without any independent monitoring of democratic performance, and no officers have been convicted for death squad crimes.[8]

The Kissinger Commission also made one other observation that should be of particular importance to those Washington policymakers genuinely concerned with the promotion of democracy. "The present purely bilateral (aid) process has its drawbacks. It factors political assessments directly into economic aid decisions. This makes the United States the prosecutor, judge and jury."[9] In such circumstances, it is extremely difficult for the beneficiaries of U.S. aid (however deep and genuine their own commitment to democracy may be) to establish their authenticity and independence of judgement, and to win the trust of the other social forces and political rivals in their own country whose cooperation they need in order to consolidate a broad-based democracy. These problems arise in the most acute form in countries where, historically, U.S. intervention has not previously served the cause of democratic government, where the imbalance of power between aid giver and recipient is extremely pronounced, and where the receiving society is polarized by social injustice and economic decline. For all these reasons, U.S. policymakers would be likely to make a more positive (or less negative) contribution to the promotion of democracy in Central America if they could refrain from making detailed and unilateral supervisions of another country's internal politics. However, this aspect of the Kissinger recommendations has received little support.

Obviously, Washington's willingness and ability to step back from overinvolvement in the internal affairs of small neighbors is bound to depend in large part on estimates of which forces are likely to expand to fill the resulting vacuum. Ideally, these would be internal democratic forces (the wide array of "potential democrats" outlined in the section above on "centrist politicians"). History suggests that almost all U.S. administrations have found it very hard to tolerate some of the more radical of these potentially democratic forces. To the extent that such intolerance is unjustified by any real threat to U.S. national interests, these reflexes of Washington must be regarded as unnecessary impediments to democratic consolidation. To the extent that politicians on the radical left fail to define fully their commitment to democracy or to communicate clearly their true democratic intentions, the responsibility lies with them.

Here there is potential scope for the United States' regional and extraregional democratic allies to play a constructive role. In principle, they might intercede, offering their good offices and perhaps even making concrete assurances that in the absence of American pressure equally effective external pressure will be applied from elsewhere to promote and protect democratization. (It is only by reasoning along such lines that one can justify the continued presence of British troops in Belize, for example). President Arévalo of Guatemala put forward some important proposals at the creation of the OAS in 1948 that would have worked in this direction, but sadly they were not adopted. The Betancourt Doctrine was another (unfortunately rather isolated) effort in the same direction put forth in the 1960s. The EEC may also be interested in playing such a role—particularly following the accession of Spain and Portugal to full membership at the beginning of 1986. (In accordance with the Birkelbach Report of 1962, the EEC managed to define and uphold very clear criteria for democratic performance that were eventually met by the new member states from southern Europe). The May 1986 and August 1987 Declarations of Esquipulas showed signs that political leaders of Central America are thinking along similar lines and the eight elected presidents from Latin America who met in Acapulco in November 1987 announced an analogous commitment.

At the time of these declarations, such a line of reasoning sounded quixotic. After all, the U.S. Congress had entrusted not just the U.S. administration, but, of all agencies, the CIA, with the prime responsibility for aiding the Contras, supposedly to bring democracy to Nicaragua. Perhaps this *was* just rhetoric, but even so the use of such language in this context undermines confidence in the strength of Washington's commitment to genuine democracy elsewhere. Whatever its other justifications, the Reagan administration's policy toward Nicaragua was widely perceived to be totally contrary to the creation of conditions for mutual accommodation and the growth of trust, conditions that are central to the promotion of democracy. Whatever the truth may be about the actual organization and conduct of the CIA, its reputation and traditions are guaranteed to taint the democratic credibility of any Latin American group it sponsors.

This final section has dwelt extensively with the problems of Central America, concentrating on those decisions taken in Washington that are ostensibly aimed at promoting and consolidating democracy there. It must be admitted that the Central American crisis poses an extreme test—geopolitical interests and ideological passions are deeply engaged. In other parts of Latin America (for example, the Dominican Republic) a more positive assessment is no doubt warranted. However, this section could only end on a Central American note, for that is the region where the United States has assumed by far the highest profile and has made the most far-reaching promises of democratization. Elsewhere in Latin America, Washington policymakers may perhaps play a useful supporting role, but the success or failure of the consolidation process will not be attributed primarily to them. In most of South America it is the indigenous political actors who will deserve and receive either the praise or the blame.[10] In Central America, on the other hand, on current form, it will be an uphill struggle for the local democrats to achieve recognition for their efforts, assuming these do come to fruition. Applying the notion of "consolidation" adopted here, it is only if Washington allows the Central American democrats to take control of their own destinies and to emancipate themselves from external sponsorship that democratic consolidation can be said to have begun. For these Central Americans to establish their authenticity, they have to emancipate themselves from all their external sponsorships, as the Esquipulas proposals (the so-called "Arias Plan") of August 1987 envisaged.

In conclusion, fragile democracies constrain all political actors to weigh their commitment to democratization against other, perhaps more urgent, concerns. The military will be preoccupied with maintaining or restoring their prestige and cohesion, shoring up their institutional autonomy, and protecting their budget. Their commitment to democracy will largely depend on what it seems to offer (or threaten) in these regards, and in particular on whether they perceive a worthwhile and well-defined role for themselves within a consolidated democratic framework. The propertied classes may not find it easy to come to terms with the new social and political forces unleashed by democratization, especially if that is accompanied by high inflation, diminished security for domestic and foreign investment, or the introduction of new social laws or constitutional reforms that weaken traditional property rights. Initial Latin American hopes that democratization might attract international financial assistance and guarantees have been largely disappointed,[11] with the result that many property owners find democracy to be more costly and risky than they had anticipated. Centrist politicians as a whole would seem to have more to gain from democratic consolidation than any of the other groups considered in this chapter, but in a fragile democracy this is a diffuse category, including many potential democrats whose initial commitment is likely to be provisional or instrumental. These forces will become more trustworthy and more authoritative as the chances of a successful consolidation improve. But equally they will tend to lose cohesion and self-confidence if the evidence accumulates that the democratization process is running off track. The radical left will be required to undertake a severe and quite possibly painful reconsideration, both of its methods and of its aims, if it is to play a constructive role. This becomes all the more difficult if the fragile democracy proves unable to protect the physical security of constitutionally minded leftists or to uphold the role of law against the unreconstructed right. Although U.S. policymakers may well regard the establishment of fully consolidated democracies as the "first best" outcome for American national interests, in the meantime they have to manage the security and foreign policy consequences of the "second best" situation created by fragile democracies. Thus they too may be constrained to adopt an equivocal, provisional, or instrumental stance that limits the chances of full democratic consolidation.

All the five strategic sectors considered in this chapter are likely to find themselves under considerable pressure to view democratization "instrumentally," rather than as an unquestionable and overriding commitment. But if each political sector concludes that the democratic commitment of the other is lukewarm, this will reduce the motivation of all, and so perpetuate the condition of fragility. For this reason, the consolidation of democracy typically requires an iterative process of confidence-building. It is misleading to think of the process as one in which a single bloc of "true democrats" imposes their blueprints on the rest of society.

Notes

1. Robert Dahl, *Polyarchy: Participation and Opposition* (New Haven: Yale University Press, 1971), pp. 8–9.

2. Jean-François Revel, *How Democracies Perish* (New York: Doubleday, 1983) and José Agustín Silva Michelena, *The Illusion of Democracy in Dependent Nations* (Cambridge: MIT Press, 1971). Both contain the seeds of potentially antidemocratic sectarianism.

3. The report rejects the allegation that the military assault took place behind the back of the civil authorities, but it states that the government failed in its legal and moral obligation to try to protect the lives of the hostages, a duty underscored by the chief justice himself before his death. Full text in *El Espectador* (Bogotá), 22 June 1986.

4. See Laurence Whitehead, "International Aspects of Democratization," in *Transitions from Authoritarian Rule: III: Comparative Perspectives*, ed. Guillermo O'Donnell, Philippe Schmitter, and Laurence Whitehead (Baltimore: John Hopkins University Press, 1986).

5. "Turkey's leading industrialists share with most of the intelligentsia the belief that membership of the European Community could provide almost a *deus ex machina* solution to guarantee the victory of liberal westernising tendencies in their country over Islamicising and oriental ones. Even the government has recently begun *sotto voce,* to argue that for Turkey—as for Greece and Spain—membership of the European Community is a legitimate way of guaranteeing a fragile parliamentary democracy against possible further military takeovers." *Financial Times*, 16 September 1986.

6. "Entrepreneurs and the Transition Process," in *Transitions* vol. III.

7. *Report of the President's National Bipartisan Commission on Central America* (New York: Macmillan, 1984), pp. 72, 124. Kissinger's reservations are stated on p. 156.

8. See, for example, "Justice Denied—Solving a Murder Case in El Salvador is Hard if Suspects are VIPs," a front-page story in the *Wall Street Journal,* 13 December 1984. Here is an extract from that detailed account:

Captain Avila's uncle is a judge on the Supreme Court. During consideration of his nephew's case, the judge happened to be filling in for the chief justice, whose office had been bombed. The uncle used his judicial position to assign to the Sheraton case judges clearly sympathetic to the officers. One such judge, for instance, allowed Lt. Lopez Sibrian to dye his hair black (from red) and to shave off his moustache prior to appearing in a lineup before a crucial witness. The witness then didn't recognize the lieutenant. It was this court that last month threw out the case against Lt. Lopez Sibrian. This reporter commented, "It is said that no officer has ever been tried in court here for murder or any other human rights violation, and some Salvadorans seek to make sure that new precedents are not set."

9. Kissinger Commission, *Report*, p. 75.

10. The eight elected presidents who signed the Acapulco Pact justifiably complained of the unconcern of the developed countries about the effects on Latin America of the debt crisis. "It is contradictory that those who call for democracy also impose, in world economic relations, conditions and adjustments that compromise that very democracy."

11. However, interesting exceptions to this generalization are provided by the $5 billion Argentine-Italian economic treaty signed in December 1987, and the $3 billion Argentine-Spanish economic treaty signed in February 1988. These two agreements are only valid provided both partners maintain democratic regimes.

7

Changing Latin American Attitudes: Prerequisite to Institutionalizing Democracy

OSVALDO HURTADO

This is the finest hour for democracy in the history of Latin America. At no other time have democracy and its institutions held such sway over this geography, covering the map of the region almost in its entirety. But this is not the first time that democracy has prevailed over dictatorial governments. What measures should be taken to ensure that democracy suffers no more setbacks and is installed as an enduring system that will guarantee the protection of freedom, the periodic change of governments through elections, the supervision and evaluation of the actions of government authorities, and the attainment of economic development and social justice?

Propensity to Conflict

Democracy is a system based on negotiation, agreements, and consensus. Even governments where the majority party is in power need the support of the opposition in order to carry out some of their policies. In a world in which the mass media and public opinion have taken on such importance, it is no longer possible to implement programs that do not have the full support of the community or that meet with overwhelming opposition. Democracy is, furthermore, a system in which power is distributed and regulated through a complex system of checks and balances that finds expression in a set of legal norms setting out the functions, responsibilities, and powers of the various organs of government.

Latin America's history provides ample proof of the apparent contradiction between the Latin American character and these facts of democratic life. The former has resulted in numerous examples of intransigent, belligerent fighting between the government and the opposition and among the various political parties. It is a character generally prone to conflict rather than conciliation, and incapable of arriving at a respectful, working relationship between the executive and the legislature. Instead, the traditional executive seeks to control the legislature and transform it into a mere vehicle for its plans, and the legislature—also reflecting the Latin American character—often tries to paralyze the presidency.

Relations between employers and workers have also been affected in a like manner, sometimes leading to radicalization. It has not been easy for either of these two groups to situate their relationship within the framework of the more general interests of society and to make of the private sector an endeavor that will benefit owners and workers alike.

Insofar as it has been impossible to find a solution to these conflicts through democratic means, and insofar as such conflicts have overstepped institutional limits, and insofar as illegal actions and measures of the authorities have stripped institutions of legitimacy, the leaders have lost control over public affairs, and the conditions have been created for a breakdown of the constitutional system. The recurrence of these patterns has made political instability a characteristic typical of the region's political life.

It is therefore not accurate to attribute sole responsibility for disruptions of the democratic order to the military. Sometimes civilians have created conditions that have led to coups d'etat. One must not forget that coups have sometimes been welcomed and applauded by broad sectors of public opinion.

In this regard, Latin America is today undergoing a positive change of attitude, some signs of which are already apparent. Relations between employers and workers appear to be less tense and conflictual, to the point that broad agreements involving the waiver of certain claims by workers and shareholders have been concluded in an effort to stave off bankruptcy by companies affected by the general economic crisis. Also, it is no longer unusual to see a degree of cooperation between the legislature and the executive.

Weakness of the Party System

Democracy requires that there be parties to represent, organize, and guide the public. Some countries of the region have not had such parties, while others have had too many parties, which has prevented the establishment of majorities capable of exercising power and organizing stable governments.

Awareness of this problem is not sufficiently widespread in Latin America. Analyses of the failure of democracy in the region frequently focus on factors of a different type and overlook the problem of parties. Despite their long history and their century and a half of frustrations in the judicial-constitutional area, Latin American democracies continue to seek a constitution that will effectively guarantee the survival of democracy. Close to one hundred constitutions have been drawn up in search of one capable of providing the ideal framework for all problems of political instability and dictatorships. For example, the question of expanding the powers of legislatures continues to be an important item in any debate among Latin American constitutional lawyers.

Every democracy requires an appropriate political constitution; laws that permit the development of a party system that would transform existing political parties into vehicles for the selection and organization of citizens, for the training of cadres and leaders, for the formulation of ideologies and policies, and for the implementation of programs and the support of governments are also needed. If one looks at the political evolution of Latin America, one can see that countries enjoying a bipartisan political system have managed to stabilize their democratic life. Such is the case with Venezuela and Colombia. Those countries that have not met this requirement, however, have suffered frequent changes of government and the onslaughts of dictatorship.

Brazil and Argentina have moved toward bipartisan systems, the former as a result of an authoritarian act of the military and the latter through the will of the electorate. A similar trend can be observed in other countries, some of which have reformed their electoral laws in order to achieve the same goal. As this process moves forward, the chances for democracy improve.

The Need for Effective Civilian Governance

The greatest challenge facing these governments will continue to be the development of their political capacity and technical ability to deal with the economic crisis facing Latin America. Their fate and that of democracy itself will be decided by the decisions they make in the economic arena.

Unfortunately, the politicians of Latin America are not always endowed with an adequate understanding of economic matters, nor do they value a technical approach. Traditionally, Latin Americans have opted for theoretical and philosophical formulas that are more closely related to the goals sought by society than to the means of their attainment, a weakness shared equally by employers and workers. It is a common occurrence for political debates to become snarled in circumstantial and personal matters, or to ignore the specific problems affecting the progress of society, the solutions of which are fundamental to the well-being of its citizens.

When one governs in times of relative wealth, mistakes in economic policy are less evident and serious. An abundance of resources can hide errors and cover up the negligence of government authorities. The situation changes dramatically when one has to govern in times of want, as is the case of the impoverished Latin America of today. Negligence and untimely or incorrect decisions have had dire consequences for society, especially for its neediest sectors. A proper economic policy is essential in times of crisis to reduce the social costs and to prevent a worsening of the prevailing uneven distribution of wealth. This situation is not sufficiently understood by political leaders.

A new, more effective style of leadership has emerged in the economic sector. It is less rhetorical and more realistic in preparing and implementing public policy and it is readier to assume costs and risks. Thanks to these new leaders, democratic governments have implemented austerity programs, and large sectors of the population have accepted or at least tolerated their consequences.

Ideology is no longer fundamental in Latin American political debate. The people, overwhelmed by the social distress that has resulted from the economic crisis, have sharpened their wits and today demand of politicians evidence that their economic measures will be effective and that their capacity to govern is credible.

Lack of Military Policy

The long and sometimes bloody fighting by democratic forces against military dictatorships has served to emphasize the barriers that have traditionally separated the civilian population from the military in Latin America. Once a democratic regime is inaugurated, it becomes impossible to reestablish adequate communication. Politicians and political parties find it difficult to forget the repressive role of the armed forces under dictatorship. For the military, their awareness of the defeat suffered and of what they call the "ostracism" and "humiliations" meted out by the new democratic regime has also precluded a positive relationship.

In other cases, democracies sometimes repeat certain practices employed by dictatorships to keep officers and soldiers under their authoritarian control. They politicize the armed forces by involving them in matters of a strictly political nature; they attempt to form personal patronage relations with the military, and seek to flatter them by granting them privileges. In short, they resort to measures that do not befit a democratic regime and that furthermore have been proven by experience to be useless as a means of ensuring the loyalty of the military establishment. The fact that the strength of a democratic regime lies in the legitimacy of its origins and actions and not in the support it receives from the military is forgotten. The gap in Latin American political thought on the subject is sad. Generally, governments and parties lack a military policy consistent with the democratic system. Worse, many democrats do not yet recognize the need for such a policy.

The traditional army that used to dominate the scene in Latin America—one composed of the followers of the dictator or *caudillo*—has largely disappeared. Most of the armies of Latin America have achieved a high degree of institutionalization; others are in the process of achieving this. If this trend is to be completed, it is important for democratic governments to foster and strengthen the institutionalization of the armed forces and of the military profession. To the degree that this is achieved, the risk of military interventionism will decrease, because institutionalization induces the armies to place themselves at the service of the nation and of democracy and to submit to the constitution, the laws, and those who legitimately govern. As a result, their loyalty becomes assured and lasting in the manner of the loyalty professed by the armies of Europe and North America to their democratic governments.

Democratic politicians should bear in mind that although the armed forces must necessarily be subordinate to civilian authority, the latter in turn must respect the military's laws, regulations, norms, and procedures, must guarantee their autonomy to make their own decisions, and must accept the respon-

sibilities they have assumed in certain areas—the economy, for example—
which, although not inherent to the military function, have become a tradition
in many countries of Latin America.

Weakness of the Bureaucratic Technocracy

The role of the state has been and continues to be an important one in the
region's development because of the significant part played by public investment
in important economic activities and in the establishment of certain services.
Unfortunately, the state and its technocracy lack an acceptable level of efficiency
and technical competence—a problem for which Latin America has yet to find
a solution.

Some parties and governments are today espousing policies directed at
reducing the role of the state. To this end, they have privatized certain economic
activities and services. In some countries, the state has taken over corporations
that would have been best left to the private sector, either because there is no
justification (not even political) for their having become public or because they
could have been managed better privately. Nevertheless, certain factors militate
against the viability of such an economic policy, particularly when the intention
is to impose it at all costs. There are parties vying for power that defend the
participation of the state in such activities. In Latin America, with very few
exceptions, there are no Weberian entrepreneurs or Schumpeterian inno-
vators—bearers of progress and change. Rather, what predominates is the type
of businessman who pursues speculative and commercial activities that pose no
risk to him. The dearth of capital and the lack of interest of the industrialized
world in investing in Latin America are insurmountable obstacles to replacing
with private capital the vast investments made to date by the state. Furthermore,
the economic crisis has forced the state to multiply its responsibilities to avoid
the bankruptcy of important productive activities, notably in the financial
sector.

If these hypotheses are true, it would not be arbitrary to conclude that the
state will in the future continue to play an important role in the continent's
development. We must, therefore, find the means to improve efficiency in public
institutions and state-owned corporations, a task that should not be belittled by
democratic politicians but rather should be accorded their highest priority. This
will ensure the continuity of certain programs. Without such continuity, it is
impossible to implement long-term policies and projects that will provide the
only real solutions to the fundamental problems of Latin America. It should be
recalled that the political instability that characterized the Fourth French
Republic, and which today characterizes the Italian Republic, was neutralized
by the stability and efficiency of the bureaucracy.

Need for Democratic Institutions

Opposition to democracy in Latin America has not been limited to some
military sectors. Certain ultraconservative economic groups, parties, and move-

ments have never felt a commitment to the democratic institutions, and they have opposed democracy when their interests were affected. Marxist parties despised what they called "bourgeois democracy" and fought it ideologically and politically. Some center parties criticized so-called "formal democracy" and championed the organization of a new "participatory democracy." Certain technocratic and leftist groups continued to seek a military messiah who would carry out the revolution they were never able to organize for lack of a following. Even the American government at times considered that military dictatorships could be its best allies and the bearers of modernization.

The last few years have shown a change in these trends. "Bourgeois democracy" and "formal democracy" have become important and even vital to a wide range of political actors, including until recently some of their most tenacious detractors. Those who have suffered the traumatic experiences of the authoritarian regimes of the Southern Cone, the brutal violations of human rights and the restrictions imposed on individual freedom, today appreciate and defend the importance and significance of their democratic freedoms. Some Marxist parties, in a fashion similar to the European communist parties, have decided to become involved in parliamentary democracy. The reformist military experiments so much in vogue in the decades of the sixties and the seventies have lost their attractiveness. The United States has committed itself to democratic institutions as never in the past; without the prodemocratic policies espoused by Presidents Carter and Reagan, some Latin American democratic processes would never have been launched or been met with such success.

As can be seen, the allies of democratic institutions can today be counted in greater numbers. Nevertheless, it is important to keep in perspective some of the historic vices that to this day exist and that express themselves in the old colonial practices at which the Spanish *conquistadores* were so adept. Today, as it was during the Spanish period, the laws and the constitution are "respected and obeyed" but are not "fulfilled" in some of the democracies in Latin America. Such is the case in countries where elections are held but are not necessarily free. The opposition is excluded from the right to govern and in this way the government falls into authoritarianism and comes close to dictatorship.

Democratic "forms" without substance degenerate, losing both legitimacy and popular support. The judicial system no longer functions; conflicts are not resolved. Instead, force is institutionalized, leaving the future of democracy to the wind. What is now taking place in Ecuador is a good example, but it is not the only case.

In addition, a new and powerful enemy of Latin American democracy has risen: violence and terrorism. In several countries, narcotics traffickers have exacerbated this problem by supporting terrorists of the right or left.

Limitations on Economic and Social Development

Perhaps the greatest obstacle to the survival of democracy lies in the slowdown and, in some cases, the reversal of Latin America's economic development. While dictatorships governed in times of abundance, the democracies have had to deal with shortages. If present conditions for the renegotiation of foreign debt are maintained and commodity prices continue to fall, there is no hope for the resumption of economic growth, at least until the end of the century. If that remains the case, the majority of the Latin American nations would not recover the level of earnings they had attained in 1970 or 1980 until the next millennium. The middle classes, long accustomed to a certain level of well-being, and the popular sectors who had managed to improve their standard of living, will hardly tolerate an indefinite period of austerity. Politicians know that no people can be asked to make continuous sacrifices without the least glimmer of light at the end of the tunnel of stagnation and impoverishment. Democratic institutions and "hemispheric security" are at grave risk.

The size of the Latin American debt had increased to more than $430 billion by 1988. It continues to be impossible to pay the principal, and the number of countries in arrears on their interest payments increases daily. Every day there are more cases of default in the adjustment programs recommended by the International Monetary Fund.

The drop in commodity prices continues, while the terms of trade deteriorate. Economic activity is still stagnant, unemployment is on the rise, and the standard of living continues to regress. The situation of the private sector has worsened as a result of overindebtedness and the danger of bankruptcy. Inflation has reached levels never before registered in Latin America. The debt-export ratio is higher today than it was before the crisis. As a result of the lack of confidence in the future of the region, capital flight continues.

The industrialized nations have repeatedly emphasized the transitory nature of this crisis and the ability of the adjustment programs to offer a definitive solution. However, the Latin American crisis continues, the results of the adjustment programs have been very relative, and the locomotive theory—that the industrialized countries would pull the poorer countries forward—has simply not worked. The governments of Latin America have demonstrated a high degree of responsibility for "putting their houses in order." The governments of the industrialized nations have remained silent, and international banking remains indifferent. Through a sort of collective self-deception, all the sectors involved seem to have decided to keep up appearances. The debtor nations resort to the most varied subterfuges in order to cover up their delinquency and to preserve their good name; the banks on their side turn a blind eye to what is happening to avoid having to register their losses and thus damage their balance sheets. Since the apocalyptic warnings of destabilization heard in 1982 and 1983 have disappeared, it is thought that the problem of the debt has been overcome.

Nevertheless, there is increasing evidence that in the current circumstances Latin American debt has become unpayable. That does not mean it should be ignored, but rather that it will not be paid despite the good will of governments and any efforts and sacrifices they might make. If we want the Latin American debt to become payable, substantial changes must be made in the conditions regulating it and to international trade. Any other approach would simply postpone the problem and defer the inevitable collapse. It must be remembered that the debts incurred by some Latin American countries in order to obtain their independence were not paid in full until the twentieth century and that the Marshall Plan absorbed 1.2 percent per annum of the U.S. gross national product. An equivalent percentage would today amount to $36 billion per year.

However, unlike the situation after WW II, there are currently more industrialized nations in a position to carry out a similar effort. The decline in capital flow toward Latin America in 1985 is the best proof of the failure of the initiatives promoted to date by the industrialized nations in an effort to deal with the debt problem, including the so-called Baker Plan. Financing for the region's development will only be achieved through public funds generated by the industrialized nations and administered directly by their governments, by the World Bank, the Inter-American Development Bank, or the International Monetary Fund. These funds should be loaned out over the long term and at low interest rates. Otherwise, the economic crises of Latin America will continue to worsen.

Given these circumstances, it would be a mistake to think that the growth of democracy in Latin America is an irreversible, consummated fact. To date, the emergence of democracies has always been an ephemeral phenomenon. To enable these democracies to become permanent is the great challenge facing not only Latin American politicians but also the North Americans. Like all human activities, democracy involves learning lessons. To learn something implies both theoretical knowledge and empirical understanding. The periods of democracy in Latin America have been short-lived, and so there has not been enough time to teach the system. When people live in dictatorships, the dictatorship's values define the political conduct of a society. The opposition should not be asked to be mature if it has never had the opportunity to acquire the experience that comes with being in government. Here lies the cause of the difficulty of the parties in establishing alliances and achieving agreements and of the mannequin-like characteristic that frequently describes the politics of Latin America. The logic behind the "extermination" of the adversary belongs in a dictatorship, not in a democracy.

This reflection takes us to one last conclusion. Latin American democracies need to be stable, but this convenience also has to do with the necessity of giving time to the idea of democracy, so that it can penetrate the conscience of the citizens and especially the principal political actors: the parties, the businessmen, the workers, the students, and the military.

8

Economic Policy and Democracy

NICOLÁS ARDITO BARLETTA

During the 1980s, several significant Latin American countries have inaugurated democratic governments, while others have reinforced their recently reestablished democracies. Argentina, Brazil, Uruguay, Guatemala, and El Salvador have joined in the promising start made by Ecuador, Peru, and Bolivia a little earlier. Unfortunately, Panama lost an opportunity after a promising start.

At the same time, the 1980s have witnessed the most dramatic sustained economic deterioration of the Latin American region as a whole since the Great Depression of the 1930s. Economic growth has been drastically reduced, per capita income has dropped to the levels of at least ten years earlier, and unemployment has risen considerably. With the population still growing at 2.5 percent per year and with rising social expectations, democratic institutions in Latin American countries face a delicate and complex challenge. The governments need to adopt economic policies to accelerate economic growth, improve social equity, and maintain political stability. This chapter reviews the economic problem and examines the political implications and some of the economic policies, both national and international, that are needed to foster development and to reinforce democracy in Latin America.

The differences in size, natural resource endowment, economic and political systems, national identity, and comparative advantage are real and important among the countries of Latin America. But there are also similarities in cultural heritage and levels of development along with a regional spirit that permits some generalizations to be made about the region's development challenge. Latin America's attempt to restore economic growth along with human development and democracy needs to be complemented by regional initiatives and international cooperation extended beyond present levels. This cooperation should take full account of the possibilities and limitations of each nation. I do not share the view that economic growth and human development are a sufficient or even a main requirement for sustaining the evolution of democratic institutions in Latin America. There are other more important variables, such as culture, political and social frameworks, and attitudes. Democracies in Latin

America sometimes survive economic stagnation, but a successful response to the economic challenge would strengthen existing democracies and facilitate the emergence of new ones.

The Development Challenge

Most Latin American countries are in the middle of a long-term development cycle shaped by the population explosion and rising social and individual expectations. For the last twenty-five years, population growth rates in at least eighteen countries in the region have been about 3 percent per year. Fortunately, the rate declined in the 1970s and 1980s to levels averaging 2.5 percent per year, but the labor force continued growing above 3 percent per year.

Four characteristics of the demographic profile should be highlighted: (1) Net employment needs in those countries will continue to grow more than 3 percent per annum for many years. To create enough jobs, the economy needs to grow at the rate of 5 percent or more each year. (2) Almost half of the population is younger than twenty years old, with expanding needs in the areas of nutrition, health, and education. (3) Rural to urban migration continues at a very fast rate. The largest eighty urban areas in the region doubled in size in the last twenty years. They will do so again in the next twenty years, posing a large urban development task. (4) About one-third of Latin America is living better; one-third is in transition to better (or worse) opportunities; but the bottom third is very poor, and their numbers (about 130 million people) are increasing the fastest. The central, long-term development challenge is how to cope with an expanding, young population that will enter the labor market at an ever-increasing rate and make formidable social demands on fragile democratic governments.

The recent economic evolution and external debt of Latin America have been intensively analyzed. Debt servicing and world deflation led to economic stagnation and adjustment. The generalized acceptance that the problem is not only one of external debt but a problem that requires a global, international economic adjustment created an international consensus supporting a three-way action program: (1) The Latin American countries would stabilize and adjust their economies to reestablish growth and establish more efficiency in resource utilization. (2) The international financial community, both official and private, would restructure debts and provide additional financial support to ease the necessary adjustments. And (3) the developed countries would restart noninflationary growth and maintain international trade with low levels of protection to permit export growth by developing countries. Increased exports would permit Latin America to service restructured debts and to have economic growth simultaneously. Each group would act within its possibilities and limitations.

The conceptual framework has been sound but the strength and timing of the actions has left much to be desired. In 1984 the new solutions had positive results. However, between 1985 and 1987 financial and trade flows as well as economic growth in the developed countries slowed. Except for Brazil, Chile, and Colombia, the region has continued to have very low levels of economic growth and, in effect, has had declining per capita incomes.

Latin America adjusted. Regional imports dropped by 40 percent in four years. The trade account improved by $35 billion in three years. Fiscal deficits have been reduced in most countries; domestic savings have increased. Domestic currencies have depreciated 25–40 percent in real terms since 1982 in eight of the largest countries (Argentina, Brazil, Chile, Colombia, Ecuador, Mexico, Venezuela, Uruguay). The net transfer of resources to the region changed from a positive $5 billion per year to a negative $30 billion per year in three years. However, at the same time, the level of social sacrifice caused by five years of stagnation is very significant: GDP dropped 12 percent in the last five years. Per capita income is no higher than it was ten to fifteen years ago. Real wages in Mexico alone declined 35 percent in three years. Private enterprise has been weakened in many countries by stagnation. Capital formation is down sharply.

The international financial community had rescheduled and restructured a good portion of the Latin debt, but it has stopped the transfer of new resources. It also received over $140 billion from the region in interest payments in four years. The developed countries as a group have not maintained 3 percent annual growth and their use of nonquantitative trade barriers has increased, blocking further growth in Latin American exports. So far, the heaviest burden has fallen on Latin America.

There is a wide consensus that adjustment should continue with renewed economic growth, not with prolonged stagnation. To have growth and external debt service simultaneously has become increasingly difficult, because of the balance of payments constraints imposed by increasing external debt service, insufficient export growth, and the use of domestic savings to service debt instead of investing in capital. Latin America's efforts need to be complemented by more vigorous international cooperation.

Economic Strategies and Policies for Growth

Economic adjustment is necessary to regain a path of sustained economic growth. The increase in national wealth is again necessary to improve social welfare.[1] For Latin America to achieve 4 percent annual growth in the next three years, the negative net transfer of resources to the region needs to be reversed by a net figure close to $20 billion per year at least for the next three years. Moreover, the international trade environment needs to be favorable, accompanied by growth of perhaps 3 percent per year in the developed world.

The new external funding can only come from new loans, a postponement of amortizations, or a reduction in interest payments. Past debt needs to be restructured to the longest possible maturities. If arrangements cannot be made to increase the amount of new lending, then perhaps a workable formula could be defined to capitalize part of the interest payments. New approaches such as conversion of debt to equity can be promoted. In some cases outright debt relief may be necessary. The capital markets of the world are already showing that the present value of Latin American debt is from 30 to 90 percent lower than book value. Some banks are finding it convenient to dispose of it at such prices, while most are building up reserves against such losses.

The economic policies that Latin America has begun to implement are politically and socially costly in the short run. Strategically, the region needs to reorient economic growth toward greater exports by maintaining competitive exchange rates and avoiding overly protective import substitution policies. In addition, Latin America should increase domestic savings by positive real interest rates, improve the efficiency of its investments, control public deficits, and direct public spending toward human capital development. It should also offer greater incentives to private economic activity by permiting markets to be flexible.

These harmless-sounding policies create a considerable amount of friction because each takes something away from some constituency or pressure group that is active in the political arena. It is difficult to sustain stabilization and adjustment policies without tangible positive results that nourish hope and expectations. Reductions of public expenditures affect public employees and the private groups benefiting from such spending. Less effective tariff protection hurts uncompetitive industries with a consequent loss of jobs. Taxes and other adjustment policies have negative effects on many politically influential groups. The comparison between the present political costs of new policies and medium-term political benefits coming from positive economic results is essential in the political negotiations that a democratic government has to undertake with different groups to adopt adjustment policies.

Renewed domestic growth and international financial and trade support would increase savings and exports gradually and lessen the need for additional external financing. To achieve that result, the countries need to keep the rate of growth of consumption below the rate of growth of income and savings. Growth would win political support for adjustment policies at home, and improved financial indicators and solvency would maintain credibility abroad.

Political Implications and the Democratic Process

Rapid implementation of austerity policies may generate immediate political costs that could endanger the functioning of democratic institutions unless there is adequate communication and understanding among critical political forces, which in many Latin American countries include the military. A democratic government that tries to please every group may maintain political capital but may lose the next election after time shows a lack of concrete results.

The international community is partly aware of these realities. For example, the Baker Plan of the U.S. government recognizes the need for substantial additional financial support to ease adjustment; the IMF has also shown some signs of flexibility in recent years. The emphasis is no longer just on stabilization policies. Nevertheless, Latin America needs more flexibility in the adjustment process if the new democratic governments are to become stronger. If power is diffuse and compromises are hard to achieve, then a slower path toward adjustment is essential.

Obviously the "political situation" is too often the excuse for countries to do nothing or to extract additional external cooperation without any significant change. Therefore, the greater the number of policies adopted for adjustment, the greater should be the external support.

The main policy effort has to be provided by Latin America, but cooperation from developed countries in trade and finance remains a critical component in order to strengthen the chances of democracy. The economic recovery of Latin American countries is also beneficial to the developed nations. For these countries, besides the success of the shared values of freedom and democracy, economic recovery also means increased trade, the safeguarding of the international financial system, and reducing migration flows into the United States.

The policy framework in the international arena will only succeed if there is policy symmetry. International trade and financial flows are important for the growth of all countries, separately and together. All countries cannot become greater exporters at the same time. Countries with trade surpluses and favorable capital movements have to increase their imports and lend part of their capital to other countries. To succeed, more outward-oriented economic strategies need to be paralleled by more open trade policies (especially on the import side) by developed countries.

The coordination of international policies would permit greater development of international comparative advantages. Consultations among the most developed countries need to be expanded and the developing countries should be included. The consultations need to go beyond the Interim and the Development Committees of the IMF and the World Bank to involve high-level representatives from Latin American countries. Furthermore, Latin American nations can contribute more to their own improvement by increasing regional coordination to integrate regional markets and facilitate transportation, communications, and information flows.

Growth and Distribution Issues

Economic growth not only provides for faster job creation and increased income per capita but also the opportunity to improve the welfare of the poor. In Latin America, the issue of growth versus distribution has been at the heart of policy actions and debate for more than two decades. The clarification of this issue is critical for the achievement of better economic performance and for the strengthening of democracy. All too often in the past, poor economic policy performance has been associated with significantly different perceptions concerning the complementarity or substitutability of the goals of economic growth and income distribution.

The goal of human development is intrinsic to a democratic system of government. It entails not only the guarantee of individual freedom but also the development of that freedom by providing opportunities to develop the talents and well-being of all individuals in society. Latin America has high levels of inequality in income distribution, but, perhaps even worse, it has given little attention to the basic needs of the poorest of the population. The success of democracy in the region will remain closely tied to the effectiveness of governments in producing concrete results for the millions of people seeking employment, housing, education, health, nutrition, electricity and water, participation, and recognition.

The key to the definition of a successful economic policy for growth and distribution is that the portion of national income that is channeled to help the poor should be sliced and allocated in the way least harmful to production efficiency and to savings and investment. This is a complex technical issue. I will highlight two essential aspects of it: First, the redistributed income would be used most effectively by investing in the permanent productive capacity of each poor person, either in terms of his self-improvement by means of education, health, culture, and motivation, or in the minimal infrastructure he needs to increase his productive capacity, such as rural roads or technical assistance programs. Productive redistribution is far more effective than consumption redistribution. An old Oriental saying expresses it eloquently: "Don't give a fish to a hungry man, teach him how to fish." Soundly, the reallocation of the income should be done in a way that is most neutral with regard to resource allocation efficiency. That means not tampering carelessly with the price mechanisms in the economy to achieve redistribution. For example, farm production should not be hurt by low prices in order to subsidize food prices in urban areas. If cheaper food is desirable, it is better to do it through the national budget or tax system and not by artificially altering the market clearing prices. Normally, neutral reallocation of resources can best be done through the national budget.

If the economies are to remain private and decentralized, then the allocative capacity of the market forces needs to be permitted to function. Economic policies work best when they guide (instead of obstruct or regulate) market forces to achieve national objectives. Even the very poorest marginal groups are hampered today in their economic and housing activities by unnecessary government regulations.[2] When there are real discrepancies between social or political goals and economic objectives then the trade-offs should be made explicit and the cost and benefits of each decision should be known.

Most successful democracies in the world work within a framework of private ownership of economic resources and market economies. Most of them also have a large middle-income group and what most observers would consider "fairly good" income distribution. In the political arena, there are ideological differences between social democratic, liberal, and conservative parties. But as democracies mature, they seem to yield to a more pragmatic, centrist approach, which oscillates between greater or lesser public regulation and public economic activism and greater or lesser emphasis on redistribution and efficiency. Perhaps the knowledge of the economic policy experiences of countries in the last three decades will contribute to achieving more political compromises around the "center," to strengthening the new democratic experiments in Latin America while they achieve higher growth and more effective improvements in human welfare.

Some critics might object that adjustment policies have worsened income distribution and human development. This is partially true, but the real cause of the worsening crisis has been economic stagnation. Growth is both the cause and consequence of social improvement.

Summary and Conclusion

The new democratic wave in Latin America is occurring simultaneously with the longest period of economic stagnation since the 1930s, while the region at large is still in the midst of a long-term population growth challenge. The stagnation forced by the reality of external debt needs to yield to a policy of economic adjustment with growth. Economic growth is necessary to sustain and strengthen the thrust toward democratic institutions. The necessary policies will only be successful if they are complemented by effective international cooperation in trade and finance well beyond the present levels. This should be possible by recognizing that the economic problem has been global. Furthermore, such additional support to Latin American recovery will produce positive concrete benefits to developed countries in particular and to the world economy at large.

The Latin American policies for renewed economic growth and human development need to emphasize:

(1) Increased orientation to world and regional markets through more exports. Exchange rates, export incentives, and protection policies need to be reviewed accordingly.

(2) Higher levels of savings and capital formation and more productive allocation of resources. Positive interest rates and more flexible market rules will contribute to this.

(3) Sounder fiscal policies that would avoid inflation and reduce excessive consumption, increase and target expenditures in human development services, and avoid the proliferation of inefficient public enterprises.

(4) More aggressive participation of the private economy through fewer government regulations and more effective incentives. These are especially relevant to the economic activities of the *marginados*.

(5) Effective utilization of the infrastructure built with external debt.

The political difficulties of implementing these policies in a democratic system are real and significant, particularly in Latin America. The careful and well-timed execution of such policies will maintain democracy in the short run and the results will sustain it in the long run. Successful implementation requires flexibility in form and substance.

Net additional funding of approximately $20 billion per year for the next three years is needed to complement national policies and achieve growth rates of up to 4 percent. Restructuring of previous debts to the longest possible maturities should continue. If no new funding is available, then the required positive transfers could be achieved by capitalization, or outright temporary forgiveness, of a portion of interest payments. External support should parallel internal efforts. Protectionist efforts in developed countries should be resisted to increase trading opportunities.

The study of the successful experiences of the last thirty years would be useful to inform leaders of the political and economic constraints and possibilities for making effective policy to encourage growth and income distribution.

Notes

1. The Inter-American Dialogue, *A Report: Rebuilding Cooperation in the Americas: 1986.* Also, see Bela Balassa, Gerardo Bueno, Pedro-Pablo Kuczynski, and Mario Henrique Simonsen, *Toward Renewed Economic Growth in Latin America* (Washington, D.C.: Institute for International Economics, 1986).

2. Hernando de Soto, *El Otro Sendero* (Peru), published in English as *The Other Path: The Invisible Revolution in the Third World* (New York: Harper and Row, 1989).

Part III

MAINTAINING
THE MOMENTUM

9

A Multilateral Arrangement to Secure Democracy

TOM J. FARER

Introduction

Article 21 of the Universal Declaration of Human Rights affirms not only that "Everyone has the right to take part in the government of his country, directly or through freely chosen representatives," but also that "the will of the people shall be the basis of the authority of government [and that will] shall be expressed in periodic and genuine elections. . . ."[1] It implies in the strongest possible terms that democracy is the basis of state legitimacy.

When it had no human rights enforcement machinery, the United Nations ignored this implication. Having acquired such machinery and reaffirmed in Article 25 of the Covenant on Civil and Political Rights[2] that the right to participate in government is indistinguishable from a competitive politics marked by free elections, the member states continue to ignore it; the alternative, of course, is to disqualify the great majority of delegates on the grounds that they represent illegitimate governments. Thus the organization maintains the principle of universality in its membership.

Both the American Declaration on the Rights and Duties of Man[3] and the American Convention on Human Rights[4] affirm a right to democracy in terms almost identical to their U.N. counterparts, but they omit a statement clearly implying that legitimate authority is inseparable from the effective exercise of that right. That inclusion might seem unnecessary because the Charter of the Organization of American States[5] recognizes the existence of democratic institutions in its member states as a prerequisite for achieving the organization's goals. Article 3 states: "The solidarity of the American states and the high aims which are sought through it require the political organization of those states on the basis of the effective exercise of representative democracy."

The Inter-American Commission on Human Rights,[6] the only self-activating enforcement mechanism established by the OAS, has self-consciously included the enforcement of democratic rights within its broad mandate[7] and has in general succeeded in obtaining support, largely though not exclusively formal and rhetorical support, for its efforts from the organization's supreme political organ, the General Assembly. The commission's special reports on the general situation of human rights in named countries have almost always included a section on political rights analyzing the freedom of the electoral process at least insofar as campaigning and voting is concerned. And where it has concluded that the process does not satisfy the applicable standards, the commission has recommended change, sometimes in very specific terms. In its 1978 report on El Salvador, for instance, it called for reorganization of the Central Election Council (which was responsible for the supervision of elections) "so that there may be equitable representation of the political parties in it, and confidence in the system may be established."[8]

The United States has led the effort to put teeth into findings of non-compliance. Unfortunately it has done so in a way that, with one exception, has carefully distinguished by omission right-wing authoritarian states from left-wing ones. In the 1959 Declaration of Santiago, adopted by the Fifth Meeting of Consultation of Ministers of Foreign Affairs, the very meeting that established the commission, the OAS foreign ministers agreed that "harmony among the American republics can be effective only insofar as human rights and fundamental freedoms and the exercise of representative democracy are a reality within each one of them. . . ."[9]

Relying in part on Cuba's deviation from the democratic norm, shortly thereafter the necessary special majority led by the United States suspended the present Cuban government from the exercise of all the rights of membership.

During the early days of the Alliance for Progress, John F. Kennedy did go so far as to deny temporarily the recognition of impeccably conservative governments established by military coups against civilian regimes. Under Jimmy Carter, the United States broke far more sharply with its traditions by allying itself with the great majority of OAS members in a call for the resignation of Anastasio Somoza at the height of Nicaragua's civil war.[10] This demand, extraordinary in the annals of intergovernmental organizations, was keyed in part to the threat to regional peace arising from the conflict within Nicaragua, in part to the grave violations of the right to life and physical security committed by the Somoza regime; but the governing resolution also cited, as a necessary element of any solution to the crisis, the establishment of a democratic government in Nicaragua.[11]

Among the Reagan administration's principal justifications for its proxy war against the Sandinista regime, a *prima facie* violation of international law, is the Sandinistas' failure to conduct free elections. While opposing U.S. actions, the Contadora countries and their support group who together comprise all the leading Latin states of the hemisphere have included in successive versions of their draft treaty the requirement that all signatories organize their political lives on the basis of fair elections.[12] In terms of the force of the democratic norm, it is significant that not one of the Central American states, the potential signatories, has labeled this provision an intrusion in its internal affairs.

Regimes chosen in relatively free elections at least nominally govern at the present time in most countries in the Western Hemisphere. Many of these regimes have succeeded military governments in countries with no tradition of civilian control over the military, in countries where the military, not the constitution, has determined the limits of policy and the tenure of civilian rule. And the extent to which several of these governments actually govern in the sense of being able to establish and implement policy in all areas of national life is modest to slight. On assuming office in Guatemala in 1986, President Cerezo said quite openly that he held about 25 percent of the real power in Guatemala. That power has not been sufficient either to end massacres in the countryside or political murder carried out by or with the acquiescence of the armed forces in the capital itself. Nor has he been able to bring to justice a single soldier for the mass murders of civilians carried out by the armed forces for over two decades prior to his accession. Later in this chapter I will return to the issue of military autonomy and its implications for the promotion and protection of democratic government.

In the remainder of this chapter I will concentrate on the role of bilateral and multilateral arrangements, both present and potential, in helping democracy in the region. For the hemisphere as a whole, we have the OAS and its peacekeeping and security arrangements elaborated in the Rio Treaty. Subregional arrangements with political elements include the Andean Pact and the Central American security system known as CONDECA. There is also the organization of the small anglophone eastern Caribbean states, which encouraged, endorsed, and according to some observers legitimized the U.S. invasion of Grenada, another venture, according to President Reagan, in democracy-making.[13]

Since none of these arrangements has demonstrated any significant capacity to produce the defense and promotion of democratic regimes, I will consider only the problems and prospects of hitherto untested means.

Even those Latin leaders with an indisputable commitment to strong democracy have been, are, and no doubt will continue to be opposed to unilateral and hence presumptively illegal military actions by the United States, whether to maintain or to install democratic government. A range of imaginable alternatives would include the following options (obviously not mutually exclusive):

(1) The United States could announce that, pursuant to its obligations under the OAS Charter and the Rio Treaty and acting in consonance with the customary law allowing one government to seek the aid of another in restoring public order,[14] in the event of the unconstitutional displacement of a democratically elected government anywhere in the hemisphere, at the request of the highest official of that government able to act without coercion, it is prepared to impose total economic sanctions and, if appropriate, to intervene militarily. In the meantime it would continue to recognize the dispossessed administration as the country's legitimate regime enjoying exclusive access to all public property, including gold and bank deposits located in the United States.

(2) The United States could announce that it was prepared to take such measures in all cases where the political organs of the OAS authorized them under the terms of the Charter and the Rio Treaty.

(3) The United States could enter into a series of bilateral agreements or one multilateral agreement with hemispheric states wishing to engage in mutual support of their respective democratic institutions. Pursuant to such agreement or agreements, each party would commit itself to nonrecognition of unconstitutional regimes and to mutual assistance including economic and military sanctions against usurpers.

(4) The United States could condition its continued participation in the Inter-American Development Bank on that institution's adoption of a policy of suspending borrowing privileges for nondemocratic regimes. A provision to that effect would be incorporated in the bank's charter. It would, however, require a vote of a majority of the bank's members for activation of the provision.

(5) The United States could encourage other democratic states to join with it in establishing a new financial institution designed to provide support exclusively for democratic regimes in the hemisphere. Loans would be callable in the event of such a regime's displacement by unconstitutional means.

(6) The United States could enter into agreements with democratic governments entitling them to special trade concessions that would be automatically suspended in the event of their unconstitutional displacement. However, the determination of unconstitutionality would be left to a committee of legal experts established pursuant to these agreements.

(7) The OAS could prepare a fair elections code and establish a list of election supervisors: Persons nominated by states obtaining an absolute majority of votes for inclusion in the list and enjoying an impeccable reputation for integrity. Governments or political parties could petition the OAS for the dispatch of electoral supervisors. The OAS could amend its charter to authorize the expulsion of members who refuse to accept supervision or, having accepted it, fail to provide the supervisors with necessary assistance or otherwise obstruct them in the performance of their duties.

Prior to examining these varied alternatives, it may be useful to underscore several obvious difficulties. First, the history of the United States, like that of any great power, does not foster belief that the United States would apply sanctions evenhandedly. Thus several of the alternatives are likely to provide convenient cover for the promotion of national interests other than defending democracy. Second, it is at least debatable whether the protection of other human rights, including such nonderogable rights as the right to life, physical security, and due process, is invariably superior in states that periodically hold free elections. Third, truly free elections involve much more than protection of the electorate from coercion during the period immediately preceding the vote and an accurate count. Hence election supervisors, while being able to affirm that the dog had a tail that wagged in the prescribed fashion, may remain (may even feel constrained by their mandate to remain) essentially ignorant of the animal's more significant characteristics. With these preliminary caveats in mind, let us turn to the clustered problems the enumerated options generate.

The Military Option

The first and third options described above have ample though not necessarily inviting precedent in contemporary international relations. In 1964, less than a year after Kenya and Tanzania achieved independence, both of these governments responded to army mutinies by calling for and quickly receiving British assistance in suppressing them. In order to reduce the risk of recurrences, both armies, but particularly the Tanzanian one, were stripped down and reassembled. Former French colonies have similarly appealed for and obtained armed intervention from the ex-metropole in order to reestablish governments displaced by military coups as well as to suppress rebellions. Both appeals and responses have occurred within the framework of mutual defense agreements. It is, however, questionable whether these agreements affect the legality of intervention.

Both before and after the adoption of the United Nations Charter, the great majority of legal scholars and most governments have regarded the power to invite foreign troops into one's country for any purpose whatsoever as an attribute of sovereignty.[15] However, where the purpose is to assist in suppressing rebellion, some scholars have argued that the need for foreign assistance implies a loss of control and hence the loss of legitimacy to act on behalf of the nation.[16]

The preclusion of intervention to suppress rebellion has two possible virtues. One, in the absence of effective democratic institutions, violence may be the majority's only means for effecting change. Since in any test of strength, the hitherto recognized government enjoys very substantial advantages, if it is nevertheless unable to overcome its opponents without the aid of foreign troops, the opponents should normally be presumed to enjoy broader and more intense popular support than the government.[17] Two, since states traditionally have intervened only in order to advance important national interests, a norm allowing intervention helps camouflage acts of sheer self-aggrandizement, i.e., aggression. The intervening state might for instance fabricate an invitation or act on the basis of an invitation from some suborned fraction of the government of the target state.

One is reminded of the joke that passed among East European dissidents in the wake of the Soviet invasion of Czechoslovakia. The spearhead of the Soviet force rumbles up to the gates of Prague when suddenly Prime Minister Dubček and his entire cabinet appear in its path. "What are you doing here on Czech soil?" Dubček asks in Russian. The young officer in the lead tank, a look of consternation spreading across his broad Slav face, signals that his interrogator should wait. Then he speaks nervously into a walkie-talkie. As the response crackles back, consternation yields to a smile of relief. Looking down with renewed confidence on Dubček and his colleagues, the officer responds: "We are here to find the people who invited us."

Obviously one key to the correct operation of the norm is the ability to identify the "legitimate government." As long as a person or persons do occupy roles defined by a state's written constitution or by long-established practice as the sources of legitimate authority, and as long as they exercise effective control throughout the territory of the state, there is no real problem because, except in time of war, the persons satisfying those conditions are certain to enjoy virtually unanimous recognition by other governments. In case of rebellion in the hinterlands, most states have continued to recognize the incumbents as the legitimate government so long as they retain control of the capital (normally, the best the rebels can hope for is recognition as belligerents, a status thought to impose an obligation of neutrality on third parties).[18] But this traditional presumption in favor of the hitherto recognized government does not have and probably by its nature could not have firm parameters. Under the conditions of civil conflict, states inevitably possess considerable discretion in choosing whom to recognize as legitimate.

Coups d'état compound the discretion of third parties and hence the potential abuse of any license to intervene. For in the generality of cases, coups create an immediate and virtually complete dichotomy between constitutionally sanctioned and effective authority. Leaders of the government might be dead or in detention. Ministers still at large are likely to lack any territorial base and may not agree whether to acquiesce or to resist the takeover. Moreover, the coup-makers may invoke a national tradition of military intervention to prevent governments from exceeding constitutional restraints, to prevent a breakdown of public order, or to combat some external threat to the political independence or basic social structure of the state; this tradition, they might argue, has become part of the constitutional scheme.

The risk of intervention in the event of a coup against a democratically elected government might encourage the coup-makers to eliminate anyone who could arguably speak on behalf of the government. And intervention itself in the face of opposition from the indigenous military establishment could cause serious human and material damage within the target state. Under those circumstances the bulk of the citizenry might prefer continued military rule.

Intervention to restore democratic rule may encounter strong civilian opposition in the target country for another reason. In cases where a democratically elected government has been unable to maintain public order or to introduce badly needed economic or social reforms or where it has launched reforms repugnant to many social groups, the coup itself may be received enthusiastically by a not-trivial part of the population. Mutual assistance pacts for the maintenance of democracy have strong moral credentials when they are contracted among states marked by support for democratic processes across virtually the entire political and class spectrum. Those are, of course, precisely the states least in need of such pacts. The demise of democracy in Chile and

Uruguay and France's close call during the Algerian War demonstrate, however, that no democratic system is immune to widespread apostasy.

Although in diplomacy as in law, the military option is deemed extreme, the option of last resort when it is a tolerable option at all as an instrument for reinforcing democracy in the hemisphere's smaller countries has certain distinct advantages over economic sanctions. While military measures might cause incidental injury to civilians, economic measures if they proceed beyond the threat stage will certainly injure the civilian population. And since they will normally work more slowly and must therefore be applied over a relatively longer period, the injury may be difficult to heal once democracy has been restored. For example: Products that have lost markets in the United States as a result of sanctions may not be able to regain them; the costs of getting up to speed again on construction projects halted by the suspension of access to the Inter-American Bank or private capital may inflate final project costs to the point where an economic return probably can never be earned.

Economic sanctions may, moreover, achieve their objective by fracturing the unity of the military or civil-military coalition that carried out the coup, thereby precipitating civil conflict and that very loss of life and property the prospect of which originally inhibited recourse to the military option. While the costs of economic sanctions may, therefore, equal or exceed those engendered by military force, the potential benefits may be smaller. Although forced back to their barracks, the armed forces will retain their fundamental character and thus remain a simmering threat to democratic government. At a minimum they will continue to exercise undue influence over the policy process. After a successful military intervention, on the other hand, a democratic government has the option of following the Costa Rican example of disbanding the armed forces and replacing them with a small constabulary under the command of officials alternating with changes in civil administration. Or it can at least purge the armed forces of their most antidemocratic elements and develop a new officer corps from young cadres of the main political parties.

Whether mutual assistance pacts between the United States and small democratic states where the popular classes have been incorporated into the political system and respect for human rights is institutionalized should altogether rule out the military option is a close question. (The only cases that come to mind are Costa Rica, Barbados, and certain other anglophone Caribbean states.) Included in pacts with larger states, the option could serve as a marginal deterrent, marginal because of the high expectation on all sides that it would not in fact be exercised. Where the prospective costs of confronting an indigenous military establishment are sufficient to discourage military means, the guarantors will then face all the difficulties associated with economic measures. They are not inconsiderable.

Economic Measures

In most cases closing U.S. markets to products of the target country will prove to be both the quickest and the most efficient measure to implement and the most severe. Since virtually all of Latin America's important exports function in highly competitive markets and therefore with low profit margins, sanctions evasion will be extremely difficult and the direct cost of sanctions to the U.S. economy extremely low. Indirect costs will vary with the size of the target state. Most of the larger Latin states are among the world's largest debtors. Sanctions cutting sharply into foreign exchange earnings—which is precisely the intent of a ban on imports—would almost certainly trigger default, with potentially serious consequences for the North American private banking community. Not all the possible ripple effects of a major default are predictable.

The debt problem would dog the heels of all economic sanctions, not just an import ban. The peculiar efficacy of a ban is attended by certain peculiar difficulties. One is legal: Assuming the target state is a member of the General Agreement on Tariffs and Trade (GATT),[19] the ban would be a prima facie violation of the GATT's organizing principle, nondiscrimination. But the GATT's ban is not absolute. There is, for instance, a national security exception.[20]

One way around the legal obstacles is the enumerated option of including in mutual aid agreements a provision authorizing if not requiring all parties to impose economic sanctions in order to restore democratic institutions in case they are overthrown. Article 58 of the Vienna Convention on the Law of Treaties provides for the "suspension of the operation of a multilateral treaty by agreement between certain of the parties . . . [if] the suspension is not prohibited by the treaty and . . . does not affect the enjoyment by the other parties of their rights under the treaty . . . [and] is not incompatible with the object and purpose of the treaty."[21] The mutual aid pacts would, in my judgment, satisfy those criteria.

Such pacts would ease some but not all the legal *problematique* of sanctions, the express purpose of which is to alter existing political arrangements in one of the parties. One of sovereignty's defining characteristics is political autonomy. Political autonomy would have little meaning if the procedures and personnel of government were not immune to external dictation. Such at least has been the generally accepted view. (The policies produced by local procedures and personnel are another matter, since there are a grand variety of ways in which they can impinge on the legitimate interests of other states. With regard to policy, in other words, there can be and not infrequently is an overlap of national jurisdictions.)

The right to determine by whom and by what means political power shall be exercised is fundamental to the idea of national sovereignty, and the protection of sovereignty is a purpose of the United Nations system that is in no way subordinate to the preservation of peace (as evidenced by the undiminished right of self-defense). Can a government bind future generations by entering into international agreements authorizing other states to enforce a particular ideology of governance? Although I have built the case for a negative answer into the question, the question is not rhetorical. For one of the most remarkable features of the post–World War II era is the extent to which states have allowed the international law of human rights to narrow the range of state discretion.

That governments can in general bind their successors by entering into agreements with other states is an indisputable proposition. If treaties became as transient as the governments that ratify them, we would face a far more disorderly and perilous world. Treaties remain binding, constraining state discretion and hence the unfettered exercise of sovereign power, just as contracts entered into by public and private corporations continue to bind the corporation regardless of changes in its board of directors and chief executive.

But there are limits; there must be limits. Within states those limits are necessary to preserve the essence of democracy. Among nations those limits are necessary to prevent the gutting of sovereignty. In the age of imperialism, such agreements were common. We had one with Cuba known as the Platt Amendment. Today they are rare because of a legal and diplomatic consensus reflected in Article 52 of the Vienna Convention that "a treaty is void if its conclusion has been procured by the threat or use of force in violation of the principles of international law embodied in the Charter of the United Nations." No uncoerced and unsuborned government would give another state a license to intervene more or less at the latter's discretion.

Option three—mutual assistance agreements to defend democracy—envisions a considerably narrower license and its objective, maintaining representative government, has the status of an internationally recognized human right. It is therefore an objective that is beneficial to all the contracting parties and to their respective peoples. Moreover, one could argue, the legitimacy of such agreements may follow *a fortiori* from the conceded power of a government to obliterate sovereignty altogether by merging with another state. On balance, it seems correct to state that international agreements authorizing intervention are neither void nor voidable if the objective is legitimate under international law and consent has not been coerced by one means or another.

Democracy: On Reality and Illusion

To be legal is not necessarily to be desirable. Among the practical obstacles to consistent and effective operation of any system of international coercion for the protection of democracy, one of the most serious is the difficulty in Third World settings of determining whether an authentic democracy either is or was functioning. Particularly in Latin America, where liberal assumptions about the popular will as the only source of legitimacy enjoy a powerful purchase in the culture, many regimes have found it useful to maintain a democratic facade while employing various means to assure that nothing endangering authoritarian rule gets built behind it. The favored means in Guatemala has been murder, not simple murder but murder preceded by unspeakable torture and followed by mutilation.[22] Thus terror becomes the accomplice of death. Before 1979, the Salvadoran military and their civilian associates were more eclectic: While not eschewing murder and lesser forms of intimidation, they also employed methods familiar to historians of North America's more notorious urban political machines; manipulation of voter rolls, lost ballots, and so forth.[23]

The wide deployment of election observers would help greatly to reduce intimidation at the polls and to produce a clean count. That may not be nearly enough to offset advantages secured over the years by murdering the cadres of opposition parties and otherwise obstructing grass-roots organizations. Much may depend on the extent to which intermediate institutions—churches, labor unions, peasant leagues—have retained their independence; where they have, they provide the opposition with a ready-made electoral base. Much may also depend on the size of the country and its level of development. In a small country it is relatively easy even in a short period to reach the entire electorate. And if a country is relatively undeveloped, the fairly simple class structure and economy will usually yield a few sharply defined programmatic cleavages that even a largely illiterate electorate can quickly grasp.

In practice, international election observance has been a very mixed bag, demonstrating at least as much capacity for authenticating as for preventing frauds. Observers tend to be impressed by the campaign and the vote and to be insensitive to structural distortions other than those they are predisposed to notice. Americans of blameless character and some considerable ideological diversity gave the good elections seal of approval to the Rhodesian election in April 1979 conducted by the white settler government of Ian Smith, although the guerrilla leaders, Robert Mugabe and Joshua Nkomo, were unable to participate. Despite their absence, the substantial turnout (64 percent of the eligible voters) and the vote (67.3 percent) for the party of the only serious black contender, Bishop Abel Muzorewa, convinced these observers not only that they had witnessed an authentic election, but that the resulting government should be recognized as a legitimate expression of popular will. Just how accurately that vote recorded the true preferences of the electorate became apparent one year later when the British administered the electoral machinery, the guerrilla leaders participated, and 93.6 percent of the eligible voters turned out. Bishop Muzorewa's followers secured 8.2 percent of the vote (compared to 62.9 percent for Robert Mugabe's party and 24.1 percent for Joshua Nkomo's), whereupon the good bishop vanished from the political scene.

Like the white settlers of Rhodesia, the French of Algeria were able to extract votes favorable to the French presence as long as they chose to stay. When de Gaulle gave Algerians a real choice, they voted overwhelmingly for independence. Precedent suggests strongly that when authoritarian governments control the electoral process, they do not often experience outcomes they are determined to avoid.

An inquiry into the authenticity of democratic forms engages issues of fact, of theory, and of value. It requires answers to two questions: Was the competition fair? Did the winners acquire and do they continue to possess the power really to govern? The respondent will answer by marshalling the facts he or she deems relevant. Theory and personal values will provide the criteria of relevance and will govern the interpretation of the facts.

Take the first question. What does "fairness" mean?[24] From a classical liberal perspective, ideally the political arena parallels the economic one. In both realms, entrepreneurs compete to identify and satisfy the demands of consumers. In both, consumers are assumed to be rational, uncoerced actors with sufficient knowledge of all the alternatives to allow them to make an informed choice. In both realms, the possibility of new entrants when existing entrepreneurs do not adequately service consumer preferences is also assumed.

Deviations from the model in the economic sphere have generated all sorts of corrective actions by governments, from pure food and drug laws to airline safety inspections to antitrust prosecutions, as well as sometimes successful demands in many countries for direct public control of key economic enterprises. Skepticism about the political model has, it seems to me, been qualitatively less intense, at least in the advanced capitalist states. Confidence in the efficacy of political laissez faire—with a few correctives primarily for the benefit of racial and ethnic minorities—together with affluence and the welfare state is the foundation of civic peace in the western world.

The liberal ethos that has shaped the intellectual formation of almost all public figures in the Americas probably is a sufficient explanation of the failure of the Inter-American Commission on Human Rights, so acute a prober beneath surfaces in most respects, to peer beyond the forms of political competition in states where civilians rule, parties alternate, and terror is not institutionalized. Moreover, the commission members' mindset mirrors that of their audience; efforts to tunnel beneath appearances would seem to be not so much quixotic as subversive. Even if the commissioners could transcend their own and their audience's predispositions, they would find their way barred by an impoverishment of means. Whether because of the hegemony of liberalism (in the Gramscian sense) or because of the intrinsically problematic nature of the subject, there exists no cluster of widely accepted criteria for identifying, much less assessing, the more subtle forms of restraint on the exercise of a free and reasonably informed political choice.

The issue is not academic. I recall clearly an important case in which the members of the commission, including myself, ignored allegations by left-wing opponents of the government that the effective exercise of political rights was being decisively inhibited by the following barriers:

(1) There was very limited access for left-wing parties to the mass media, which were controlled by a few wealthy families and powerfully influenced by the government;

(2) Voting "correctly" was a condition of neighborhood and village access to government services;

(3) Leaders of the two major parties maintained a "gentlemen's agreement" to keep potentially popular reform measures that were deemed radical off the agenda of issues over which they would compete;

(4) The parties shared power at all levels of government, regardless of the outcome of the competition between them and they excluded representatives of the left.

The point was so evident that left-wing critics who labeled the political system under which they lived a "facade democracy" did not even bother mentioning the vast disparity of resources between them and the political elite.

How could the commission have come to grips with these charges when they were not qualitatively different from those that could be leveled at most Third World democracies and when to some degree more than one of these barriers can be found even among the industrially advanced capitalist democracies? The commission's substantive standards are not utopian. It is able to find violations of the right to participate in government only in two sorts of cases: Those in which votes are stolen and voters are terrorized and those in which the real substance of power is not in the offices of government, but rather in the cantonments of the armed forces.

The second set of cases is common enough in Latin America. In the spirit of the colonial administrators who responded to the avalanche of edicts descending on them from Madrid with the immortal line, "*Obedezco pero no cumplo*" (I obey but I do not comply)[25] the officer corps in most countries have remained intractably independent of civilian control. Regarding themselves as the true guardians of the national interest, and treating the unity and autonomy of the military institution as the highest value, they comply with the orders and exhortations of elected officials to the extent that they deem appropriate and remain prepared to displace any government that threatens either their autonomy or their conception of the national interest. The enduring power of this awful constraint on the exercise of democracy is suggested by the fact that of all the Latin states where real party competition has at least arguably flourished at one point or another during the past four decades, only Costa Rica and, arguably, Venezuela, have succeeded in firmly subjecting their armed forces to civilian control, the former by virtually disbanding them.

Because the latitude allowed elected officials by their military establishments varies according to time and place across a broad spectrum and because encroachments on civilian rule not infrequently are gradual, subtle, and masked both by loosely drawn constitutional language and by collaborators in the civil administration, determining when encroachment has so eviscerated civilian rule as to constitute a violation of political rights is very difficult. Complicating the identification of delinquency are constitutional provisions in many countries that allocate to their governments a broad discretion to suspend most civil and political rights in times of emergency and that allow trials of civilians by military courts, particularly during states of emergency.

Military establishments can suck out the substance of democracy in ways far more subtle than the mass detention without charge or trial of civilians or their subjection to courts manned by serving officers. For instance, as a condition for allowing the restoration or continuation of civilian government, they may enter into pacts with the political elite in which the latter delegate to the former the selection of the minister of defense and exclusive jurisdiction over crimes attributed to military personnel. Party leaders may also feel compelled to issue amnesties to members of the armed forces for every sort of crime and to commit a percentage of the national budget to arms purchases. They also submit to military dictation on such questions as whether independent labor unions, peasant associations, and left-wing political parties shall be allowed to organize, whether criticism of the military shall be treated as a criminal offense, and on such issues as tax and land reform. What is left of democracy?

Yet another dilemma confronts those who would organize interstate arrangements in order to succor democracy. What if a government freely chosen by a majority of the voters, rather than acquiescing in a reign of terror by the country's security forces as a condition of remaining in office, initiates it? The idea is not farfetched. Hitler secured office through constitutional means and with the assurance that persecution of the Jews would enjoy wide popular support. And Germany is hardly the only country in which majorities have evinced supreme disinterest in the human rights of some discrete minority.

Conclusion: A Basis for Skepticism, But. . .

If the United States or any other country wants to concentrate aid of one sort or another on regimes that have (1) an authentic electoral mandate, and (2) the will and freedom to exercise it, and (3) are not themselves violating human rights, the task of finding appropriate subjects for assistance may seem slightly less formidable than the one ascribed by George Bernard Shaw to metaphysicians. They, said he, are looking in an unlit cellar at midnight for a very black cat who is not there.

Can one nevertheless find comfort in Dr. Johnson's observation that "the fact of twilight does not prevent us telling day from night"? While to gods, sitting in awful detachment on Olympus, cases may be clear, strategic interests and ideological passions have a way of clouding the minds of mere mortals, particularly those who preside over the destinies of great powers. What guide do we have other than experience?

This hemisphere's experience with one hundred years of North American hegemony offers rather slight grounds for belief that political leaders in the United States, taken as a group, are immune to the occupational confusions of the powerful. In this connection it is useful, indeed it is essential, to recall that states with morally elevated domestic arrangements have sometimes displayed considerable ruthlessness in dealing with the inhabitants of other states. After all, it was Athens which denied Melos the choice of neutrality in the Peloponnesian War, secured its surrender through a relentless siege, and thereafter put to death all the city's grown men and sold the women and children for slaves.

To be frank, I have hardly greater confidence in the objectivity of weak states. When World War I released the so-called suppressed minorities from the sinking hulk of the Austro-Hungarian Empire, no sooner did some of them manage to form states than they began suppressing their own minorities and battling with each other, all in the grand name of national self-determination. Unilateral intervention by any state is suspect, intervention by a superpower being merely the *a fortiori* instance.

Schemes for international action to foster democracy that are not truly multilateral in character will end up serving as fig leaves for the raw thrust of great power interests. The participants in such schemes must include states with long democratic traditions and the capacity for independent judgement. As a practical matter, then, they must include at least some of the North Atlantic democracies in addition to the United States. Mutual licenses for intervention negotiated among the United States and a handful of weak Caribbean basin countries, although invoking the great name of democracy as their inspiration, would certainly look like nineteenth-century protectorates in twentieth-century drag.

Can it be that in this case looks are deceiving, that the body of interests and values under the costume has to some degree changed? Certainly the trading monopolies that protectorates have sometimes fostered are not a present or prospective goal of the United States. At least in the Caribbean basin, the United States promotes economic ties to discourage coups and revolutions that would be objectionable for geopolitical rather than economic reasons. Economic influence, in other words, is a means rather than one important end. But because of ideologically fixed doubts that are prevalent in the U.S. foreign policy community about the political "soundness" of leftist reformers, institutionalized channels of intervention will tempt Democratic as well as Republican presidents to use them in ways that tend to freeze the political agenda in Caribbean basin countries and to deflect the natural trajectory of their political systems as they respond to shifts in their economies and societies.

While some degree of intervention is likely to occur with or without benefit of a legal fig leaf, the leaf may be necessary to marshall domestic political support for high-profile and decisive interventions in states on the cusp of radical political change. Nevertheless, the ultimate impact of licensed intervention on opportunities for citizens to participate in the processes by which they are governed is conjectural.

It is conjectural in part because developments within the United States—including a better-educated and more sophisticated electorate, a Congress better equipped in terms of infrastructure and psychology to review the executive handling of foreign policy, and the proliferation of human rights monitoring groups with elite sponsors and some media and grass roots support—make it considerably more difficult today than it was in either the early years of this century or during the first phases of the Cold War for the executive branch to subvert democracy in the name of democracy. Because of these recent incentives to make policy conform to rhetoric, and because of the indigenous threats to the continuance of democracy where it now exists and to its successful gestation where it has only recently been inseminated, institutions tending to induce or to facilitate United States involvement could on balance promote participatory politics in the Caribbean basin. A superpower agreement pursuant to which the Soviet Union explicitly recognized the basin as a zone of United States influence and committed itself to eschew military relations with incumbents or rebels (other than the present government of Cuba, which would be required to adopt a policy of strict neutrality in relation to internal conflicts in the hemisphere) would ease U.S. geopolitical anxieties and enhance the prospects for a positive U.S. role in fostering democracy in the region. But as I have already suggested, West European participation in any system for the defense and promotion of democracy would reduce the risk of abuse, as it enhances the chance of success.

Success on a scale not previously known could result from strategies not previously tried. Because the obstacles to success are qualitatively different in the hemisphere's larger states and because neither the United States alone nor that country in conjunction with its allies is prepared to assume the risks or bear the potential costs of serious economic sanctions, much less military intervention, in such states, and because the potential targets are unlikely to associate themselves with any institution that poses even a theoretical risk of intervention, there is a strong case for two quite separate arrangements.

One arrangement would link the capitalist democracies with the smaller states of the Caribbean basin. At a minimum it would provide well-established democracies—principally Costa Rica, the anglophone islands, and Belize—with military guarantees against foreign aggression and domestic coups. Such an organization might even earmark a rapid-response force, analogous to the units France deploys in or for assignment to Africa, which could be dispatched at the request of a recognized member government, subject, however, to a veto by a majority of the other members. By majority vote the members could also impose a ban on exports from any nation experiencing an interruption in democratic government.

To enhance the attractiveness of such an arrangement, such an organization should have at its disposal financial resources to support development projects and to ease crises such as balance-of-payments shortfalls resulting from crop failures or from a price collapse in the market for a key commodity. Obviously these resources must augment those that would otherwise be available through established intergovernmental financial institutions.

The organizational arrangements could include a category of "associated states." These would be states without fully developed democratic institutions, generally states in which the military continues to exercise decisive power, whose governments wished to access the organization's exchequer while being unwilling or because of political obstacles at home unable to accept the vulnerability to economic sanctions or military intervention stemming from full membership. The organization could fund projects in associated states tending to strengthen their democratic potentials.

An institution linking industrially advanced capitalist democracies with the larger Latin states now governed by elected regimes could not be organized, I am convinced, unless its architects were prepared to forgo any coercive means other than suspension and expulsion for influencing the internal politics of its members. It could pursue its goals in part by funding improvements in the democratic infrastructure of states: projects tending, for example, to increase the competence, prestige, and independence of the judiciary, or to increase equality of opportunity and generally to broaden the middle-class economic base, or to strengthen civilian involvement in military education and strategic planning, or to diversify the media, or to facilitate the organization of traditionally underrepresented groups. In addition, it would strengthen transnational contacts among elites with a natural democratic bias (for example, intellectuals, teachers, peasant and labor leaders) and it would use its resources and prestige to encourage constructive yet relatively informal contacts between elites normally separated by deep fault lines of ideology and organization (for example, generals and intellectuals, business and labor leaders). Through the networks created by means of a plethora of conferences, seminars, fellowships, and secondments, it would seek to disseminate the economic, political, and administrative strategies of modern welfare capitalism along with its skeptical, empirical, and more-or-less libertarian ethos. But to have much immediate impact, I believe that like its counterpart organization for the smaller hemispheric states, it would have to dispose of substantial financial assets on which the members with relatively low per capita incomes could draw.

Aside from (and perhaps in some measure as an measure of) their capacity to accelerate the consolidation of democratic regimes, by legitimating and institutionalizing a large role in the Western Hemisphere for our principal democratic allies and thereby requiring Washington to consult and coordinate policy with them rather than merely announce it and demand support, these two organizations would tend to stabilize U.S. policy and to reduce our paranoid anxiety about developments south of the border. Because such paranoia has periodically inflamed our politics and distorted our priorities, one can only welcome the mellowing effect that a larger role for other democracies could produce.

Notes

1. Approved by Resolution 217A (III) of the General Assembly, 10 December 1948. Three (pt. 1) GAOR, Resolutions (A/810), pp. 71–77.

2. Adopted by Resolution 2200 (XXI) of the General Assembly, 16 December 1966. GAOR, XXI, Suppl. No. 16 (A/6316), pp. 52–58.

3. Resolution XXX, adopted by the Ninth International Conference of American States, held at Bogotá, Colombia, 30 March–2 May 1948. Pan American Union, Final Act of the Ninth Conference of American States 38–45 (Washington, D.C. 1948).

4. Signed at the Inter-American Specialized Conference on Human Rights, San José, Costa Rica, 22 November 1969. Entered into force 18 July 1978. OAS Treaty Series, No. 36, at 1–21 (OAS Official Records, OEA/Ser.A/16, (English).

5. 30 April 1948, 2 U.S.T. 2394, T.I.A.S. No. 2361, 119 U.N.T.S.

6. For a description of the commission's activities and an effort to locate its work within the context of inter-American relations, see Tom Farer, *The Grand Strategy of the United States in the Western Hemisphere* (New Brunswick: Transaction, 1987), Section 3. An excellent compilation of the commission's normative framework, doctrine, cases and report summaries can be found in *Inter-American Commission on Human Rights: Ten Years of Activities 1971–81* (OAS, Washington, D.C., 1982).

7. See, e.g., its *Report on the Situation of Human Rights in Argentina*, OEA/Ser.L/V/II.49, doc. 19 corr. 1, 11 April 1980, pp. 245–50 (English version). In its *Annual Report* for the period 1979–80, the commission declared as follows: "The right to political participation leaves room for a wide variety of forms of government; there are many constitutional alternatives as regards the degree of centralization of the powers of the state or the election and attributes of the organs responsible for the exercise of those powers. However, a democratic framework is an essential element for establishment of a political society where human values can be fully realized. The right to political participation makes possible the right to organize parties and political associations which, through open discussion and ideological struggle, can improve the social level and economic circumstances of the masses and prevent a monopoly of power by any one group or individual."

8. OEA/Ser.L/V/II.46, doc. 23 rev. 1, 17 November 1978, p. 176.

9. Fifth Meeting of Consultation (Santiago, Chile, 12–18 August 1959), Final Act, OAS Official Records, OEA/Ser. C/II.5, pp. 4–5.

10. An illuminating case study of Carter's human rights policy can be found in Richard Lillich and Frank Newman, *International Human Rights* (Boston: Little, Brown, 1979) p. 824.

11. The Seventeenth Meeting of Consultation of Ministers of Foreign Affairs, Resolution II, approved at the seventh plenary session, 23 June 1979, see Inter-American Commission on Human Rights, *Ten Years of Activities*, p. 396.

12. See "Declaration of the Presidents of Colombia, Mexico, Panama and Venezuela on Peace in Central America," OEA/Ser.G, CP/INF. 2021/83, 19 July 1983; Stephen Kinzer, "Nicaraguans Say They Would Sign Proposed Treaty," *New York Times*, 23 September 1984; Jim Morrell and William Goodfellow, "Contadora Under the Gun," *International Policy Report*, Washington, D.C., May 1986.

13. In defense of the legality of the invasion, see, *inter alia*, letter (dated 10 February 1984) of Davis Robinson, the legal adviser of the Department of State, to Professor Edward Gordon, chairman, Committee on Grenada of the American Bar Association's Section on International Law and Practice and the statement by Langhorne Motley, assistant secretary of state for inter-American affairs, before the House Armed Services Committee, 24 January 1984 (*Current Policy* No. 541, "The Decision to Assist Grenada"). For a fence-straddling view, see Daniel Hill Zafren, "The Intervention in Grenada: A Brief Analysis Under International Law of the Justifications Asserted by the United States," Congressional Research Service, the Library of Congress, 27 October 1983. For more critical views, see Abram Chayes, "Grenada Was Illegally Invaded," *New York Times*, 15 November 1983; Burns Weston, "U.S. Invasion of Grenada Violates International Law," *Des Moines Register*, 1 November 1983; and *Report of the Committee on Grenada*, American Bar Association, Section of International Law and Practice, 10 February 1984.

14. See generally Tom Farer, "Foreign Intervention in Civil Armed Conflicts," *Recueil des Cours* 2 (1974): 297, 318–30. See also Hersch Lauterpacht, *Oppenheim's International Law*, 2 vols. (Cambridge: Cambridge University Press, 1952) 2:250.

15. Ibid.

16. See William Edward Hall, *International Law*, 3d ed. 1914 (Oxford: Clarendon Press), p. 34, and Norman J. Padelford, *International Law and Diplomacy in the Spanish Civil Strife* (New York: Macmillan, 1939) p. 8.

17. I have developed this point in Farer, "Harnessing Rogue Elephants: A Short Discourse on Foreign Intervention in Civil Strife," *Harvard Law Review* 82 (January 1969): 511, 516–18.

18. See Lauterpacht, *International Law*, 248–53, and Gerhard von Glahn, *Law Among Nations* 2d. ed. (1971), p. 551.

19. General Agreement on Tariffs and Trade, 30 October 1947, 61 Stat. (5), (6), T.I.A.S. No. 1700, 55–61 U.N.T.S.

20. Article XXI: "Nothing in this Agreement shall be construed . . . to prevent any contracting party from taking any action which it considers necessary for the protection of its essential security interests . . . taken in time of war or other emergency in international relations . . . [or] to prevent any contracting party from taking any action in pursuance of its obligations under the United Nations Charter for the maintenance of international peace and security."

21. U.N. Doc. A/CONF. 39/27, at 289 (1969).

22. See *Report on the Situation of Human Rights in the Republic of Guatemala*, Inter-American Commission on Human Rights, (1981) OEA/Ser.L/V/II.53, doc. 21 rev. 2., especially pages 19–38 and 48–55. See also *Guatemala: A Nation of Prisoners*, Americas Watch Report (New York, 1984).

23. See *Report on the Situation of Human Rights in El Salvador*, pp. 148–58 (English version).

24. I have examined this issue at some length in "Human Rights and Human Welfare in Latin America," *Daedalus* 112 (Fall 1983): 139.

25. See Christopher Dickey, "Obedezco Pero No Cumplo," in *Central America: Anatomy of Conflict*, ed. Robert Leiken (New York 1984), p. 33.

10

The Future of Democracy:
An Analytical Summary

THOMAS E. SKIDMORE

This is clearly a crucial moment for Latin American democracy. In the words of Argentine President Alfonsín, "we have witnessed a vigorous rebirth of democracy in Latin America." Argentina, Brazil, and Uruguay, for example, have emerged in the mid-1980s from repressive military regimes that degraded their political institutions and demoralized their people. Chile shows signs of moving out of its dictatorship. How can these trends to democracy be extended and reinforced?

Former Ecuadorean President Hurtado saw the Atlanta meeting that produced this volume as "an ideal forum for reflection on the measures that should be taken to ensure that democracy suffer no more setbacks and be installed as an enduring system that will guarantee the protection of freedom, the periodic change of governments through elections, the supervision and judgement of the actions of government authorities, and the attainment of economic development and social justice." The key questions to be faced are: (1) how to strengthen the newly created democracies; (2) how to prevent a regression to dictatorship; and (3) how to extend democracy to those countries still nondemocratic.

The pages that follow draw especially on the paper commentaries (which are not included in this volume) and discussions at the Atlanta meeting, thereby supplementing the formal papers that can be found in the preceding chapters.

A swing to democracy is nothing new in Latin America. There was a democratic wave in the late 1950s and early 1960s, for example, but it was soon followed by the military coups of the late 1960s and early 1970s. Can we learn from that past how to strengthen democracy in the future?

This chapter is a synthesis based on the papers, commentaries and discussions that took place at the consultation in Atlanta in November 1986. Readers should note that references to political events and opinions are as of that date. Those wishing to find a more detailed version of the papers should consult the preceding chapters. Speakers are quoted primarily in the present tense to retain the flavor of the discussions.

Defining Democracy

Democracy has lent itself to widely varying definitions. Nothing has made that clearer than the fierce controversy that has raged over the nature of governments in Central America. The current preoccupation with Central America is logical, because this region presents one of the greatest challenges to the growth of democracy. Should the priority be on individual freedom, social welfare, or the defense of the state? Pragmatic Americans and reform-minded Latin Americans disagree on answers to that question. Samuel Huntington argues for a "modest meaning" of democracy, a government whose decision-makers are periodically selected in free, competitive elections with universal adult suffrage. Further, argues Huntington, democracy is incompatible with "gross inequality" or a highly controlled and centralized economy.

Many Latin Americans would contest that definition. Former Belize Prime Minister George Price has questioned the implication that a market economy is a necessary condition for democracy.* Belize, for example, has carried out a "major reconstruction of the social order" within a system of adult suffrage and constitutionally guaranteed human rights. Former Costa Rican President Oduber defines democracy as the best means to accomplish social change. Nicaraguan Vice President Sergio Ramirez argues that an authentic democracy must involve effective and widespread participation. Dictatorships, he continues, have for too long manipulated democratic institutions to benefit the few. Democracy must correct the unjust distribution of economic benefits. Ramirez sees U.S. support for the Contras as a "tragic error" and predicts that the Contras could never win, however many millions of dollars they get from Washington.

Former Speaker of the House Jim Wright also finds Huntington's definition too "modest." Political democracy, argues Wright, is only a starting point. It remains "unfulfilled without social and economic democracy." Yet Wright also believes that Americans expect democracy to include freedom of the press and of religion. President Carter agrees with Wright's concerns, noting that they are shared by other countries and not simply the United States. He pointed to the Contadora process as the best hope for peace and urged Nicaragua to lift its emergency laws and adopt the Contadora principles.

The debate over Nicaragua serves to underline how external actors such as the United States deeply influence today's prospects for democracy. Past U.S. interventions in Central America and the Caribbean, for example, have left a legacy of angry nationalism that often prevails over democratic aspirations.

In judging democracy's prospects, we need to distinguish between internal and external factors that strengthen or weaken democracy. There are at least five internal factors.

---

*Huntington replied that at the minimum, democracy required a measure of economic pluralism.

The need for consensus on the rules of the democratic game: No democracy can survive if the contenders for power are not prepared to accept the outcome of such democratic processes as elections, court decisions, and congressional votes. Powerful politicians or interest groups cannot think in zero-sum terms—indeed, democracy might be defined as a system that never produces a zero-sum solution. Latin Americans report that this democratic mentality is growing.

The dramatic discrediting of recent authoritarian regimes, such as the one in Argentina, has helped to speed this trend. Guerrilla movements have also been discredited in many countries, such as Brazil and Uruguay. Both the extreme left and extreme right have undermined their credibility and given the advocates of democracy a favorable climate in which to organize.

Yet most countries lack a strong democratic tradition. Former President Hurtado even suggests that "the Latin American character" might be antithetical to democratic qualities. Without accepting that reductionism (which North Americans once used to justify their interventions), one can concede that the mental habits of democratic life are at best fragile in Latin America.

Anyone who doubts that fragility need only look at Chile. Until the early 1970s Chile appeared in political science textbooks as one of Latin America's most solidly based democracies. The Communist Party, for example, had long been legal, a rarity in Latin America. Presidential candidates of the right, center, and left had been elected between 1958 and 1970. Chileans and their foreign friends shared a faith in the resiliency of her political institutions. Yet Chilean democracy disappeared in 1973.

Today Chile is making slow progress toward democratization. (Paraguay is, too, but Cuba is not. Neither is considered here.) A decade and a half after the 1973 coup, those Chileans working to restore democracy face the widespread fear that Pinochet's departure might create a winner-take-all scene. The zero-sum problem arises again. What irony that Chile should now need lessons in democracy. And those lessons are needed elsewhere. In Guatemala, for example, President Cerezo's government faces a formidable task in seeking to establish civilian power.

The need for a strong political party system: Strong political parties are essential for democracy. Vigorous parties are an all-important vehicle for channeling power and fixing government responsibility. But they are another tradition notably lacking in much of Latin America.

Colombia and Venezuela are the strongholds of party stability. Both have parties that greatly predate the recent democratization. Might their success stem from the fact that both countries have two-party systems? But most countries of Latin America have multiparty systems. Can they create the basis for lasting democracies?

Argentina has certainly enjoyed a democratic rebirth. Alfonsín's Radicals unexpectedly won an absolute majority in the 1983 presidential election, but the prospects for a viable pluralistic party system are far from clear. Much of Peronism, for example, is at best equivocal in its commitment to democracy.

Professor Juan Linz has argued that Latin America would be better served by a parliamentary rather than the presidential system. The latter favors all-or-nothing solutions (that theme again), while the parliamentary system is more flexible. Changing cabinet ministers and developing political cadres can be done in a parliamentary system in ways that are impossible in presidential governments. Notwithstanding the merits of this analysis, it appears to have few adherents in Latin America.

The need for economic growth: Virtually all governments want economic growth, which generates gains that can be distributed without any group losing in absolute terms. It also facilitates individual and group mobility, thereby generating political loyalties. Yet Latin America (with Brazil only a partial exception) actually lost economic ground as measured by per capita income over the last decade. The causes, both internal and external, are complex. Although acknowledging internal causes (inefficient state enterprises, poor planning, unwise subsidies) Latin Americans point to the international economic climate. The major culprit is the foreign debt. Without major debt relief, all agree, the Latin American economies will be unable for at least a decade to deliver the welfare that their electorates have the right to expect.

Lest anyone should assume that there is a simple positive correlation between democratic regimes and economic prosperity, former Undersecretary of State William D. Rogers presents sobering evidence. The recent wave of democratization has occurred in the face of highly unfavorable economic circumstances. Commodity prices have plunged, the relative cost of debt has mounted, and per capita income has declined. Yet the democratic urge has prevailed. Latin Americans are not opting for democracy because of fattening pocketbooks.

Professors Stepan and Linz point to the experience of post-Franco Spain where the democratic system has continued to enjoy massive support despite a declining economy. Is that experience relevant for Latin America? Or will the authoritarians again use economic failure as a pretext for closing the political system? Economic austerity is presenting (and will continue to present) a harsh test for all the Latin American democracies.

The need for a democratic military: Every politically aware Latin American knows that the military are crucial political actors. Many of the participants in the Atlanta meeting had suffered persecution or worse at the hands of the military. How the democratic governments should deal with the authors of such horrors gets no single answer. Argentina is at one extreme, sending to prison top military officers for their gross violations of human rights. At the other extreme is Brazil, preferring to sweep the record of torture under the rug of a general amnesty.

But those are differences in handling the past. How can the military be encouraged to change their role in the future? How can they become the effective guardians of a democratic order? Stepan and Linz suggest steps that civilian governments can follow to develop routine oversight procedures and thus move toward making the military more continuously accountable to the elected government.

The need for social reform: This crucial dimension of democratization was a major tenet in the Alliance for Progress and in the platforms of many of the democratic movements now in power. But it is frequently neglected in present-day debates. Why? Perhaps because attention is now fixed on consolidating the political institutions of democracy. Perhaps also because U.S. promotion of internal reform has lost favor, both in the United States and Latin America. The ubiquitous USAID mission is now a relic of the past, except in Central America and the Caribbean. Former Canadian Prime Minister Pierre Trudeau, a strong supporter of social reform, notes that capitalism failed to help the poor in pre-Castro Cuba or pre-Sandinista Nicaragua. It is therefore not surprising, argues Trudeau, that those countries do not give liberal democracy their highest priority.

External Factors

Any estimate of Latin America's democratic potential must also focus on the way outside factors influence Latin American political development. Two themes are especially important: the international economy, which I will discuss here, and the role of the United States and Latin American and European democracies, which was discussed by Tom Farer and will be analyzed by Robert Pastor in the concluding chapter.

The international economy: the foreign debt: Latin Americans rightly see their countries' huge foreign debts as major obstacles to economic growth. President Alfonsín calls it an "unbearable burden," and points to the fact that "during the last five years Latin America has transferred to the developed countries more than one hundred billion dollars, drastically decreasing our investment possibilities to restart the economic growth that we desperately need." Former Costa Rican President Oduber calls the debt problem "the most important issue until the year 2000." Former Panamanian president Ardito Barletta suggests that the U.S. policymakers ought to consider Latin American debt relief to be at least as worthy a cause as the rescue of the Chrysler Corporation.

Most of Latin America sees the current terms for servicing its debt as not only economically suffocating but politically illegitimate. Democratic voices from Argentina, Brazil, and Peru, for example, ask why they should bear the burden of paying off loans incurred by irresponsible military regimes. No matter how many times it has been said, the Latin Americans say it again: the greatest current threat to Latin American democracy is the foreign debt burden. Month after month, year after year, the tocsin sounds. Yet only short-term, ad hoc solutions are being tried.

A cynic might conclude that the creditors have no interest in restructuring the debt. Today's high loan profits (when paid!) help reinforce the commercial bankers' apparent disinterest in Latin America's long-run economic health. If the debtor countries were ever to unite, then the story line could rapidly change. The lack of any effective effort in that direction is notable. Despite the rhetoric, muddling through remains the order of the day.

The international economy: the trading system: Latin Americans see other factors in the international economy as troublesome. One is the slump in primary product prices on the world market. This complaint seems unlikely to get the attention from the developed countries that it got in the 1950s, when major commodity agreements were in fashion. Trade barriers are another matter. Latin American exporters (and the politicians whom they helped elect) are outspoken critics of U.S. and West European protectionism. But as Indiana Senator (and former Chairman of the Senate Foreign Relations Committee) Richard Lugar reminds us, the United States has its own record trade deficit it must try to reduce. Nonetheless, the United States has kept its markets relatively open and its interest rates down, thereby partially easing the debt repayment burden.

Latin American economic cooperation: The hope of Latin American union goes back to Simón Bolívar. It recurred in the 1960s with the hope for a Latin American common market. Although the effort failed, along with the smaller Central American and Andean versions, the hopes live on. President Alfonsín urges that "we start creating—quickly, seriously and efficiently—a large Latin American economic space." He argues that "Latin American economic integration" offered an attractive option "within a world where one horizon after another is being closed." The Argentine president can point to one success: the rapidly growing number of Argentine economic agreements with Brazil.

Alfonsín views the spread of democracy as offering a new opportunity for Latin American economic integration; it could also improve the chances for political cooperation. Such a future, however, would come to naught if the pendulum returns to dictatorship, and as Osvaldo Hurtado warned: "It would be a mistake to think that the growth of democracy in Latin America is an irreversible, accomplished fact. To date, the emergence of democracies has always been an ephemeral phenomenon. To enable these democracies to become permanent is the great challenge facing not only us Latin American politicians, but also the North Americans."

11

How to Reinforce Democracy in the Americas: Seven Proposals

ROBERT A. PASTOR

Inside and Outside

Arguments about whether the United States can or should export democracy—like those about Cuba exporting revolution—miss the point.[1] Ideas as compelling as democracy or as seductive as revolution know no boundaries. What matters is not the export of such ideas, but the nature of the market into which they are imported. Democracy is purchased only when the local market is hospitable and consumers want it.

Outsiders can hurt or harm the prospects for democracy, but almost always, the internal balance of political forces is more important than outside influences in determining whether democracy emerges and survives. Of course, all other things being equal, the smaller the country the heavier the impact of external factors—whether these be changes in the prices of commodities like sugar or oil, Communist subversion, capitalist exploitation, or superpower intrigues.

But a product that is bought is also sold. It is rare that one can draw a line between demand and supply or between internal and external factors and conclude that one is determining—that, for example, the United States alone caused democracy to succeed or fail in country "X." The relationship between an outside government and an inside group might be so close as to be practically symbiotic, and thus the nature and direction of influence might be difficult to discern. The United States or Cuba might be responding to an invitation for help from a local group or government, or the local group might be suborned by the foreign power. More likely, a local group and an outside power will judge that they share an interest and will help each other in pursuit of that interest.

In assessing the relative influence of external versus internal factors in shaping political change, two contradictory forces need to be understood. First, the sheer wealth and power of an outside nation like the United States affects the internal struggle in a small country even if it has no policy toward the conflict. Between 1933 and 1936, the United States opposed the gradual but persistent attempts by Nicaraguan National Guard Commander Anastasio Somoza to undermine and eventually overthrow the elected government, but the State Department was so concerned that any action on its part to resist Somoza would reinvolve it in Nicaraguan politics that it did not even raise its voice in protest. Only Somoza understood that the United States had disengaged; everyone else was looking for a signal that never came. The United States, in brief, continued to exert a psychological effect on the actors in Nicaragua that was separate from the physical effects of policy.[2]

The other force—nationalism and the deepening of sovereignty—runs in the opposite direction. Whereas the psychological impact of dominance translates into influence even where the large power is not trying to exert any, this second force makes it more difficult for outside powers to influence internal events in small Third World nations. When the issue is political change in a small nation, this second force of nationalism can prove more potent than threats and sanctions by the larger power. One only needs to consider the impact of U.S. actions against Nicaragua and Panama during the latter half of the Reagan administration. Short of using direct force, U.S. actions often strengthen nationalist forces and thus have an effect contrary to U.S. goals.

Democracy can be imposed and indeed was imposed in the aftermath of war by the United States in Germany, Japan, and in Grenada. But while democracy may be a salutary consequence of war, and it is often used for propaganda purposes to mobilize support within a democracy for a war effort, it has never been the principal cause of war, nor should it be. If the pursuit of democracy were a reason to go to war, U.S. troops would be fighting in dozens of countries, and the world would be a decidedly less safe and democratic place.

The United States has often tried to use indirect force to promote its security objectives. Again, it has claimed its goal is to promote democracy, and while that has been *a* goal, it is never *the* reason that the United States employs force. For one thing, overthrowing a government risks making a bad situation worse. As John F. Kennedy put it: "We cannot force out any duly constituted government, however repugnant its methods or views may be—particularly when we have no guarantee that its successors in the long run will be a real improvement. Imported democracy is never as meaningful or viable as the domestic brand."[3]

A second reason why a guerrilla war is not a good instrument for promoting democracy is that twentieth-century history and logic suggests that revolutionaries do not make democrats. Samuel Huntington has made that point:

"Revolutionary coercion" may bring down an authoritarian regime, but, except again for Costa Rica in 1948, guerrilla insurgencies do not inaugurate democratic regimes. All revolutionary opponents of authoritarian regimes claim to be democrats; once they achieve power through violence, almost all turn out to be authoritarian themselves, often imposing an even more repressive regime than the one they overthrew.[4]

It is not hard to explain why revolutionaries create new dictatorships. To persevere in their struggle against a vastly superior force, rebels need to believe that they have a monopoly on truth and goodness and that their enemies are evil. To survive, revolutionaries should be wary of, perhaps even paranoid toward everyone. Guerrilla wars are not the place to acquire the habits of compromise and conciliation that make democracy possible.

The essence of democracy is the recognition of legal and constitutional limits. Before discussing ways to nurture democracy, therefore, it is essential to state what should not be done. Democracy should not be promoted by "all means necessary," that is, by violence. Neither the United States nor Latin American governments should arm guerrilla groups in the name of democracy to overthrow a government. A policy that promotes democracy internationally should also forswear violent methods.

If one excludes the use of force by a foreign power to change another nation's political system, then internal factors are unquestionably more important than any others in determining whether democracy is possible. Those internal factors include the democratic values of compromise and mutual respect, a military that is neutral politically and subordinate to elected civilians, and the existence of institutions and groups that are partial to the incremental changes inherent in democracy rather than the deceptive stability of dictatorship or the seductive transformations of revolution.

The struggle for democracy is not one that merely pits democratic against undemocratic groups. As Whitehead, O'Donnell, and others point out in this volume, democratic groups can sometimes behave undemocratically (motivated by hatred against another group), and undemocratic groups, for example in the military, sometimes facilitate a democratic process. Nonetheless, it is useful to conceptualize a balance of political power between democratic and undemocratic forces, and the policy question is how to tilt this balance in favor of democracy.

External assistance to promote either democracy or dictatorship is more likely to be effective when the local political equation is delicately balanced. When dictators are deeply entrenched, international actions are unlikely to produce democracy, at least in the short term. Such actions can help sustain local democratic groups, but they cannot help them to prevail. When democracy is strong, international actions are unnecessary. When the local political equation is delicately balanced, however, international actions either on behalf of democracy, such as in the Dominican Republic or in Ecuador in 1978, or against democracy, such as in Guatemala in 1954 and Chile in 1973, may be determining. In brief, local actors are more important than international actors in building or undermining democracy, but when internal politics are roughly balanced, outside actors or actions may become more important.

The principal purpose of this chapter is to explore how outside actors and actions can reinforce those "internal" democratic actors who are either struggling to replace a dictatorship or to consolidate a democracy. Before describing a number of proposals, let me briefly define two key terms. By "democracy," I mean the definition developed by Robert Dahl as including two dimensions, "public contestation in elections and the right to participate." Democracy means government by the consent of the governed; people have the right to choose, and more importantly, to replace their leaders at regular intervals. Secondly, when I refer to a possible role played by the "inter-American community" in reinforcing democracy, I mean the citizens of the Western Hemisphere and any informal or formal group of citizens or nations within the region.

The Climate

The economic, political, and strategic environment can either facilitate or impede democratization. To the extent that promoting democracy abroad is an important criterion for a nation's foreign policy, then the objective ought to be to contribute to the environment most conducive to democracy.

It is commonly believed that an economic crisis threatens democracy—as, for example, with the collapse of the Weimar Republic in Germany during the depression, but Franklin Roosevelt showed that democracy can also be rejuvenated by such a crisis. If the economic deterioration is prolonged, as was the case with Uruguay, it will undoubtedly have a corrosive impact on democracy. While the debt crisis has been the longest and worst economic setback since the depression, the new democracies will not inevitably collapse if a durable solution is not found. How governments address the problem, as Stepan and Linz write, may be at least as important as whether the problem is solved.

Nonetheless, there can be no question that over the long term, nations that pay one-third to one-half of their foreign exchange earnings each year to service their debt rather than invest in their future will find themselves with diminishing political space. If the standard of living in a democracy continually deteriorates, democracy may survive, even though the government is changed in each election, but it will become much more fragile. Therefore, to the extent that democracy is an important goal, the inter-American community ought to try to negotiate a long-term solution to the debt crisis that will reduce the debt burden, particularly of the new democracies. Such a solution should include new concessional loans mostly from the international development banks, internal economic reforms, new efforts at regional integration, and debt relief.[5]

The regional political environment also can help or hurt the cause of democratization. The existence of so many vigorous democracies in the English-speaking Caribbean undoubtedly reinforces democratic inclinations—or the "logic of democracy," in the region, as Anthony Maingot described it.[6] Several of the Andean Pact nations played an important role in the late 1970s to gradually expand and consolidate democracies in the region. Though these subregional groups have reinforced democracy by their logic or by ad hoc decisions, there have been few attempts to devise new norms or institutions to secure democracy.

The psychological environment is also important. The momentum of democracy throughout Latin America has undoubtedly aided democrats. Perhaps most profound was the transition toward democracy in Spain and Portugal in the mid-1970s. If Spain and Portugal—the sources of Latin America's culture—could become democratic, then that political culture itself was not immutable or static. Latin America could free itself from tyranny. Carlos Fuentes, the Mexican novelist, wrote of the wondrous impact that the transformation of the old world had on the new:

> Throughout Spanish America, we used to see Spain and say: Look at the toothless hag, sitting on the church steps, reeking of incense, dressed in rags and begging alms. We shrugged in resignation: We are as we are because Spain is what she is.
> No longer. Fifty years after the Battle of Spain, the lady is sleek, modern, beautiful and, we hope, willing to admit us into her bright new abode.[7]

Finally, the strategic context can influence the balance of political forces within a country. During periods of strategic confrontation, dictators use the excuse of the global struggle against Communism (as Castro uses the struggle against imperialism) to suppress dissent in the name of nationalism. Democracy is also more difficult to maintain during civil wars for a similar reason: the state insists that its security must take precedence over political pluralism. It becomes more difficult to make this argument during a period of relative détente or in the absence of an insurgency.

In summary, the economic, political, psychological, and strategic climate matters; it sets the context within which democratic and undemocratic forces struggle for power, and it reinforces one side or the other.

The Challenge

In exploring ways to reinforce democracy, the inter-American community builds on a firm philosophical and constitutional foundation. The Charter of the Organization of American States begins by stating that "American solidarity and good neighborliness can only mean the consolidation on this continent, within the framework of democratic institutions, of a system of individual liberty and social justice." Article 20 of the American Declaration of the Rights and Duties of Man, adopted at the Bogotá Conference in 1948, declares:

> Every person having legal capacity is entitled to participate in the government of his country, directly or through his representatives, and to take part in popular elections, which shall be by secret ballot, and shall be honest, periodic, and free.

To implement this goal, it is necessary to reinforce democrats and democratic institutions and processes, and conversely, to deny legitimacy to dictatorships and undemocratic processes and institutions. Described in terms of the three phases of the democratization process, the inter-American community's objectives should be: (1) to facilitate, in legitimate ways, the breakdown of dictatorships; (2) to prevent the breakdown of democracy (in the transition); and (3) to strengthen democracies (consolidation).

From the case studies of the breakdown of democracy (see the appendix), several lessons emerge. First, during the transitional phase, political parties that win power by a large margin should not consider themselves any more secure than those that win by a small margin. A one-sided triumph tends to seduce the ruling party into thinking that it can rule alone and does not need to compromise with the opposition. The government then addresses too many controversial issues and makes too many enemies. The democratic opposition feels excluded and before too long it begins acting undemocratically. The proximate cause of the breakdown is the invitation and legitimation of military intervention by elements of the democratic opposition.

Secondly, it is a mistake to see the breakdown of democracy as a single act— a military coup—in a political vacuum. More often than not, the act is the culmination of events in which the civilian opposition and the media identify the ruling party with the political system and decide to overturn the system rather than wait for the next election.

Third, "pacts" negotiated between the major political parties have been an important device for reinforcing embryonic democracies in Venezuela and Colombia. The pacts have kept the political debate within legitimate bounds and thus have denied the military any legitimacy for intervening to overthrow a regime.[8] But it appears that the most important elements of a successful transition are the intangible traits that Hurtado describes in his chapter: flexibility and a willingness to negotiate, compromise, and share power.

Seven Proposals

Let us now consider seven sets of proposals to facilitate both the transition from dictatorship to democracy and the consolidation of democratic governments:

(1) "NATIONAL COMMITTEES TO DEFEND DEMOCRACY"

Human rights organizations emerged in the 1970s to awaken the conscience of the Americas to the gross abuses of human rights that had become almost routine in many countries. With great courage, leaders of these organizations became the voices of the voiceless, and they alerted the world to the discrepancy between proclaimed values and actual behavior. International human rights organizations and leaders from other nations relied on these voices and magnified their impact. The most effective human rights groups were nonpartisan, that is, they did not support any particular party or political group.

As so much of Latin America has embarked on the transition toward democracy, there is a need for new organizations to support the democratic process, much as the human rights organizations have defended the rights of the individual. The emergence of *Conciencia* in Argentina is an encouraging sign. Similar to the U.S. League of Women Voters, *Conciencia* is composed of about eight thousand members whose goal is to train Argentines, particularly women, to participate actively and effectively in political and community life. The model has been extended to Uruguay and Brazil.[9]

Organizations like *Conciencia* serve an important purpose of encouraging participation in the political process, but other groups are needed to tackle the specific tasks of defending democratic institutions. Using the very effective model of national and international human rights groups, new "National Committees to Defend Democracy" should be established. The objective of these committees should be to oversee the democratic transition and to remind citizens of the importance of respecting the democratic system even if they disagree with some of the government's specific actions. The national committees could include respected leaders who are committed to democracy but not interested in participating in partisan politics. These could be elder statesmen, judges, professors, respected former military figures, or human rights activists.

Based on indicators developed from previous cases of democratic breakdown, the committees would monitor the democratization process and issue warnings when the process seems to be endangered. Such warnings would attract the attention of international groups, who could visit the country, reinforce democratic groups, and raise the costs to those who would disrupt democracy. The committees could also write reports that evaluate the state of democracy—its substance as well as its form—using standards and a scale proposed by an international group but tailored by the national committees to the particular country.

As the threat of a military coup always hangs over a new democratic experiment, special measures should be considered to reduce that threat and at the same time to establish a modern, professional relationship between the military and the civilian government. One measure would be to establish a special committee composed of civilian and military leaders to meet periodically and exchange views of the evolving relationship and the progress of democratization. This group could be used both as a vent to release pressures building as a result of a lack of communication between the military and civilian leaders and also a catalyst for forging a new relationship between the military and the new civilian government.

(2) TRANSNATIONAL BONDS TO REINFORCE PLURALISM

A vigorous democracy needs independent organizations that reflect the interests and concerns of business, labor, the press, consumers, universities, churches, professionals, and the full range of specific interests in a country. Such organizations need to be free and strong enough to articulate the concerns of their constituents and, to the extent possible, meet their needs. In the competition between such groups, there is an inevitable tendency for the stronger and wealthier groups to try to use their disproportionate power to gain a larger share of public goods. In many democracies, checks and balances are built into the system to prevent the accumulation of too much power by certain groups and to prevent the disenfranchisement of other groups. But in small countries (or towns for that matter), weaker groups have a more difficult time.

In the last two decades, a number of transnational organizations have begun to assist in the development of various interest groups in the Third World. Business associations and labor unions were among the first to assist their counterparts, but the Socialist International and the Christian Democratic International now play similar roles to help their associated parties in Latin America and throughout the world. The three main political parties in West Germany—Social Democrat, Christian Democrat, and Liberal—established foundations to help democracy in the Third World by assisting their associated parties.

In 1983, the U.S. Congress established the National Endowment for Democracy to strengthen democratic pluralism through assistance to nongovernmental institutions abroad. Under the umbrella of the endowment, four institutions were created: the Free Trade Union Institute of the AFL–CIO, the Center for International Private Enterprise of the Chamber of Commerce, and two political party institutes, the National Democratic Institute for International Affairs and the National Republican Institute for International Affairs.

All of these institutes are designed to support democracy over the long term. They aim to build the pluralistic foundation on which democratic institutions, attitudes, and processes depend. Each institute has a different focus and has chosen a different path to accomplish that goal. Using the model of the Christian Democratic International, the Republican Institute has chosen to support and work with like-minded conservative political parties in the world. The Democratic Institute has decided to support the democratic *process* instead of identifying with individual political parties in the Third World. It has played a leading role in monitoring and reinforcing the electoral process in the Philippines, Haiti, and Chile and has worked with democratic groups in Nicaragua, Panama, El Salvador, and many other countries.

The National Democratic Institute has also tried to develop and operate its programs multilaterally, working with political parties and groups from Europe and from established democracies in Latin America like Venezuela and Costa Rica. In just a few years, the Democratic Institute and the National Endowment have overcome considerable skepticism in the region about their impartial commitments to pluralism and democracy, and their support is now sought by groups representing almost the entire democratic political spectrum.

In the 1970s, some victims of abuse were supported by international human rights organizations. In the 1980s and 1990s, it is just as important that pluralistic groups and democratic institutions in Latin America be reinforced by outside encouragement and assistance.

(3) AN INTERNATIONAL ELECTION-MONITORING ORGANIZATION

For democracies to be secure, elections need to be free and fair. When questions are raised about the fairness of elections—whether in Panama, Mexico, Nicaragua, or El Salvador—the government that takes office is flawed; its legitimacy and power is diminished. Some governments no doubt would prefer to be accused of fraud than to risk free elections, but in the long term, such a strategy is self-defeating. The loss of credibility in honest elections inevitably leads to a loss of governmental effectiveness.

The issue is how to demonstrate that an election is genuinely free. It is unlikely that a national electoral organization that is controlled by the ruling party could reestablish its credibility. Nor should any one nation, especially the United States, monitor another country's election in the Western Hemisphere. However, an international election-monitoring organization could be established. Such an organization should define its mandate broadly rather than just observing the polls on election day. The organization should visit the country for an extended period before, during, and after the election. Such an organization should have sufficient staff, resources, and experience to ensure that it can be effective, and it should issue periodic reports on whether evidence of fraud was found. The organization can either be intergovernmental, like the Inter-American Commission on Human Rights, or it can be nongovernmental, such as Helsinki or Americas Watch.

No doubt such a group would be charged with intervention, much as occurred with the human rights commission. But the international rebuttal is the same as it is for human rights: the concern for democracy is universal, and it is protected by numerous international treaties to which most of the nations of the Western Hemisphere are signatories.

A radical, but perhaps necessary approach would be for all governments in the hemisphere automatically to issue an invitation to this organization to oversee elections. If the organization has grounds for believing that the election might be tainted, based on complaints that it has received, the group would accept the invitation. (This is essentially the method used by the Inter-American Commission for Human Rights.) But the decision whether it would observe the election would be the group's prerogative.

The composition of the election-monitoring organization could be determined in a number of different ways. Larry Garber suggests that it have five commissioners from different countries and backgrounds (that is, members of election commissions, judges, and political leaders).[10] Larry Diamond and Seymour Martin Lipset recommend "the establishment of a formal, multilateral organization to monitor and certify the integrity of all national elections in the hemisphere that purport to be democratic."[11] They suggest that the organization be composed of an equal number of appointees from each democratic country, perhaps appointed by the supreme court of each.

Diamond and Lipset also recommend that each government look to the Costa Rican Supreme Elections Tribunal as a possible model of a thoroughly credible, autonomous election agency. The international organization can provide technical assistance and international observers. In fact, the Inter-American Institute of Human Rights established CAPEL (Centro de Asesoría y Promoción Electoral) in 1983 to provide technical assistance, though not to monitor elections. Based in San José, CAPEL has been influenced by the Costa Rican model and it has trained people in several countries to run elections. CAPEL should be strengthened. Also important is the existence of private, nonpartisan citizens' organizations to monitor elections, like NAMFREL in the Philippines. In two cases, Costa Rica in 1948 and the Philippines in 1985–86, dictators were defeated when such independent organizations were able to demonstrate fraud.

The reports of the international organization could be presented annually to the OAS General Assembly, like the reports of the Inter-American Commission on Human Rights. The report should include recommendations on what the individual government and the inter-American community should do with regard to the next and future elections. Another alternative would be to bring specific charges against a country before the Inter-American Court of Human Rights. The court has broad advisory powers and could be asked to decide on such matters. In brief, there are many different ways to establish an international election-monitoring organization. What is interesting, and disappointing, is that no such organization currently exists.

(4) GOVERNMENT POLICIES: A NEW BETANCOURT DOCTRINE

For international organizations to be established and effective, changes are necessary in each government's policies. All democracies routinely and rhetorically defend democracy, but few if any have specific policies for implementing that defense.

The United States has the longest history of professing to base its Latin American policy on support for democracy, but many Latin Americans view such a claim as masking a desire to intervene for other reasons. No one articulated the combination of conviction and interference better than President Woodrow Wilson. In his first statement on Latin America on 12 March 1913 Wilson declared that "we shall lend our influence of every kind" to promoting democratic and constitutional government. "The United States," he insisted, "has nothing to seek in Central and South America except the lasting interests of the peoples of the two continents." And yet in pursuit of this goal, Wilson sent marines to Mexico, Nicaragua, the Dominican Republic, and Haiti.[12]

His policy of withholding recognition of governments that came to power by force had a more salutary effect. A study of Latin American elections concluded that "U.S. influence and dominance helped to increase voter participation in Latin America."[13] Of course, not all these elections were free or fair, but they nevertheless compelled leaders to acknowledge the norm of regular elections.

Since Wilson, the periods of greatest U.S. involvement in Latin America have tended to coincide with the most strident affirmations of democracy. While pursuing U.S. security concerns, Americans have felt the need to view their goals in idealistic terms. An interesting window into the U.S. government's debate on democracy can be found in a declassified top secret memorandum describing meetings of the National Security Council during the Republican administration of Dwight D. Eisenhower.

Though many Latin Americans perceived Eisenhower as preferring dictators to democrats, an NSC meeting on 17 February 1955 revealed a cleavage within the administration and a different presidential policy. Secretary of Treasury George Humphrey argued that "whenever a dictator was replaced, Communists gained." He therefore urged Eisenhower to "back strong men in Latin American governments." Nelson Rockefeller, who was then a special assistant to the president, called Latin dictators "a mixed blessing. It is true," he argued, "in the short run, that dictators handle Communists effectively. But in the long run, the U.S. must encourage the growth of democracies in Latin America if Communism is to be defeated in the area." Eisenhower agreed with Rockefeller and set the policy. And yet despite his clear statements of support for democracy, no one in the administration even raised a question when the conversation shifted to the subject of Guatemala, where the Administration had supported a successful effort to overthrow a democratic government—albeit one perceived as Communist—just seven months before.[14] The discussion illustrated the gulf between the democratic intention that has probably been held by all U.S. presidents and an actual reaction to a perceived security threat.

The support for democracy experienced a rebirth under John F. Kennedy, a partial decline under Presidents Johnson, Nixon, and Ford, and then the latest reincarnation under Presidents Carter and Reagan. Despite differences between the Carter and Reagan administrations, a State Department publication during the Reagan administration asserted that a bipartisan consensus existed based on the fact that both Carter and Reagan "sought to encourage democratic transitions in Latin America."[15]

The United States has not been the only government in the hemisphere supporting democracy. There have been numerous efforts by Latin American leaders to strengthen democracy by denying recognition to regimes that take power unconstitutionally. In 1907, Carlos Tobar, an Ecuadorean diplomat, enunciated a doctrine that would subsequently bear his name. He recommended that governments not recognize any regime that came to power by violent means until it was regularized by a free and popular election. This doctrine preceded Wilson's policy and was imbedded in a set of treaties designed to bring peace to Central America, but their effect was transitory.[16]

Perhaps the clearest and most determined policy for assisting other nations to achieve democracy was developed and implemented by Romulo Betancourt, who was elected president of Venezuela in 1958, after Venezuelans had overthrown a brutal dictator. Betancourt rejuvenated and modernized the Tobar principle. He urged nonrecognition of de facto regimes and their expulsion from the Organization of American States. In his inaugural address, President Betancourt said:

> Regimes which do not respect human rights, which violate the liberties of their citizens and tyrannize them with political police ought to be subjected to a rigorous cordon sanitaire and eradicated by the collective peaceful action of the Inter-American juridical community.[17]

And in the Venezuelan constitution, the preamble urges all Venezuelans to "uphold the democratic order as the only and unrenounceable way of assuring the rights and dignity of its citizens, and favor its pacific extension to all the peoples of the earth."[18] Thus, Venezuela is as interventionist in theory as the United States. In practice, Betancourt and other Venezuelans have found—as the United States has—that it is difficult to translate these goals into policy or to influence democratic trends abroad.

(5) MULTILATERALIZING THE BETANCOURT DOCTRINE: DEMOCRACY IN THE
INTER-AMERICAN SYSTEM

In August 1959, Betancourt proposed that the OAS only recognize "regimes
born of free elections and respecting human rights." He urged the other
governments to begin implementing this new approach by excluding Dominican dictator Rafael Trujillo. Although Eisenhower had decided several months
before to give "special encouragement" to democracies in the region, his
Secretary of State Christian Herter opposed Betancourt's resolution on the
grounds that it violated the OAS charter's principle of nonintervention. "History has shown," Herter told the OAS in a message reeking with irony, "that
attempts to impose democracy upon a country by force from without may
easily result in the mere substitution of one form of tyranny for another."
Mexico and Argentina aligned with Herter and defeated the Venezuelan initiative.[19]

Exactly one year later, after the radicalization of the Cuban revolution and
the growing prospects that it could spread to the Dominican Republic,
Eisenhower's policy on democracy changed again. At an OAS meeting to
condemn Trujillo's attempted assassination of Betancourt, Herter called for the
OAS to supervise a political transition in the Dominican Republic. Specifically,
he proposed an end to Trujillo's reign, the establishment of political parties,
and the holding of free elections. Most of the Latin Americans were shocked by
the proposal, and it never came to a vote.[20]

Betancourt's doctrine proved impractical in 1959 when few Latin democracies existed, and U.S. policy was contradictory; but today, when the vast
majority of Latin American governments are democratic but still endangered,
and a bipartisan consensus for supporting democracy exists in the United
States, there are grounds for reopening the issue. Of particular relevance is the
Esquipulas Accord signed by the five presidents of Central America in August
1987. As a result of that accord, the five leaders accepted a shared responsibility
to implement, maintain, and monitor all the rudiments of democracy—such as
elections, free press, and participation—in all of their countries, and to provide
international verification of the plan's provisions.

The question arises whether the Latin and Caribbean democracies today can
agree to develop new norms and policies that could unite them to raise the costs
of military coups and bring their moral pressure to bear on the remaining
dictatorships in the hemisphere. Given the new bonds that connect these
democracies, they might want to concentrate their energies on ensuring that
there is no slip backwards toward dictatorship by any one of them. (It might be
easier to build a cordon around the new democracies and prevent such backward slippage than to push old dictators toward democracy.)[21]

Consideration should be given to calling a special OAS Summit Meeting to
assess the state of democracy in the region and to develop recommendations on
ways to strengthen it where it exists and promote it where it is absent. While
there is some skepticism at the present time as to the utility of the OAS, the

existence of democracy in so many of the member states of the organization might permit the development of a new and important purpose for the organization. It is possible, for example, that the members of the OAS could negotiate a treaty that would provide for the collective security of democracy. Such a treaty would have to be very carefully written to prevent abuses.

During the 1970s, the United States adopted a range of policies to promote human rights in Latin America. These policies ranged from private diplomacy, public statements, the reduction or elimination of aid, votes against loans in the international development banks, and the reduction of Export-Import Bank credits, to the withdrawal of diplomatic personnel. The Reagan administration utilized many more instruments—including a trade and financial embargo and covert support of insurgents—against the Sandinista government and later the military government of General Manuel Antonio Noriega in Panama. Despite the severity of these actions, the administration did not achieve its objectives. The question for the inter-American community is whether a unified effort by some or most of the region's democracies might not achieve more with less.

There are other approaches to solidifying democracies in the region. Argentine President Alfonsín signed agreements for economic cooperation with Spain and Italy that are contingent on the maintenance of democracy in Argentina. If the military overthrew the government, Argentina would lose valuable programs.[22] The basic concept underlying these agreements can be replicated. Great Britain could negotiate an agreement on the Falklands/Malvinas that would be contingent on Argentina maintaining its democracy. Ecuador and Peru could reach a similar agreement on their border dispute; the same could hold for El Salvador and Honduras. One of the missions of the military has been to defend the nation's borders. Territorial disputes have often been used to justify both the defense budget and the large role played by the military in political affairs. If coups were to cancel territorial agreements, the military would be hard-pressed to pretend that they were acting on patriotic grounds.

(6) GROUP OF DEMOCRATIC PRESIDENTS

An alternative approach would be to establish a group of democratically elected presidents outside the OAS. Since the resurgence of democracies in the region, inaugurations of new presidents in the Americas have become occasions for incumbent presidents of Latin America to meet and discuss a range of contemporary issues. These meetings have permitted the presidents to know each other better than has been the case in the past, and this in turn has permitted them to remain in contact in moments of special need.[23]

No greater need for such top-level consultation exists than to prevent the breakdown of democracy in any country. The question is whether a more formal network of communication—with perhaps a secretariat—might be more effective in the case of a genuine emergency. The Group of Eight, which is composed of the four Contadora countries and the four members of the Support Group—Argentina, Brazil, Peru, and Uruguay—would be a logical core for such a group. The secretariat could be linked to National Committees to Defend Democracy. The United States, Canada, and the Caribbean countries might also be included in the network.

Such a group could coordinate their governments' policies toward threats to any democracy. They could, for example, decide jointly not to recognize a military coup, or to adopt national sanctions against a regime that overthrew a democracy. They could decide to vote jointly in the multilateral development banks against loans to such regimes.

The power of outside actors to reinforce democracy is magnified when they are independent, democratic, and act in concert. It is clear that the predominance of democracies at this moment offers the inter-American community a unique opportunity to reinforce democracy by modifying norms, structures, and institutions to serve a dual purpose: to prevent the breakdown of democracy and to multiply moral pressures to permit its expansion.

(7) A COUNCIL OF DEMOCRATIC HEADS OF GOVERNMENT

When governments find it difficult to pay their commercial debts and there is a possibility of "imminent default," they meet with a group called "the Paris Club" of debtor governments to negotiate debt reschedulings; by this process, they preserve their financial credibility and the banks continue to get paid. At the conclusion of the conference at the Carter Center in November 1986, twelve current and former presidents met and discussed what they could do individually and collectively to reinforce democracies at fragile moments. They decided to establish the Council of Freely Elected Heads of Government, a kind of "Paris Club" to assist democracies. The council is an informal group composed of current and former democratically elected presidents and prime ministers of the Americas.[24]

The council sent a telegram on 21 November 1986 to the secretaries-general of the Organization of American States and the United Nations and to incumbent democratic presidents and prime ministers of North and South America. The presidents said that they were moved to establish the Council to ensure that the democratic openings of the 1980s not be lost. They offered their assistance whenever a president judged that democracy in his country was threatened. They offered to be "on call to existing international organizations and to those democratic heads of government who need help in alleviating threats to their democracies." They have already lent their voices to support President Alfonsín in the spring of 1987 when several military officers threatened a coup. They have tried to assist parties to the conflict in Panama and Nicaragua. They have observed the electoral process in Haiti and in Panama and have raised their voices when the military denied the people a free election.

There is much else that the group could do. In chapter 5, Guillermo O'Donnell notes that softliners in the military play a critical role in the transition toward democracy, yet not only are such military leaders not recognized for their contribution, they are often treated like pariahs by the new civilian government. A Council of Freely Elected Heads of Government could have the moral authority and the detachment to perform two critical tasks regarding the military. First, the group could offer awards—and other incentives—to military leaders who have distinguished themselves by respecting human rights and promoting transitions to democracy. Leaders such as General Francisco Morales Bermudez of Peru, Admiral Alfredo Poveda of Ecuador, and Generals Ernesto Geisel and João Figueiredo of Brazil ought to be candidates for such an award.

Secondly, a new civilian-military relationship is necessary.[25] If the new democracies are to endure, the military will have to find a mission that will be subordinate to the new civilian leaders but will also be important and legitimate. The council could also include some former military presidents, who might be well-positioned to assist in developing such a new relationship. The council could function as a catalyst for establishing national committees, the international election-monitoring organization, and other institutions, and it could function as a bridge between these various organizations, which would send "warning signals" of democratic fragility.

In summary, there is much that can be done by outside groups, institutions, and individuals to reinforce those democrats in the Americas who are determined to prevent the pendulum of democracy from swinging back toward dictatorship.

Notes

Although I assume responsibility for any flaws in the proposals offered in this chapter, I gladly share the credit, as I tried to integrate and develop numerous ideas offered by a number of the contributors of this volume as well as many others who wrote short memoranda for the workshop preceding the conference. I refer to several of these memoranda in the chapter. They are listed in the bibliography of this book, and are available from the Carter Center. I am also grateful to the following people for comments on an earlier draft of this chapter: Thomas Buergenthal, Alfred Stepan, Albert Fishlow, Dayle Powell, Jennifer McCoy, Eric Bord, Richard Sinkin, and Abraham Lowenthal.

1. For a discussion of the first question, see Howard J. Wiarda, "Can Democracy Be Exported? The Quest for Democracy in U.S.–Latin American Policy," in *The United States and Latin America in the 1980s,* ed. Kevin J. Middlebrook and Carlos Rico (Pittsburgh: University of Pittsburgh Press, 1986).

2. This thesis is developed in my book *Condemned to Repetition: The United States and Nicaragua* (Princeton: Princeton University Press, 1987).

3. Speech by Senator John F. Kennedy in San Juan, Puerto Rico, 15 December 1958, published in John F. Kennedy, *The Strategy of Peace,* ed. Allan Nevins (New York: Harper and Row, 1960), p. 137. Kennedy was talking about overthrowing "friendly" right-wing regimes. His support for the Bay of Pigs invasion suggests that his comment did not apply to overthrowing unfriendly leftist regimes.

4. Samuel Huntington, "Will More Countries Become Democratic?" *Political Science Quarterly* 99 (Summer 1984): 213. Octavio Paz made a similar point: ". . . the logic of terror is mirror-logic; the image of the murderer that the terrorist sees is not his enemy's

but his own. This psychological and moral truth is also a political truth." In "Latin America and Democracy," *Democracy and Dictatorship in Latin America* (New York: Foundation for the Independent Study of Social Ideas, 1983), p. 15.

5. For a catalogue and analysis of proposals for addressing the debt crisis, see Robert A. Pastor, *Latin America's Debt Crisis: Adjusting to the Past or Planning for the Future?* (Boulder: Lynne Rienner Publishers, 1987), chap. 15.

6. Anthony P. Maingot, "A Logic of Democracy Approach to Cuba, Guyana, and Suriname," paper prepared for the Conference on "Reinforcing Democracy in the Americas," The Carter Center of Emory University, Atlanta, 17–18 November 1986.

7. Carlos Fuentes, "Homage to Mother Spain," *Newsweek International,* 21 July 1986.

8. See Terry Karl, "Petroleum and Political Pacts: The Transition to Democracy in Venezuela," *Latin American Research Review* 22, No. 1 (January 1987): 63–94.

9. For a brief description of these organizations, see U.S. Department of State, *Democracy in Latin America: The Promise and the Challenge* (Washington, D.C., March 1987), p. 7.

10. Larry Garber of the International Human Rights Law Group proposed an international election-monitoring organization in a memorandum prepared for the conference.

11. Larry Diamond and Seymour Martin Lipset, "Ensuring Free, Fair and Peaceful Electoral Competition," memorandum prepared for the conference.

12. See Lloyd C. Gardner, *Safe for Democracy: The Anglo-American Response to Revolution, 1913–23* (New York: Oxford University Press, 1984).

13. Enrique C. Ochoa, "The Rapid Expansion of Voter Participation in Latin America: Presidential Elections, 1845–1986," in *Statistical Abstract of Latin America, Vol. 25,* ed. James W. Wilkie and David Lorey (Los Angeles: University of California, Los Angeles Publications, 1987), pp. 862–910.

14. U.S. Department of State, *Foreign Relations of the United States, Vol. 6, 1955–57* (Washington, D.C., 1987), pp. 2–5.

15. U.S. Department of State, *Democracy in Latin America,* p. 7.

16. For an essay on the Tobar Doctrine and why it failed in Central America in the first two decades of the twentieth century, see Charles L. Stansifer, "Application of the Tobar Doctrine to Central America," *The Americas* 23 (January 1967): 251–72.

17. Cited in Charles D. Ameringer, "The Foreign Policy of Venezuelan Democracy," in *Venezuela: The Democratic Experience,* ed. John D. Martz and David J. Myers (New York: Praeger, 1977), p. 337.

18. Cited by Marcial Pérez Chiriboga, "The National Security Problem for Latin America: The Superpower's Reaction to Revolution," prepared for the World Peace Foundation, November 1986, p. 12.

19. Cited in Stepen G. Rabe, *Eisenhower and Latin America: The Foreign Policy of Anticommunism* (Chapel Hill: University of North Carolina Press, 1988), pp. 104–6.

20. Rabe, *Eisenhower and Latin America,* pp. 158–59.

21. For a further elaboration of this approach, see Robert A. Pastor, "Securing a Democratic Hemisphere," *Foreign Policy* 73 (Winter 1988–1989): 41–59.

22. "Argentina/Spain Signs $3 billion Cooperation Deal: Treaty is Similar to the Recent Accord with Italy," *Latin American Weekly Report,* 11 February 1988, p. 10. For the text of the Spanish agreement, see *Foreign Broadcasting Information Service,* 5 February 1988, pp. 32–33.

23. Bradley Graham, "Latin Leaders Consult on Problems: Informal Network in South America," *Washington Post*, 5 October 1985.

24. The twelve leaders that decided to establish the council included Jimmy Carter, Gerald Ford, Raul Alfonsín, Errol Barrow, Vinicio Cerezo, Nicolás Ardito Barletta, Fernando Belaúnde, Rafael Caldera, Osvaldo Hurtado, Daniel Oduber, George Price, and Pierre Elliot Trudeau. Since the meeting, Carlos Andrés Pérez, Michael Manley, and Erskine Sandiford (of Barbados) have become associated with the group.

25. For some specific proposals, see the papers written by Virginia Gamba and Ricardo Arias Calderon for the conference at the Carter Center.

Appendix

CASE STUDIES
OF DEMOCRATIZATION

Nine Cases of the Breakdown of Democracy

EDWARD GIBSON

VENEZUELA, 1945–1948:
The *Trienio*

Chronology of Key Events

18 OCTOBER 1945: Coup deposes government of President Isaías Medina Angarita. A *junta* led by Provisional President Rómulo Betancourt, three other Acción Democrática leaders, and two military officers takes office. Major political and economic reforms are enacted.

JANUARY 1946: The Christian Democratic party, Comité de Organización

Política Electoral Independiente (COPEI) is established and becomes the most important party in opposition to Acción Democrática.

15 MARCH 1946: Electoral reform law is passed granting universal suffrage.

14 DECEMBER 1947: Rómulo Gallegos, Acción Democrática presidential candidate, wins the presidency with 74 percent of the vote. Congressional elections are also held, giving Acción Democrática a 70 percent legislative majority.

24 NOVEMBER 1948: Military coup overthrows government of Rómulo Gallegos.

Introduction

The period between 1945 and 1948, known as the *trienio*, marked Venezuela's first experimentation with mass political democracy. As such, it provides a fascinating case study of the problems and potential pitfalls facing the founders of new democratic regimes. The abrupt termination by the military of Venezuela's tumultuous democratic experiment in November 1948 yielded powerful lessons for the inexperienced leaders of the regime—lessons that were applied by that leadership when it built one of Latin America's most stable democracies upon its return to power after 1958.

Politics during the *trienio* were characterized by an absence of trust between major contenders for power and by a lack of agreement on legitimate criteria for gaining power and for the resolution of conflict. In large part the lack of a framework for democratic cooperation between political groups can be traced to the actions of the party in power, Acción Democrática (AD). Possessing uncontested control over the political process, AD was in a unique position to create conditions for democratic cooperation between government and loyal opposition,[1] and to strengthen the democratic regime's fragile legitimacy within Venezuelan society. However, its actions in power destroyed the regime's legitimacy among non-AD sectors. Specifically, AD's socioeconomic policies alienated powerful interests in civil society whose support for democracy was tenuous at best. This was compounded by the alienation of non-AD political parties, through their exclusion from the policymaking process, the partisan implementation of government programs, the monopolization of the government bureaucracy, and the intolerance of dissent. While the coup that overthrew the AD government was carried out by the military high command, it enjoyed the widespread support of many non-AD sectors in civil and political society.

Acción Democrática in Power

Acción Democrática's rise to power in a military coup in October 1945 marked a radical change in the rules of the political game and the currencies of

political power in Venezuela. Conflicts over the regime's legitimacy were therefore probably inevitable. The new political system placed a premium on mass
organization and electoral strength as criteria for political power. Of all organized groups in the country, only AD possessed these resources to any considerable extent. Thus, social and political groups that had felt secure under
previous political regimes were suddenly unequipped to defend themselves or
to seek political power under the new regime. When they perceived their
interests to be threatened by the AD government, they readily sought alliances
with disloyal forces seeking to overthrow the democratic regime.

The AD government's policies soon alienated traditional centers of power in
Venezuela. The government attempted to enact an educational reform law that
threatened the Catholic Church's preeminence in private education. This, combined with the public anticlericalism of many of AD's prominent supporters,
galvanized opposition to the regime from the Catholic Church, and sparked
one of the *trienio*'s most bitter conflicts. The AD also put leaders of previous
governments on trial for abuses and for their illegal enrichment while in office.
This kind of action, perceived by many in political society to be a sign of
government vindictiveness (exercising, as Juan Linz would put it, a "politics of
resentment"), isolated AD from much of the traditional political establishment.

AD's active support of trade unionism alienated powerful industrial interests,
particularly in the oil industry. Its land reform program and support of rural
unions threatened agrarian elites. The party's revolutionary rhetoric, its appeals
for popular mobilization, and its constant electioneering also created insecurity
among established interests and the military.

The alienation of conservative interests was possibly an inevitable feature of a
government committed to broad political and economic reform. While undermining the regime's legitimacy among such interests, it need not necessarily
have provided the basis for an authoritarian coup d'état. The regime enjoyed
strong support from labor, the peasantry, and much of the middle class.
Furthermore, the new regime should have counted on the support of non-AD
political leaders who shared the same commitments to democratic rule as the
AD. Most importantly, they shared a political stake in the preservation of
civilian constitutional government. The loss of support within political society
was to prove AD's most critical failing. This loss of support was caused by a
number of factors.

As other case studies in this volume show, the exclusion of the opposition
from the political process by a party in power is often a major factor in a
democratic regime's loss of legitimacy. The overwhelming advantages possessed
by AD in mass political organization during the *trienio* gave opposing parties
little chance of capturing political power through electoral means. Their frustration was compounded by the fact that AD offered them little opportunity to
share political power through such other avenues as legislative coalitions, senior
government appointments, or systematic consultations on key policy decisions.
In addition, the resulting detachment of non-AD parties from the government's
fundamental socioeconomic reforms meant that, outside of AD, no political

groups were publicly committed to their implementation. This facilitated a convergence between disaffected party leaders and disloyal interests in opposition to the regime.

AD's extensive party network, which tied it closely at the local level to a variety of sectors, allowed it to adopt partisan criteria for the implementation of government programs. This greatly enhanced its electoral base, which grew as sectors adhered to the party in the hopes of benefiting from government resources. Yet it also undermined the government's legitimacy among competing electoral groups.

Juan Linz notes that one characteristic of new democracies is that governments and their supporters tend to "identify democracy with their own particular social and cultural policies." He further suggests that "on that basis, any opposition to those policies is perceived as antidemocratic action rather than as an effort to change the decisions of the temporary majority."[2] These observations accurately describe AD's relations with the rest of political society. Impressed by its huge electoral mandates, AD sought to singlehandedly reshape Venezuelan society. Instead of attempting to broaden support for the democratic regime, AD sought primarily to pursue programmatic goals and sectoral interests. It also responded bitterly to criticism, often questioning the democratic integrity of non-AD parties opposed to the government's policies. While the top leadership of AD often attempted to moderate the tone of the debate, it had little control over its rank and file.

In return, the opposition parties criticized the government in tones that with increasing stridency threw its legitimacy into question. Charges of government harassment, corruption, inefficiency, and ineffectiveness were the order of the day during the latter part of the *trienio*. Since the democratic regime was in its formative stages and was tightly controlled by AD, such criticisms were detrimental not only to the legitimacy of AD as a governing party, but to the democratic regime itself. In the final weeks of the *trienio*, opposition party leaders openly called for the ouster of the government. The military, dissatisfied with the AD government and fearful of divisions the political strife was causing within its own ranks, launched a successful and bloodless coup on 24 November 1948.

Conclusion

The democracy that entered into being between 1945 and 1948 did so on an extremely fragile base of legitimacy. The country had never before experienced democratic government. Few organized social or political groups possessed the skills or resources of mass organization necessary to contest power under the new regime. Furthermore, several important sectors, particularly those whose interests had been protected under previous regimes, had not relinquished their affinities for more authoritarian forms of rule.

Under these conditions a critical task for the democratic leadership was to strengthen a minimum consensus among the opposition on the desirability of continued constitutional rule. This required the building of a diverse coalition that would integrate the semi-loyal opposition into the democratic process and counter the disloyal opposition bent on destroying the regime. However, AD's *partido único* strategy isolated it from potential allies in political and civil society, eliminated any stakes that non-AD groups might have possessed in the continuation of the constitutional regime, and helped crystalize a broad coup-coalition that included virtually every non-AD sector in Venezuelan society.

A lesson the *trienio* provides to the leaders of fledgling democratic regimes is the illusory strength of electoral support as a legitimizing power resource when most other effective power resources lie in sectors that are at odds with the electoral majority. AD interpreted its huge electoral support as a mandate for partisan rule. Yet in a society where the acceptance of democratic norms was weak, such electoral majorities did little to give the government legitimacy among the excluded and threatened sectors that were able to overturn the government through military force.

Annotated Bibliography

Betancourt, Rómulo. *Venezuela, Política y Petroleo.* 2d. ed., Caracas: Editorial Senderos, 1967. This work provides an obviously partisan yet very detailed and revealing exposition of AD's program and objectives during the *trienio*. It also reviews Venezuelan politics during subsequent periods. Also published in English, as *Venezuela, Oil and Politics,* Boston: Houghton Mifflin, 1979.

Burggraaff, Winfield J. *The Venezuelan Armed Forces in Politics, 1935–1959.* Columbia: University of Missouri Press, 1972. A descriptive analysis of the role of the military in Venezuelan politics from the end of the Gómez dictatorship to the overthrow of the Pérez Jiménez government. This book provides one of the most thorough accounts in the literature of the military's role in the *trienio*, and of the process that led it to overthrow the AD government of Rómulo Gallegos.

Levine, Daniel H. *Conflict and Political Change in Venezuela.* Princeton: Princeton University Press, 1973. A study of the evolution of norms and institutions of democratic coexistence in Venezuela since 1936. The book focuses primarily on the successful process of democratic consolidation after 1959. However, it offers suggestive insights into the breakdown of democracy during the *trienio* and the ways in which the errors committed during the *trienio* shaped the successful consolidation in the 1960s. A shorter version of Levine's argument is presented in Juan Linz and Alfred Stepan, eds., *The Breakdown of Democratic Regimes: Latin America,* Baltimore: The Johns Hopkins University Press, 1978.

Martz, John D. *Acción Democrática: Evolution of a Modern Political Party in Venezuela.* Princeton: Princeton University Press, 1966. An excellent study of the role of *Acción Democrática* in shaping Venezuelan democracy. This work focuses on *Acción Democrática*'s evolution as a political party, its program, doctrine, links to civil society, and on the dynamics of Venezuela's party system. Martz's study of Venezuelan party politics also provides the basis for more general insights into modern political parties in Latin America.

COLOMBIA, 1949: Elite Conflict and Societal Violence

Chronology of Key Events

1945: Reformist Liberal President Alfonso López Pumarejo resigns from the presidency in the midst of interparty strife and opposition to his rule from Conservatives and moderate Liberals. He is succeeded by an interim "National Union" coalition under Liberal President Alberto Lleras Camargo.

1946: Conservative candidate Mariano Ospina Pérez wins the presidential election. He forms a "National Union" coalition, with Liberal Party leaders in prominent cabinet positions. Interparty violence mounts in the countryside. Strikes and riots in urban areas also increase.

MARCH 1948: Citing a list of grievances for alleged Conservative persecution of Liberal Party members, the Liberals withdraw from the National Union coalition.

APRIL 1948: Liberal Party leader Eliézer Gaitán is assassinated by a lone gunman. His assassination sparks the *bogotazo*, a massive urban riot in the nation's capital.

APRIL 1948: A second National Unity coalition is formed under the Ospina government.

MAY 1949: Citing the government's failure to enact reforms and continued persecution of party members, the Liberal Party withdraws once again from the National Union coalition.

NOVEMBER 9, 1949: Following an effort by the Liberal-controlled Congress to impeach him, President Ospina closes Congress and declares a state of siege.

Introduction

In 1949 Colombia's democratic system was formally overturned and the country continued a slide toward fratricidal violence that would ultimately claim two hundred thousand lives. The origins of the democratic breakdown and the *"violencia"* that followed it lay in the interactive relationship between socioeconomic change and the unique features of the Colombian political system.

The profound socioeconomic changes brought on by development in the 1920s, 1930s, and 1940s put strains on a political system characterized by informal norms of consent, accommodation, and bipartisanship within an oligarchic political elite. These changes altered the balance of power between the dominant Liberal and Conservative parties in favor of the Liberal Party. The resulting Liberal attempts to forge a Liberal hegemony over the political system threatened the Conservative Party with permanent minority status.

It also violated an implicit and critical understanding in Colombia's political system: that no party would be denied access by any other to power and to the spoils that accrued from control of the administrative apparatus of government. In Colombia, party affiliation and partisan access to administrative spoils had penetrated deeply into the country's political fabric. Interparty conflict was therefore felt at all levels of national life.

Ultimately, the hardening of partisanship and the rising level of political conflict overwhelmed a political system based on informal mechanisms of agreement between party elites. Those that frantically sought agreement in the final moments of Colombian democracy exercised little control either over their parties' rank and file or other members of the top party leadership. When President Ospina Pérez closed Congress and declared a state of siege in 1949, little disagreement existed within the political elite that all avenues of conciliation through the existing rules of the game had been exhausted.

The Erosion of Bipartisanship

The democracy that collapsed in 1949 had its roots in the Republican Union of 1909. Putting aside differences that had caused two large-scale civil wars in the nineteenth century, the Liberal and Conservative Parties united to overthrow the dictatorship of Rafael Reyes. They subsequently formed a coalition government and inaugurated a democratic regime tightly controlled by members of the two-party elite. This "oligarchic democracy" was predicated on a series of understandings between the Conservative and Liberal leaders. The most important of these was the bipartisan nature of the system. Not only would the system be dominated by the two parties, but power in essence would be shared between them, no matter which party controlled the executive branch of government. Thus, in what was known as *convivencia*, the party out of power was regularly granted a share of government portfolios by the party in power. Implicit in this arrangement was the idea that no party would become a permanently excluded minority. Another assumption was that party leaders exercised control over their parties' rank and file. This was an essential ingredient in the closed and informal system of interelite bargaining.

The erosion of the norms that held the system together first surfaced in the 1930s. Colombia was undergoing rapid economic development. With modernization, the role of the state and its importance in terms of power and patronage grew. Rural-urban migration accelerated and popular participation in political life increased. These changes favored the Liberal Party, whose historic strengths lay in the cities and the more modern sectors of Colombian society. Populism became a growing factor in Liberal Party politics, and labor unionism became a new power resource for elements within the party leadership. As a result, the ideological content of party rhetoric, muted in the past for the sake of *convivencia*, became intensified. The leadership and the constituencies of the Conservative Party found their stakes in the system increasingly threatened.

During the 1930s the Liberal Party sought to institutionalize its hegemony over the political system. In 1933 it won election victories that demonstrated clear Liberal majorities for the first time in the century. Claiming electoral fraud, the Conservatives announced their abstention from future electoral competitions. Reformist Liberal governments instituted major electoral reforms that further strengthened the Liberal electoral position. As the Liberals consolidated their hegemony and their control of governmental institutions down to the municipal level, interparty conflict intensified. Violence in the countryside, as party followers struggled over local administrative spoils, also grew. As importantly, the framework of trust and conciliation between the members of the party elite, the mainstay of the oligarchic system's stability, was steadily eroding.

During the second presidency of reformist Liberal President Alfonso López Pumarejo (from 1942 to 1945) interelite strife reached crisis proportions. Leaders of both parties openly questioned the legitimacy of the political system. Conservative Party leader Laureano Gómez declared the need for a "revolution" against the Liberal-dominated regime. Populist Liberal leader Eliézer Gaitán attacked the corruption and inefficiency of the oligarchic political system. Following López's resignation, two attempts were made by moderate leaders to restore *convivencia*. The interim government of Alberto Lleras Camargo forged a "National Unity" coalition that endured until the 1946 presidential elections. Conservative President Mariano Ospina Pérez (who won the elections following an internal split in the Liberal Party) also formed such a coalition, assigning prominent cabinet positions to Liberal leaders.

However, interparty conflict intensified during the time of the Ospina government. As the Conservatives took charge of governmental institutions, violence flared up in the countryside. Liberal leader Gaitán's ambivalent posture toward labor strikes against the government, and his sporadic harassment of Liberal members of the National Union government, reinforced Conservative distrust of the Liberal leadership. Elite strife paralleled violence in the countryside. In March 1948, after presenting a list of grievances for alleged government-sanctioned persecutions of Liberal Party members, the Liberals withdrew from the coalition government.

An important element in the progressive breakdown of Colombian democracy was the factional and disorganized nature of the two dominant parties. Although party affiliations were strongly felt at all levels of society, party leaders in reality had little control over their diverse factions or over the actions of local party leaders. This contributed to the erosion of trust between party elites. Acts of violence carried out in the name of one party or the other strained relations between party leaders. Yet, for fear of losing vital partisan support, they were reluctant to condemn such actions. Similarly, moderates were torn by the conflicting imperatives of preserving the system through compromise and retaining the support of hard-line factional leaders in the party. This often explained the ambivalence of party leaders during critical stages of interparty negotiation.

The Breakdown

The final phase of the crisis of Colombian democracy came with the assassination of Liberal leader Eliézer Gaitán on 8 April 1948. His assassination sparked what came to be known as the *bogotazo*, one of the largest urban riots in western history.

While the *bogotazo* helped to harden partisan antagonisms, it also awakened moderate party leaders to the need for compromise to save the political regime. A second effort to forge a bipartisan National Unity government was made by President Ospina. Liberal leaders were given prominent cabinet positions, and the government embarked on the drafting of major political reforms.

The second National Union coalition broke down, however, when the Liberal Party withdrew from it in May 1949. The ostensible reasons for the Liberal Party's withdrawal were the government's failure to carry out a reform of the police forces and partisan purges by Conservatives of the armed forces. However, the breakdown of the National Union can be attributed largely to the fact that loyal moderate leaders seeking a bipartisan solution no longer controlled the bulk of effective power and resources in their parties. They were unable to guarantee the adherence of party followers to agreements made with the other party, or to control actions by rival party leaders that disrupted their peace efforts. As a result of the mounting violence and hatred of the preceding years, the power centers of both parties had moved into positions of disloyalty to the regime. Laureano Gómez, the effective leader of the Conservative Party, attacked the regime's legitimacy from exile in Spain. This made it virtually impossible for President Ospina to mobilize Conservative support for peace efforts. Moderate Liberals were torn between the desire to save the system and the need not to be isolated from their fractionalized party following. Their ambivalence heightened Conservative suspicions and further eroded the framework of trust needed for negotiations.

The final months of Colombian democracy were characterized by an all-out struggle for control of the executive branch. This took the form of an institutional battle between the Liberal-controlled legislature and the Conservative-controlled executive. During this period both parties made full use of the institutions under their control for partisan ends. These included such "neutral" institutions as the courts and the military. As a result, decisions or initiatives emanating from the nation's highest political institutions were treated with contempt by adversely affected parties. For practical purposes, the political system had lost all authority. On 9 November 1949 President Ospina, in response to a congressional motion to impeach him, closed Congress, suspended civil liberties, and declared a state of siege.

Conclusion

The Colombian case provides a demonstration of the shortcomings of informal elite-based mechanisms of conflict resolution in a modernizing society. In order for such mechanisms to work, elites must exercise control over their constituencies. While such might have been the case during the earlier years of Colombia's oligarchic democracy, Colombian society in the 1930s and 1940s was far more mobilized and differentiated. Parties had developed deep linkages into society, yet they exercised little control over their constituencies. This made it very difficult for party elites to maintain commitments entered into through the ad hoc and informal system of interelite bargaining. The lessons of this experience were well applied during the democratic restoration of 1958, when those same elites formalized previously implicit power-sharing guarantees and integrated them into the political system.

Another lesson this case provides is one that has often appeared in other case studies in this series: the danger of one party seeking to institutionalize its hegemony over the political system. In other countries, where the norms of democratic coexistence are weak, this often leads excluded parties to move into positions of disloyalty to the regime. In Colombia, the political system's legitimacy was based on the understanding that the power-sharing norms of *convivencia* would be respected. The threat of an institutionalized "Liberal Republic" led Conservative elites and their powerful constituencies to withdraw legitimacy from the system. This, combined with the particularities of the Colombian party system, ensured that political conflict would spread throughout the country.

Annotated Bibliography

Dix, Robert H. *Colombia: The Political Dimensions of Change.* New Haven: Yale University Press, 1967. Dix analyzes several facets of the Colombian political system, including its institutions, interest groups, and decision-making processes. His interest is how the Colombian political system manages the process of modernization and development. Contrasting it to other types of modernizing regimes in Latin America, he categorizes the Colombian system as "rule by a modernizing elite." This work was recently revised and updated in *The Politics of Colombia,* New York: Praeger and Hoover Institution Press, 1987.

Oquist, Paul. *Violence, Conflict, and Politics in Colombia.* New York: Academic Press, 1980. Oquist's central concern is to explain the causes of *la violencia.* He suggests that a major cause of the violence of that period was "the partial collapse of the state." He provides a highly useful interpretation of events leading to the democratic breakdown as well as of how the political system shaped the character of the violent conflict during that period.

Wilde, Alexander. "Conversations Among Gentlemen: Oligarchical Democracy in Colombia," in *The Breakdown of Democratic Regimes: Latin America,* ed. Juan Linz and Alfred Stepan. Baltimore: The Johns Hopkins University Press, 1978. In this article, Wilde provides an analysis of the breakdown of the Colombian democratic regime. This case study uses his argument that the causes of the crisis originated in the inadequacy of informal mechanisms of power-sharing and negotiation between party elites.

Sanchez, Gonzalo, and Ricardo Peñaranda, eds. *Pasado y presente de la violencia en Colombia.* Bogotá: Fondo Editorial CEREC, 1986. A compilation of some of the most current work on *la violencia* by Colombian and North American scholars.

Once ensayos sobre la violencia. Bogotá: Fondo Editorial CEREC y Centro Gaitán, 1985. A collection of some of the original and most influential articles on *la violencia,* including articles by E. J. Hobsbawm and Camilo Torres.

GUATEMALA, 1954: Regime Breakdown and Foreign Intervention

Chronology of Key Events

1944: Rebellions break out against the thirteen-year-old dictatorship of Jorge Ubico. A three-person *junta*, which includes reformist officer Jacobo Arbenz and conservative officer Jorge Arana, assumes power and calls for elections.

DECEMBER 1945: Juan José Arévalo is elected president with 85 percent of the vote. A Democratic-reformist regime is inaugurated.

JULY 1949: Jorge Arana is assassinated; Arbenz associates are implicated in the murder. Armed clashes break out between the government and Arana's supporters.

MARCH 1951: Jacobo Arbenz assumes the presidency.

JUNE 1952: The most extensive agrarian reform law in Guatemalan history is enacted. Part of land held by the U.S.-owned United Fruit Company is expropriated. Other measures are taken to counter U.S. economic influence in Guatemala.

JANUARY 1953: Dwight D. Eisenhower is inaugurated President in the United States. Conflict with the U.S. government grows.

MAY–JUNE 1954: The United States exposes Czech arms shipment to Guatemala and denounces the government as a communist beachhead in the Americas. An anti-Arbenz invasion force, covertly supported by the U.S. government, enters Guatemala.

27 JUNE 1954: Arbenz resigns from the presidency following an ultimatum from his military high command.

Introduction

The 1954 overthrow of the constitutionally elected President of Guatemala, Jacobo Arbenz Guzmán, presents a clear case of a democratic regime breaking down through foreign intervention. The government of President Arbenz was overthrown following an extended campaign of political and economic destabilization by the government of the United States, and an invasion of rebel forces armed, trained, supported, and reportedly directed by the U.S. government. The lessons offered by the Guatemalan case thus differ somewhat from those offered by most South American cases, where the United States played a far less important role.

Yet this difference should not be overestimated. In an analysis of the process that led to the breakdown, the United States must be considered an important power contender in the domestic political arena. Beyond that, however, the Guatemalan case shares with its counterparts the incremental nature of the process of breakdown, where the actions of political leaders, particularly those in the incumbent government, led to the crystalization of a disloyal opposition that eventually overthrew the regime. In 1954 it is probable that opposition to the Arbenz government from the domestic economic elite (including the United Fruit Company) and from conservative elements of the military was not sufficient to overthrow the democratic regime. The decision by the United States to join them in that effort provided the "critical mass" for such an endeavor. Yet it should also be noted that efforts by the United States to overthrow the Arbenz government could not have succeeded without opposition to the government from important sectors of Guatemalan society, and without the loss of active support for the government by sectors that could have rallied to the regime's defense in the final stages of the crisis. The most important of these were loyal and semiloyal military elements that could have countered conservative disloyal officers within the military institution. The fact that actions by the Arbenz government led to a simultaneous loss of support for the regime from powerful actors both domestic and foreign accounts for the success of the anti-regime forces in 1954.

The Crystalization of Domestic Opposition

The conditions surrounding Jacobo Arbenz's ascent to power in 1951 were hardly auspicious. The democratic regime inaugurated in 1944 was unstable and beset by coup conspiracies. The government of Juan José Arévalo, which preceded Arbenz's government, had been reportedly the object of twenty-five coup attempts.

Two factors clouded the Arbenz government's legitimacy when it took power. The first was the 1949 assassination of Colonel Francisco Arana, Arbenz's chief conservative adversary. A number of Arbenz's close associates were implicated in the assassination. Arana's death was followed by a virtual state of civil war in which forces loyal to the government defeated pro-Arana military elements. The second factor was the 1950 presidential election, which was marred by violence and reports of electoral fraud.

The fast pace of social change and mobilization that had first developed under Arévalo's reformist regime intensified under the Arbenz government. Arbenz committed himself to a broad range of structural changes, the centerpiece of which was land reform. His economic program threatened powerful economic interests, particularly Guatemala's landowning oligarchy. Furthermore, Arbenz legalized the Communist Party, appointed a handful of communist leaders to secondary posts in his administration, and actively sought the support of communist-controlled rural and urban labor unions. These actions, as well as the revolutionary rhetoric often used by Arbenz and his supporters, solidified opposition to the regime from such traditional bastions of conservatism as the Church, the agrarian elite, and segments of the military.

Yet, while a strong base of opposition existed against the Arbenz government, several important sectors had benefited from its policies and offered a potentially important base of support. These included a growing domestic entrepreneurial sector, which had benefited from the government's nationalistic and stimulative economic policies, nationalist and reformist elements of the military, which formed an important part of the military institution, and also the increasingly mobilized lower socioeconomic groups.

In the latter part of his administration, as his economic and political problems intensified, Arbenz came to rely on his supporters on the left and in the labor movement for support. This was to have a number of adverse consequences. In spite of increased popular activity during the democratic regime, leftist and working-class groups were the weakest and least organized of Guatemala's power contenders. They were to prove ineffective against organized conservative forces seeking to topple the regime. Also, calls for popular mobilization by the government and its supporters increased the insecurity of non-working-class sectors and intensified the climate of instability in the country.

Of equal importance was the effect that calls by government supporters for the formation of popular militias and the arming of workers had on the military. Arbenz never fully disassociated himself from those calls. Fears of the creation of parallel armies affected loyal and disloyal officers alike, who shared an interest in the preservation of the institutional integrity of the armed forces. Arbenz's inability to deal decisively with those fears contributed in great measure to the failure of loyal and semiloyal military officers to rise to the defense of the regime during the final stages of the crisis.

Crystallization of U.S. Opposition

Arbenz's land reform program directly challenged the interests of Guatemala's largest landowner, the U.S.-owned United Fruit Company. The Arbenz government expropriated eighty-three thousand of the company's two hundred thousand hectares. The Arbenz government also sought to reduce the company's control over the country's ports and internal transportation system through the construction of alternative roads and port facilities. In addition, the government sought to diminish U.S. economic influence in such other areas as public utilities and oil exploration. These actions were protested by the U.S. government. With the advent of the Eisenhower administration, the U.S. government actively pressured the Guatemalan government on behalf of U.S. economic interests.

While the Arbenz government's economic policies created friction with powerful U.S. interests in Guatemala, its independent foreign policies brought it into direct conflict with the U.S. government. Guatemala took the leadership in hindering U.S. efforts in international forums to increase international participation in the Korean conflict. It also challenged U.S. objectives in other foreign policy areas. These actions took place at the height of the Cold War and were viewed with intense hostility and suspicion by the U.S. government. Compounding them was the high visibility of the Communist Party in Guatemala, as well as the presence of Communist officials in Arbenz's government. Convinced that Guatemala was serving as a "beachhead" for international Communism in the Americas, the U.S. government embarked upon a major campaign of political and economic destabilization. Through the Central Intelligence Agency, it recruited and built a small armed force to topple the Arbenz government, and it mounted a massive antigovernment propaganda campaign aimed at creating discontent within the Guatemalan armed forces and other sectors of society.

In June 1954 the CIA-supported invasion force entered Guatemala. It suffered very heavy losses against Guatemalan forces. Toward the end of the month the invasion force had captured one departmental capital, but it was apparent that it had no chance of a military victory as long as the Guatemalan armed forces remained united behind their government. Arbenz's major problem, however, was not the invasion force, but his own rebellious military. In early June senior military officers, concerned by the government's policies and worried by growing leftist-led agitation, had demanded that Arbenz remove leading Communist officials from his government. They also demanded that he reject calls by his supporters for the formation of armed peasant and worker militias to defend the government. Arbenz did not act upon their demands.

On 25 June President Arbenz received an ultimatum from his senior officers on the front that demanded his resignation; these officers threatened to come to an agreement with the invasion force if he refused to resign. Arbenz immediately ordered the army chief of staff to distribute arms to his supporters in the labor unions and political parties. The army, however, refused to carry out the president's orders. On 27 June, Jacobo Arbenz resigned from the presidency.

Conclusion

The ouster of the Arbenz government provides important lessons to democratic leaders who must contend with opposition from both foreign and domestic quarters. The gravest threat to such a regime's survival lies in a potential alignment between domestic interests and a hostile foreign power. The Arbenz government had little chance of surviving as long as its policies threatened both the interests of powerful domestic sectors and the global interests of their potential foreign ally, the United States. In retrospect, therefore, it seems that the pursuit of an aggressively independent foreign policy, which brought little material gain to Guatemala but aroused the hostility of a highly suspicious U.S. government, was a tactical mistake. While the Arbenz government acted within its rights as a sovereign power, its primary interests, preserving the democratic regime and protecting its socioeconomic achievements, required that compromises be made to temper the hostility of its powerful northern neighbor. The success of Bolivia's revolutionary leaders in gaining the acceptance—and support—of the Eisenhower administration during that same period is instructive in that regard.

Arbenz's other critical error was in not solidifying a strong base of support within the military, the one organized entity capable of defending the regime against disloyal forces. The proximate cause of Arbenz's fall was not the U.S.-backed invasion force, but a coup launched by elements in his own high command. In a sense, Arbenz's pattern was similar to the one followed by João Goulart ten years later in Brazil. He placed inordinate reliance on the mobilization of his supporters on the left (who were far weaker than their conservative adversaries), and in so doing he alienated potential supporters in the military. His ambivalent position on the formation of popular militias diminished his support within the officer corps and created conflicts of loyalty for his military supporters. As Juan Linz and Alfred Stepan have noted, a democratic regime requires not merely the passive support of its followers, but their aggressive support in times of crisis. For Arbenz, the final line of defense for his regime in June 1954 was the armed forces. The passivity of potential military supporters in the final days of the crisis sealed the fate of the democratic regime.

Annotated Bibliography

Adams, Richard N. *Crucifixion by Power: Essays on the Guatemalan National Social Structure, 1944–1966.* Austin: University of Texas Press, 1970. Whereas the body of literature on the Guatemalan democratic experience of 1945–54 focuses largely on the U.S. intervention, this book provides a useful and highly needed examination of the role of domestic power structures in perpetuating authoritarianism in Guatemala.

Blasier, Cole. *The Hovering Giant: U.S. Responses to Revolutionary Change in Latin America.* Pittsburgh: University of Pittsburgh Press, 1985. This book provides highly useful comparisons of U.S. responses to revolutionary governments in such countries as Mexico, Bolivia, Guatemala, and Cuba. It contains one of the most useful short treatments of the interplay between domestic and international factors that led to the overthrow of the Arbenz government.

Immerman, Richard. *The CIA in Guatemala: The Foreign Policy of Intervention.* Austin: University of Texas Press, 1982. Immerman provides a detailed account of the U.S. policymaking process that led to the overthrow of the Arbenz government. He places the U.S. intervention in Guatemala within the context of the Cold War and draws linkages between the 1954 Guatemalan intervention and latter interventions in Cuba and the Central American region.

Schlesinger, Stephen, and Stephen Kinzer. *Bitter Fruit: The Untold Story of the American Coup in Guatemala.* New York: Doubleday and Company, Inc., 1982. As with Immerman, Schlesinger and Kinzer focus on the U.S. role in the overthrow of the Arbenz government. However, they are less restrained in the use of undocumented evidence and assertions. They also claim a far more direct connection between the interests of United Fruit company and the motives for intervention by the U.S. government.

ARGENTINA, 1955–1966: A Case of Aborted Legitimacy

Chronology of Key Events

SEPTEMBER 1955: The Government of Juan D. Perón is overthrown.

JANUARY 1958: After two-and-a-half years of military rule under General Pedro Aramburu, presidential elections are held, inaugurating Argentina's experiment in limited democracy. All Peronist parties are banned from political activity. Arturo Frondizi, in large part through a secret arrangement with the Peronists, wins the election with over 50 percent of the vote.

MARCH 1962: Arturo Frondizi is overthrown by a military coup following Peronist victories in congressional elections.

SEPTEMBER 1962; APRIL 1963: Armed clashes take place between the *gorila* faction of the armed forces, favoring the establishment of a military government, and the "legalist" faction. Clashes result in decisive "legalist" victory.

JULY 1963: Arturo Illia is elected to the presidency.

MARCH 1965: Peronists score decisive gains in congressional elections.

JUNE 1966: President Illia is overthrown by a military coup. General Onganía is named president by the military junta.

Introduction

In contrast to the Chilean case, which involved the breakdown of a highly institutionalized regime with widespread legitimacy, the regime in Argentina from 1958 to 1966 was characterized by the disloyalty, or, at best, the semi-loyalty, of most influential sectors in society. The overthrow of President Illia in 1966 was thus less a culmination of a process of breakdown for an established democratic regime than the culmination of the failure by democratic leaders to institutionalize the norms and procedures of democratic coexistence within Argentine society.

The key task of democratic leaders between 1958 and 1966 was to expand the legitimacy of a system whose consolidation represented their only long-term hope of preserving political power. Their failure to do so lay largely in the constraints imposed on them by the military and other powerful sectors. The prevailing alignments of power compelled democratic leaders into coalition-building and conspiratorial activity with disloyal actors. However, democratic leaders also eroded whatever fragile legitimacy they, as a political class, could have imparted to the system. Deep antagonisms between democratic leaders, who tended to place a greater premium on the pursuit of power than on their common stake in constitutional government, precluded cooperation between them and helped to discredit the democratic process. The resulting loss of prestige suffered by the democratic regime fostered the rise of alternative political ideologies in civil society and the military. As the final vestiges of democratic legitimacy disintegrated in the mid-1960s, these other ideologies gained acceptance within society at large and paved the way for the most smoothly executed military coup in Argentine history.

"Birth Defects" of the Regime Inaugurated in 1958

The two most distinguishing features of the constitutional regime inaugurated in 1958 were the military's dominance over the political process and the banning of Peronist parties from political activity. These two factors provided the democratic regime with a very narrow base of legitimacy from the start.

Another factor compounding the regime's inherent instability was a bitter split between two factions of the Radical Party, Argentina's largest non-Peronist movement and the only possible agent of a majoritarian non-Peronist coalition. This split divided the movement into two parties, the *Radicales Intransigentes* (UCRI), led by Arturo Frondizi, and the *Radicales del Pueblo* (UCRP), led by long-time Radical leader Ricardo Balbín. It effectively prevented cooperation between the two largest political groups that shared a stake in the preservation of constitutional government. It also contained the seeds of the eventual collapse of the Argentine democratic experiment.

The Frondizi Government

The electoral strategy that brought Arturo Frondizi to power in 1958 was based on a populist electoral platform, as well as a secret agreement with the exiled leader, Juan Perón. This agreement gave Frondizi the support of Peronist voters in exchange for legalizing the Peronist Party by a Frondizi government. While it was instrumental in his election victory, Frondizi's strategy carried a number of costs that eventually impaired his ability to govern.

First, it created expectations in much of the voting public that, given the limitations on his government, Frondizi would be unable to fulfill. Second, it placed him under deep suspicion within the armed forces, which further limited his range of action in office. Third, it created a political debt to Perón and his followers, most of whom were openly disloyal to the regime, which he lacked the resources to repay. His government was soon accused by Peronist leaders with virulence of "betraying" their movement. This immediately threw the government's legitimacy into question among sectors that had hoped to be reincluded in the political process by the Frondizi administration.

Largely as a result of military pressure, Frondizi reversed many of his electoral promises and enacted an orthodox economic austerity program in 1959. This action, as well as other aspects of economic policy, shattered his electoral base of support. As a result, he came under the increasing control of the armed forces. His repeated tactical efforts to build new bases of support through popular appeals were thwarted by the military and served only to heighten suspicions in the officer corps against his government.

The one option that would have given the Frondizi government an electoral majority was a coalition with the other large political entity with a direct stake in the system: the UCRP. However, this option was precluded by the intense rivalries existing between the top leadership of the two parties. Following Peronist victories in the 1962 congressional elections (Frondizi had lifted the electoral ban), the president appealed to UCRP and other, minor party leaders to form a coalition to avert a military coup. They rejected his appeal, citing his government's "antinationalistic" economic policies and other factors. In the words of one observer, "So great was their distrust of Frondizi that they preferred to risk the breakdown of civilian government rather than do anything that would enable him to serve out his term."[3] The UCRP actively supported the military faction that overthrew Frondizi's government in March 1962.

The Illia Government

The 1963 election of UCRP candidate Arturo Illia followed a series of armed clashes between two military factions over the nature of the political order that would follow the overthrow of the Frondizi government. They resulted in the victory of the "legalist" faction of the armed forces, led by General Juan Carlos Onganía, which permitted the holding of presidential elections and the assumption of power by Arturo Illia.

The inauguration of Illia's presidency was marred by an additional set of factors. He was elected president with a mere 26 percent of the vote. His election was due less to his own charismatic appeal than to the proscription of Peronism and the divisive nature of the non-Peronist opposition (the UCRI, with Frondizi under detention, had split into two antagonistic factions). Furthermore, Illia's party, the UCRP, was closely allied with the military faction defeated by Onganía's forces in the clashes mentioned above. Thus, as with the Frondizi government, the Illia administration entered office under deep suspicion from the dominant leaders of the armed forces.

Nevertheless, President Illia "gave liberal democracy one of its fairest tests in Argentine history."[4] To an extent greater than any of his predecessors, he allowed freedom of the press, tolerated union activism, respected the rights of opposition political parties, and limited policymaking to constitutional decision-making channels.

Nevertheless, two characteristics of his rule undermined his efforts to build the foundations for a democratic regime. The first was his lackluster leadership. In a period during which competing authoritarian ideologies that promised dynamic leadership were gaining support in growing segments of society, the Illia government focused primarily on short-term initiatives, offering no long-range programmatic vision. Juan Linz writes of the importance for a new democratic regime of setting and controlling an "initial agenda" to galvanize its following and build support for the regime. The Illia government's failure to do this provided valuable ammunition to disloyal elements that offered alternatives to a democratic system increasingly perceived as ineffective.

Secondly, in spite of its obvious minority status, the Illia government rejected the formation of governing coalitions with the leadership of other parties. Determined not to share power after over thirty years in opposition, even with parties sympathetic to its program, the UCRP isolated itself from constitutionalist elements that could have provided support against a military coup. A telling remark was made by a Christian Democratic legislator only days before the coup: "The country does not deserve a military coup, but this government does."[5]

The media played a central role in eroding the legitimacy of the Illia government and the democratic regime. In increasingly strident tones, influential newspapers and magazines denounced the government's leadership, praised the virtues of potential leaders of a military coup, ridiculed the president and his cabinet, and questioned the effectiveness of democratic institutions. These attacks and the intellectual climate they created were instrumental in generating public support for a coup. Political leaders, including the leaders of deposed constitutional governments, also called openly for the Illia government's ouster. Former President Frondizi himself announced the dawning of a "great revolution" just days before the coup.

All this clamor accompanied the growth of new ideologies in the armed forces. The proponents of these ideologies saw the armed forces, whose hierarchy and cohesion had been restored under Onganía's leadership, as leading a new political order characterized by social discipline, centralized authority, and rational industrial development.

On 28 June 1966, the armed forces announced the ouster of the constitutional government of Arturo Illia. Shortly after that, Juan Carlos Onganía was named president by the military junta. No public protest followed the coup. Several political party leaders pledged their support for the coup and offered their services to the new government. They soon learned, however, as did their Chilean counterparts several years later, that they would be allowed no role in the new authoritarian regime whose birth they had eagerly awaited.

Conclusion

A major reason for the failure of the 1958–1966 democratic regime was the restriction imposed on democratic leaders by the permanent specter of military intervention. This created what Guillermo O'Donnell has called an "impossible game" for democratic elites: popular appeals to expand the regime's legitimacy sparked the hostility of the armed forces; submission to military demands eroded electoral support. However, within this restricted political context there was space for democratic leaders to gradually build the foundations of a democratic order.

The first obvious step in such a direction was cooperation between non-Peronist political parties. As the only political entities with a stake in the constitutional regime, the burden of preserving it fell heaviest on them. Unity between Radicals and other moderate non-Peronists could have provided a basis for a majoritarian coalition, or at least for a common front opposed to military intervention. It also offered the most realistic hope for a gradual (and nonthreatening) reincorporation of Peronist parties into the democratic process. In large measure, it was the divisiveness of non-Peronist forces that gave the military so much influence over Argentine political life.

Another factor that facilitated the coup of 1966 was the discredit suffered by the democratic process from the violation by party leaders of constitutional norms and procedures. The pursuit and maintenance of power by democratic elites seemed to rely more on *golpismo*—encouraging military coups—and factional military alliances than on election strategies and democratic coalition-building. The fact that all political elites had been parties to such behavior severely eroded whatever legal legitimacy they might have possessed once in office. The positive impact that Arturo Illia's constitutionalist government could have had on the regime's legitimacy was mitigated by his party's involvement in Frondizi's overthrow, its past affinities with *gorila* elements in the military, and the partisan nature of its rule. The cumulative effect of these patterns of behavior was a generalized disdain in Argentine society for the class of elites linked to democratic procedures and institutions. It is a condition that persists to this day, and presents a formidable challenge to the consolidation of democracy there.

Annotated Bibliography

O'Donnell, Guillermo. *Modernization and Bureaucratic Authoritarianism: Studies in South American Politics*. Institute of International Studies. Berkeley and Los Angeles: University of California Press, 1978. O'Donnell provides an important theoretical contribution to the explanation of the "bureaucratic authoritarian" phenomenon in Latin America, basing his analysis on the Argentine and Brazilian experiences. This book also contains a very interesting analysis of party politics in Argentina from 1955 to 1966, as well as an interpretation of the 1966 coup.

Potash, Robert. *The Army and Politics in Argentina, 1945–1962*. Stanford: Stanford University Press, 1980. Potash provides a minutely detailed description of political events in Argentina during that period, focusing particularly on the military's involvement in politics and on political dynamics within the military institution.

Rouquié, Alain. *Poder militar y sociedad política en la Argentina*. Buenos Aires: Emecé Editores, 1978. This is an excellent (if at times polemical) analysis, full of valuable empirical material and interpretive insights, of the interaction between the military and political society in Argentina from the birth of the republic to 1973. Originally published as French, as *Pouvoir militaire et société politique en Republique Argentine*, Paris: Presses de la Fondation Nationale des Sciences Politiques, 1978.

Rock, David. *Argentina, 1516–1982: From Spanish Colonization to the Falklands War*. Berkeley and Los Angeles: University of California Press, 1985. A valuable contribution to an understanding of the historical roots of modern Argentina's social, political, and economic problems. Contains a detailed examination of pre–1955 events, as well as a less thorough yet interesting interpretation of more recent events.

Wynia, Gary. *Argentina in the Post-War Era: Politics and Economic Policy Making in a Divided Society*. Albuquerque: University of New Mexico Press, 1978. Wynia examines the relationship between political regimes and policymaking between 1945 and 1976. He presents interesting contrasts of the types of strategies, coalitions, and policy options available to political leaders under different types of regimes.

BRAZIL, 1964: The Failure of Popular Mobilization

Chronology of Key Events

AUGUST 1961: Jânio Quadros, president of Brazil, resigns unexpectedly after only seven months in office.

SEPTEMBER 1961: João Goulart, Quadros's vice-president, assumes the presidency. However, his powers are sharply curtailed by Congress.

JANUARY 1963: Following prolonged effort by Goulart to have his full presidential powers restored, a plebiscite restores a full presidential system.

MID-1963: The economic crisis grows as the government's stabilization plan fails. Political instability and mobilization affect most parts of the country.

13 MARCH 1964: At a large rally, President Goulart calls for fundamental reforms in the nation's constitution and economic structure. He calls for massive demonstrations and nationwide strikes to pressure Congress to enact the reforms.

26 MARCH 1964: An enlisted men's naval mutiny takes place in support of the Goulart government. The government grants amnesty to the mutineers.

31 MARCH 1964: A military coup overthrows the government of president João Goulart.

Introduction

The collapse of the Brazilian constitutional regime in 1964 was a direct result of actions taken by the incumbent leadership, particularly during the final weeks of the regime, which eroded the legitimacy of the government and generated a "critical mass" of support for a military coup.

Long-term pressures on the Brazilian political system had created an open crisis of regime as far back as 1961. Influential leaders from all parts of the political spectrum called for substantive changes in the constitutional regime, and vocal sectors on the left demanded a restructuring of the socioeconomic order. Yet the final outcome of the crisis—military overthrow of the regime rather than reform through constitutional channels—was by no means foreordained. It was the direct result of decisions taken by the political leadership, particularly President Goulart's deliberate use of popular mobilization as a political strategy, which alienated regime supporters and created the conditions for disloyal elements within the armed forces to overthrow the constitutional regime.

The Goulart Government

João Goulart assumed power in 1961 amid strong opposition to his rule from Congress, as well as widespread questioning of the political regime's capabilities for coping with Brazil's fundamental problems. Much of that questioning came from the regime's top leaders. Goulart's presidency followed the abrupt resignation of President Jânio Quadros, who had resigned in a failed bid to expand the prerogatives and powers of the presidency. Goulart himself assumed office with his powers greatly curtailed by Congress, and he spent much of his first two years as president attempting to get those restraints rescinded.

Throughout Goulart's tenure, support for an overthrow of the regime existed in the military and the economic elite. Yet this support was not in itself sufficient for the crystallization of a coup coalition capable of overthrowing the constitutional regime. Several factors impeded such a development. Among these were the powers inherent in the office of the presidency and the vested interest of powerful politicians in preserving constitutional forms of government. A number of these politicians commanded a wide following within the electorate, and they hoped to reach the presidency in future elections. Their support was critical to the success of a potential coup coalition.

There were also divisions within the military institution. While powerful military elements, disenchanted by civilian rule and influenced by what one observer has called "new professionalist" ideologies[6] actively conspired to launch a coup, they were countered by a strong legalist tendency within the armed forces.

These regime-sustaining forces, however, were to be rapidly eroded by events that took place in the final weeks of March 1964. They were set in motion by a decision by President Goulart to break the deadlock in the system through a deliberate intensification of the political crisis. By means of this effort Goulart hoped to bring about a realignment of political powers that would allow him to expand his presidential powers and to enact fundamental reforms in Brazil's socioeconomic structure. At a political rally on 13 March Goulart outlined a series of proposals for constitutional and economic reform and called for massive demonstrations and strikes throughout the country to pressure a reluctant Congress to enact his proposals.

While Goulart's strategy succeeded in intensifying the crisis, it led ultimately to the downfall of his government. Its results were to mobilize disloyal forces into action against the government, and to alienate actors whose active support Goulart needed for the defense of the constitutional regime.

The structural reforms proposed by Goulart threatened powerful economic interests and helped to shift those who had either been uncommitted or semiloyal into a position of disloyalty toward the democratic regime. In addition, the apprehension of the middle classes caused by rampant inflation and an erratic economy was aggravated by the rhetoric of revolution and mass mobilization that accompanied statements by Goulart and his supporters. The insecurity of the middle classes was joined to the fear of more powerful sectors in society. Disparate and often antagonistic groups became linked in opposition to the Goulart government.

Goulart's decision to resort to popular mobilization also had a number of adverse effects on the position of his government. By relying on what was basically an extraconstitutional channel for advancing his objectives, he neglected and alienated moderate centrist and leftist supporters within political society that could have served as allies in a constitutional effort to pass his reforms or to block a potential coup. Several leaders within political society, alarmed by his rhetoric and political tactics, also began to suspect that he had anticonstitutionalist intentions of his own. They therefore saw it in their interest to oppose his initiative, and they moved into a position to support elements committed to his overthrow. Although loyal to the political regime in which they had a vested interest, their opposition to the government shifted them into supporting a coup coalition whose leaders were bent on doing away with the democratic system.

The regime's loss of legitimacy was to a great extent accelerated by Goulart's own statements on the need for constitutional reform. His attacks on the constitution as archaic and obsolete undermined his own claims, as a constitutional president, to obedience from the public and the military. Statements by close supporters of the president that denigrated the constitution and the nation's political institutions compounded the problem. Such statements, made by individuals whose authority was based on the legitimacy of constitutional institutions, helped remove the air of illegality that might have surrounded plotters against the regime.

Another consequence of Goulart's actions serves as a powerful lesson to other democratic leaders considering the use of popular mobilization as a political tactic. Unless carefully controlled, popular mobilization can acquire a momentum of its own that, particularly in times of crisis, will move beyond the political leadership's control. Leaders in political society must retain the initiative in the political process. Transferring that initiative to highly mobilized groups in civil society can lead people to believe that constitutional leaders have lost control of the political process. In the final weeks preceding the 1964 coup, there were many in Brazilian society who felt that such a point had been reached.

The Role of the Media and Foreign Actors

The media played an active role in galvanizing support for a coup in the final weeks of the regime. Following the rally of 13 March, some of the more important newspapers adopted editorial positions that were decidedly pro-coup. Most of the editorials called on the military to assume its traditional role as defender of the constitution against a government that seemed bent on subverting it. Few, however, actually called for the permanent abolition of democratic rule in Brazil. Nevertheless, the pro-coup stance of much of the media facilitated matters for the anti-regime plotters within the military.

The United States also played a visible role in destabilizing the Goulart government. Angered by Goulart's populist policies, the U.S. government greatly reduced its economic assistance. It also gave encouragement to pro-coup elements within the military with whom it was tied through military assistance programs. Military training programs sponsored by the U.S. government, which emphasized anti-subversive internal security doctrines, also influenced the ideological development of officers who would lead the coup against the constitutional regime. Finally, the U.S. government provided strong political and economic support to the military regime after the coup.

Final Decisions

The decisive step in the breakdown process occurred during the enlisted men's naval mutiny of 26 March. In an expression of support for the Goulart government, more than one thousand sailors and marines seized a naval armory in Rio de Janeiro. During the mutiny, Goulart exhibited extreme indecision. He finally delegated the decision on how to respond to the uprising to a naval minister, who opted for granting amnesty to the mutineers.

Goulart's response to the mutiny galvanized support for a coup among important elements of the military, who now feared the disintegration of discipline within the military institution. Just as important, it diminished the aggressiveness with which his military supporters might have defended the regime, because they were now torn by conflicting loyalties to the government and to the integrity of the military institution. Their ambivalent support was no match for the intensity of the coup coalition that overthrew the democratic regime on 31 March, and launched twenty years of bureaucratic-authoritarian rule.

Conclusion

The breakdown of Brazilian democracy in 1964 demonstrates how the actions of a political leader can compound the structural weaknesses of a regime and precipitate its downfall. In early 1964 the overthrow of democracy was not an inevitability. Several factors existed that countered the destructive tendencies in the political system and offered the possibility of a constitutional solution to the crisis. However, deliberate decisions taken by the president and his supporters gradually eroded support for the regime.

Specifically, Goulart's resort to popular mobilization had a number of adverse consequences for the regime. It created a climate of instability that, far from serving as a manifestation of the president's popular support, gave the impression that the political process was no longer being controlled by the constitutional leadership. It aggravated fears in the middle and upper classes of an imminent radical takeover of the government. As an extraconstitutional bid to pressure the legislature to enact reforms, Goulart's action alienated important segments of political society. It also threw the government's own commitment to constitutional procedures into question and prompted many regime supporters into an alliance with disloyal forces. The last weeks of the Goulart government provide a fascinating case study of the dangers of the use of popular mobilization as a political strategy by democratic leaders.

Goulart's final critical error was in not recognizing that fears for the integrity of the military institution would weigh far more heavily on the minds of his military supporters than concerns for the survival of the constitutional government. In this error he would join the company of such other Latin American leaders such as Yrigoyen, Perón, Arbenz, and Allende. Goulart's failure to take decisive measures to assuage such fears in the final stages of the crisis made the erosion of support for the democratic regime complete.

Annotated Bibliography

Roett, Riordan. *Brazil: Politics in a Patrimonial Society.* New York: Praeger Publishers, 1984. This book provides an interesting introductory overview of Brazilian history and politics from the colonial period to the present, including the recent transition to democratic government. The author describes the Brazilian political system within the context of a "patrimonial" social order that has placed limits on the growth of popular participation and national integration.

Skidmore, Thomas E. *Politics in Brazil, 1930–1964: An Experiment in Democracy.* Oxford: Oxford University Press, 1967. A thorough treatment of Brazilian politics from the rise of Vargas to the fall of João Goulart. Skidmore pays extensive attention to the Goulart government and the collapse of the democratic regime in 1964.

Stepan, Alfred. *The Military in Politics: Changing Patterns in Brazil.* Princeton: Princeton University Press, 1971. Stepan analyzes the causes of the breakdown of Brazilian democracy in 1964, focusing specifically on evolving patterns of civilian-military interaction. Stepan also examines internal military dynamics, such as changes in military ideologies and organization that contributed to the 1964 military coup and to the imposition of extended authoritarian rule. An abridged version of Stepan's argument is presented in his chapter on Brazil in *The Breakdown of Democratic Regimes: Latin America,* ed. Juan Linz and Alfred Stepan, Baltimore: The Johns Hopkins University Press, 1978. This case study uses Stepan's argument that the popular mobilization strategy employed by Goulart in the final days of his presidency was decisive in crystallizing support for anti-regime forces.

Stepan, Alfred, ed. *Authoritarian Brazil: Origins, Policies, Future.* New Haven: Yale University Press, 1973. A valuable collection of essays by prominent scholars that discusses political origins, political economy, and the possible evolution of authoritarianism in Brazil.

CHILE, 1973: Fragmentation of Political Center

Chronology of Key Events

SEPTEMBER 1964: Eduardo Frei, leader of the Christian Democratic Party, is elected president with 56.1 percent of the vote. His election is supported by Chile's two main conservative parties. The Christian Democratic "Revolution in Liberty" is inaugurated.

MARCH 1965: The Christian Democrats win an unprecedented majority in the Chamber of Deputies during congressional elections.

SEPTEMBER 1970: Leftist *Unidad Popular* (UP) candidate Salvador Allende wins presidential elections with 36 percent of the vote.

DECEMBER 1971–OCTOBER 1972: Popular mobilization intensifies, followed by countermobilization by the middle class and established interests.

Truckers' strike gains wide adherence by professionals, shopkeepers, and other groups. Allende invites senior military officers into his cabinet.

MARCH 1973: Congressional elections fail to break the political deadlock.

JUNE 1973: A coup attempt is crushed by the constitutionalist chief of staff of the army. Further talks between the government and the opposition break down.

AUGUST 1973: Chamber of Deputies adopts a resolution declaring UP government unconstitutional.

SEPTEMBER 1973: A military coup deposes the government of Salvador Allende.

Introduction

The breakdown of democracy in Chile resulted from the erosion of traditional norms of accommodation and compromise between political leaders at the center of the political spectrum. The failure to arrive at centrist compromises by leaders of diverse political parties resulted in the decline of mediating institutions and procedures that for generations had provided stability in an ideologically polarized society. As a result, the democratic leadership lost the initiative in Chilean political life, giving way to mobilization politics and undermining the regime's legitimacy among the military and important sectors of civil society.

Early Indicators of the Breakdown

The early signs of a shift in the basic patterns of Chilean politics came with the displacement of the pragmatic Radical Party by the Christian Democrats as Chile's most important center party. The Christian Democrats rejected the Radicals' nonideological strategy of pursuing power through coalitions with the left and the right, and sought to build an ideological centrist majority committed to moral renewal and gradual social change. While the party's *partido unico* and "Revolution in Liberty" strategies responded to deeply felt needs within Chilean society, their unintended consequence was to harden the political system's ideological poles. Opposition parties on the right and the left were excluded from much of the policymaking process. Deprived of the possibility of sharing power through traditional coalition-building mechanisms, they sought to consolidate their own bases of support in the electorate by means of sharply defined ideological and partisan appeals.

During the 1970 elections, party leaders rejected the formation of preelectoral coalitions between the center parties and the parties of the left or the right. The inevitable outcome of that decision was the election of a minority president. Furthermore, the failure of centrist leaders to structure a preelection compromise created the likely possibility that the minority president would come from one of the more extreme ideological ends of the political spectrum.

The Unidad Popular *Government and the Growing Crisis of Regime*

Tensions in the political system following the 1970 election victory of the leftist *Unidad Popular* coalition surfaced immediately. A coup attempt by elements of the military was aborted, and the opposition forced Salvador Allende to sign a "Statute of Guarantees," committing himself to preserving constitutional liberties while in office. The demand that an experienced and respected parliamentarian formally commit himself to what should have been an implicit part of Chilean political life was a strong manifestation of how strained the patterns of trust and consensus between members of the political elite had become.

The Allende government was soon beset by a series of destabilizing problems. The first of these was an economic crisis in large part generated by its own policies. The government granted massive wage increases and embarked on the takeover of large numbers of industrial firms. These measures led to spiraling inflation and severely taxed the Chilean economy. They also aroused powerful opposition from several social sectors. While the difficulties and opposition generated by those policies undermined the UP's ability to implement other aspects of its program, they were probably politically unavoidable. Given the expectations generated by its election victory and the absence of a moderating effect of a coalition with important centrist parties, the new UP government was compelled to make bold moves in pursuit of its socialist strategy to preserve the support of important elements in its coalition. Such moves, however, confirmed the early fears of the opposition and intensified the sense of crisis in the country.

Another problem that undermined the government's legitimacy early in its tenure was popular mobilization. It took the form of strikes, demonstrations, and unauthorized industrial takeovers (often encouraged by elements within the UP coalition), and a countermobilization was instituted by the middle class and established interests. The inability to maintain order is often one of the most serious threats to the legitimacy of a democratic government. In a highly polarized context, in which many believe the government itself is responsible for much of the violence, the threat is particularly grave. Salvador Allende's reluctance to disassociate himself from radical elements in his coalition involved in the violence compounded the suspicions of the opposition about the intentions of his government.

Between March and June 1972, moderate leaders of the UP and the opposition parties met repeatedly to negotiate a resolution to the political crisis. In the final phase of these negotiations, both sides reached substantial agreements on a number of disputes, including key aspects of the UP's economic program and relations between the government and the opposition. These agreements would have represented substantial compromises by the Allende government. They would, however, have permitted a continuation of the process of socioeconomic change that it sought, albeit at a moderated pace.

The negotiations broke down, first in April, when the UP canceled talks under pressure from its left wing, and finally, in July, when the Christian Democrats withdrew in response to pressure and parliamentary maneuvers by their conservative faction. The breakdown of talks resulted from the reluctance of centrist leaders to risk losing support in their parties by forging compromises for the sake of the political system. Their failure to take that risk during the critical negotiations of March–June 1972 had devastating consequences for Chile's democracy. One author has noted that "in retrospect, the negotiations appear to have been the last chance to prevent the polarization which terminated in the 1973 coup."[7]

The Role of Other Actors

Outside of Chilean political society, two actors that played visible roles in the breakdown of democracy were the media and the United States government. While neither of these two actors played a decisive role in the breakdown, they did contribute to the intensity of the crisis that led to the overthrow of the Allende government. The broadcast media and influential newspapers, particularly the daily *El Mercurio,* played an important and increasingly strident role in opposition to the UP government. In the final days before the coup, *El Mercurio* and other publications openly called on the military to overthrow the *Unidad Popular* government. While most of the media acted independently of the political leadership, their reporting and editorializing tended to be highly partisan, often conveying inaccurately the positions of leaders on the other side. As traditional political mechanisms of bargaining and compromise broke down, political leaders resorted to the media to advance their positions, contributing further to the climate of rhetorical excess and conflict.

The role of the United States government in the overthrow of the UP government has been the subject of considerable political and scholarly debate. The U.S. government played an active role in supporting the rise of the Christian Democratic movement, both overtly, through the Alliance for Progress, and covertly (allegedly unbeknownst to the Christian Democratic leadership) through substantial CIA financing and propaganda during the 1964 and 1970 elections. More significantly, the U.S. government embarked on an open campaign of destabilization of the Allende government through economic sanctions and covert aid to opposition groups, including *El Mercurio* and the striking truckers. While less important as determinants of the breakdown than the internal crisis of the Chilean political system, these actions contributed substantially to the climate of crisis and instability that pervaded Allende's years in office.

Final Decisions

The stalemate in political society led finally to the politicization of "neutral" powers in the state. During 1972 leaders resorted to such politically neutral branches of government as the court system and the *Contraloria General de la Republica* to resolve disputes between the president and the legislature. In Chile's highly institutionalized political system, these branches of government commanded great respect as bastions of impartiality, legality, and fairness. By calling upon them to rule on political issues that were matters for the executive and legislature to decide, political leaders threw their neutrality into question. It was no longer possible for those branches to rule on key issues without appearing either "reactionary" or "revolutionary." Their politicization was a further manifestation of the erosive effect of the political crisis on the country's democratic institutions.

In the second half of 1972 political leaders made a decision that in other countries has often preceded the breakdown of democratic institutions: the politicization of the military. In return for an end to a nationwide strike, the UP government agreed to appoint the commander in chief of the army and a number of other military officers to key positions in the cabinet. While the measure was designed to bring stability to the system until legislative elections could be held, it effectively put an end to the neutrality of the last "neutral" institution in Chile.

Participation in government opened deep cleavages within the military institution. After legislative elections failed to break the political deadlock, the armed forces left the UP government. Their departure left a power vacuum that the government was unable to fill.

On 29 June 1973, an attempted military coup was crushed by the loyalist commander in chief of the army, General Carlos Prats. This led to the final effort by moderates to structure a centrist consensus. Although they came close to reaching an agreement on the formation of a new cabinet, the government refused to accede to the Christian Democratic demand that military officers be appointed to the cabinet at all levels of government. Talks once again broke down. On 22 August the Chamber of Deputies adopted a "Sense of the House" resolution declaring that the Allende government was unconstitutional.

The failure of the final centrist attempt at compromise in an atmosphere where calls for the overthrow of the government or the arming of the workers were the order of the day made it inevitable that the last loyal and semi-loyal elements in the military and political society would quickly move into disloyalty to the democratic regime. The military coup that overthrew the government of Salvador Allende on 11 September thus came as little surprise to anyone. Involved in the decision by centrist democrats to support the coup was the fatal miscalculation that the military would return power to them once the immediate problem of the UP government was resolved. Few imagined that they, as had so many other abdicating democrats in Latin America, would be so absolutely excluded from the new political order inaugurated by the military.

Conclusion

The Chilean case illustrates, as do the Colombian and Venezuelan break-downs, the potential costs to a democratic regime of hegemonic quests by individual political parties. In Chile's highly developed and ideological party system, where power sharing and coalition-building norms were essential ingredients in the maintenance of a fragile center consensus, the cost was retrenchment by parties on the left and the right around ideological and maximalist agendas. Had the Christian Democratic victories of the 1950s and 1960s actually represented the emergence of a permanent and dynamic centrist majority, the exclusion of noncentrist parties would not have had as destabiliz-ing an effect. However, as the 1970 elections showed, (when the Christian Democrats received only 28 percent of the vote), the maintenance of centrist majorities still required coalitions with parties on either end of the political spectrum. By 1970, however, the parties at the two ends were determined to seek power on their own.

The experience of the Allende years also illustrates the burden that centrist leaders must carry in preserving the viability of democratic institutions in times of crisis and polarization. The need to make clear and unambiguous moves in defense of the system, even at the expense of losing the adherence of supporters on extreme ends of the political spectrum, is critical in periods of high in-stability. Ambiguity in the quest for a centrist consensus will be interpreted in the worst possible light by other moderates, whose perceptions will be clouded by the events and passions of the moment. Such conditions will lead, as they did in Chile, to an erosion of the framework of trust that is a requisite of democratic negotiation.

Another important lesson concerns the cost to a democratic regime's legit-imacy of the politicization of such nonpolitical institutions as the courts or the military. The decision by political leaders in Chile to move in that direction resulted from a stalemate in the political decision-making process. Resort to other sources of authority—not tarnished by the partisan struggle—seemed the only way of resolving crucial problems. However, it removed the impartiality that gave those institutions the substance of their constitutional legitimacy. Politicization of the armed forces pushed them into open conflict with groups involved in the political struggle. It was also an admission by civilian elites that they no longer controlled the political process. Both of those factors gave the military ample incentive to remove civilians from office and launch a campaign of repression against opposition in society.

Annotated Bibliography

Boorstein, Edward. *Allende's Chile: An Inside View*. New York: International Publish-ers, 1977. An American Marxist economist's description of the workings of the *Unidad Popular* government and the obstacles that hindered the implementation of its strategies. This work focuses far more on the impact of U.S. intervention, and places greater primacy on its role in the breakdown, than the other works cited below.

Sigmund, Paul E. *The Overthrow of Allende and the Politics of Chile, 1964–1976.* Pittsburgh: University of Pittsburgh Press, 1977. Sigmund provides a detailed account of the events that led from the election of the Frei government to the overthrow of Allende. In a portrait that is generally sympathetic to the Christian Democratic leadership, Sigmund's book is particularly valuable in describing the internal tensions and divisions within the Christian Democratic and *Unidad Popular* movements that shaped many of the decisions leading to the breakdown of democracy.

Valenzuela, Arturo. *The Breakdown of Democratic Regimes: Chile.* Baltimore: The Johns Hopkins University Press, 1978. This book is part of the series of studies on Latin America and southern Europe entitled *The Breakdown of Democratic Regimes,* edited by Juan Linz and Alfred Stepan. In what has become one of the most influential interpretations of the breakdown of Chilean democracy, Valenzuela provides a balanced and theoretically grounded analysis. He places the primary burden for the breakdown on the failure of the political system to maintain the politics of accommodation that for generations had maintained stability in a polarized society. His arguments on the role of the Christian Democratic Party's rise in that process is advanced in this case study.

Whiting, Van. "Political Mobilization and the Breakdown of Democracy in Chile," *Latin American Issues* 1, 1 (1984). In a suggestive article that challenges Valenzuela's interpretation of the causes of the Chilean breakdown, Whiting argues that its primary cause was the unprecedented degree of popular mobilization that began in the 1960s and eventually overwhelmed the political system's absorptive capacities. He thus counters Valenzuela's assertion that the breakdown of the political system preceded destructive popular mobilization.

URUGUAY, 1973: Democratic Abdication and the Militarization of Politics

Chronology of Key Events

NOVEMBER 1966: A plebiscite is held that approves a new constitution abolishing the collegial executive. Presidential elections are also held, which result in the election of Colorado candidate Oscar Gestido. Upon his death one year later, he is succeeded by Vice-President Jorge Pacheco Areco.

JUNE 1968: The government declares a state of siege, under *Medidas Prontas de Seguridad* (Prompt Security Measures), in response to strikes and attacks by the Tupamaro guerrilla group. Regular suspension of constitutional guarantees and censorship of the press follow under the *Medidas* during subsequent years.

MID-1970: Tupamaro guerrillas kidnap and assassinate Dan Mitrione, a USAID official working with the Uruguayan police. Congress agrees to declare a twenty-day suspension of constitutional guarantees.

SEPTEMBER 1971: The government transfers responsibility for combating the Tupamaro guerrillas from the police to the armed forces.

FEBRUARY 1972: Juan María Bordaberry assumes the presidency.

FEBRUARY 1973: Following an attempted coup by military elements, Bordaberry agrees to the formation of a military-dominated National Security Council to oversee government decisions.

JUNE 1973: President Bordaberry announces the dissolution of Congress. Military-authoritarian rule is imposed on Uruguay.

Introduction

The breakdown of Uruguayan democracy in 1973 followed a prolonged period of decay in the nation's democratic institutions. As far back as the 1950s when economic decline put an end to decades of prosperity, the political system, particularly the legislature, showed signs of immobilism in the face of pressing needs for reform and for a programmatic vision. The decline of Uruguay's political democracy accelerated dramatically in the late 1960s when protest and political violence from civil society sparked repressive counter-measures from the state. Between 1967 and 1973, as states of siege became almost routine and constitutional liberties eroded, the Uruguayan legislature became irrelevant to the political process. The military gained incremental control over most aspects of political life. When President Bordaberry announced the dissolution of Congress and the imposition of military-authoritarian rule in 1973, he was merely adjusting the nation's formal political structures to the realities of political power in Uruguay.

Early Crisis of Regime

The decline of international demand for Uruguay's traditional exports in the 1950s plunged the country into an economic crisis from which, up to the present date, it has not recovered. The nation's industrial development strategy, its extensive social welfare system, and even its highly developed clientelistic party system were predicated upon the prosperity of its agro-export sector. When that sector failed to adapt to changing international markets, stagnation gripped virtually all other sectors of society.

The economic depression set in motion a crisis of regime. At the root of the crisis was the visible lack of efficacy—the ability to identify solutions to fundamental problems[8]—of the Uruguayan political system. Deeply entrenched in society through clientelistic party networks, mired in allocative politics, and controlled by a factional, aging, and noninnovative party leadership, the national legislature seemed unable to provide any new programmatic vision for the country. Legislative paralysis was compounded by the collegial nature of the executive branch, which was divided between the two dominant parties, the Colorado and Blanco parties.

By the 1960s the crisis of regime was being manifested in widespread questioning of the nation's political institutions and by calls for constitutional reform. A new constitution was enacted in 1966, which among other changes replaced the collegial executive branch with a single-executive presidential system. This put an end to the formal supremacy of the legislature in Uruguayan politics.

A long-term process that intensified after 1966 and contributed to the breakdown of the democratic regime was, to use one of Juan Linz's concepts, an "abdication of democratic authenticity" by the Uruguayan legislature. Linz notes that this happens when democratic leaders, rather than taking responsibility for resolving intractable problems, postpone such tasks or delegate them to the executive or a technocratic elite or to such neutral bodies as the judiciary or the military. It often leads to a concentration of power in the executive and to an erosion of the "authenticity" of the nation's formal democratic institutions. The failure of the Uruguayan party leadership to respond to the economic crisis, its preoccupation with clientelistic politics over innovative policymaking, and its resort to the restoration of executive power as a means to resolving the crisis, are examples of that phenomenon.

The restoration of executive power after 1966 accelerated the abdication of democratic authenticity by the Uruguayan legislature. This was not a result of the constitutional reforms themselves, which provided for congressional oversight over the executive branch. Rather, it resulted from legislative inaction before a deliberate arrogation of power by the executive branch, and the growing influence of the military over the policymaking process.

Executive Arrogation of Power and the Militarization of Politics

The presidency of Jorge Pacheco Areco saw a marked increase in political unrest, strike activity, and violence. One of the more visible and destabilizing challenges to the constitutional regime came from the urban guerrilla group, the Tupamaros. The Pacheco government responded to protests and guerrilla violence with an unprecedented degree of repression. One week after he assumed office, President Pacheco outlawed a number of leftist parties. He also ordered the closing of two newspapers, *El Sól* and *El Día,* thus reversing Uruguay's long free-press tradition. In mid-1968 President Pacheco declared a limited state of siege, invoking his constitutional power to institute *Medidas Prontas de Seguridad* (Prompt Security Measures). The *Medidas,* which were to be used repeatedly by the president, permitted the government to suspend constitutional guarantees, impose censorship measures, and carry out arrests and searches of suspected subversives. Between 1968 and the 1973 coup, they became a regular weapon the executive used to silence the press and to intimidate the opposition.

While the Congress had the power to nullify the *Medidas,* it rarely did so. At times this was due to successful parliamentary maneuvering by the president. At other times it was due to direct intimidation of the Congress. In 1969 the Congress attempted to rescind an executive order conscripting striking bank workers into the armed forces. Following a threat from the government's defense minister, who claimed to be speaking on behalf of the armed forces, the

Congress acquiesced to the president's action. The effect of these actions was to further remove the legislature from effective oversight of key policy decisions.

Subsequently, the president used his special security powers and ruled by decree throughout the remainder of his term. The Congress also agreed to suspend constitutional liberties for extended periods on two occasions. One of these followed the assassination by Tupamaro guerrillas of Dan Mitrione, a USAID official working with the Uruguayan police. During the later part of President Pacheco's tenure, torture and brutality against dissidents by the military and the police increased.

A critical turning point in the political process occurred in September 1971 when the president agreed to transfer the responsibility for dealing with the urban guerrillas from the police to the military. The government declared the existence of a state of "internal war." For captured suspects, military justice would be formally substituted for civil procedures and protections.

With this action the government surrendered its constitutional responsibility for the maintenance of order to the armed forces. By subordinating constitutional procedures to military justice in the battle against the Tupamaro guerrillas, it severely eroded the legitimacy of the regime's legal norms and institutions. Most importantly, it gave unquestioned control over the resolution of a vital political issue to the armed forces. The defeat of the Tupamaros strengthened the perception in the military and society that the armed forces were better able to resolve pressing political problems than the civilian leadership. Following the elimination of the Tupamaro threat, military control was extended to other governmental functions, culminating in the presidency itself.

The concentration of power in the executive branch and the militarization of the nation's political institutions entered their final phase during the presidency of Juan María Bordaberry. The government maintained its repression against the press and the opposition. Military influence over the political decision-making process, veto power over presidential decisions, and defiance of congressional authority were exercised far more openly than they had been in the past. Attempts by Congress to question the military's role in political affairs were met by the imprisonment and harassment of congressional leaders.

In February 1973 elements of the armed forces rebelled against the constitutional government. In the negotiations that followed, President Bordaberry agreed to the formation of a National Security Council (COSENA), whose members would include the chiefs of the three military branches, to oversee government policy. This represented the formal elevation of the armed services to the highest levels of the executive branch of government. On 27 June, following a series of congressional challenges to the president and the armed forces, President Bordaberry announced the closing of Congress and the formal imposition of authoritarian rule over Uruguay.

Conclusion

The case of Uruguay provides a demonstration of how even a highly institutionalized democratic regime can lose legitimacy and give way to authoritarian political alternatives. In contrast to the Chilean case, where democratic institutions were a major arena for the political struggle, in Uruguay by the end of the 1960s they were almost irrelevant to the political process. Political initiative was located, first, in violent opposition from civil society, and later, in an increasingly militarized executive branch.

The events that led to that situation took place over a long period of time and had their roots in the political system's inability to reverse the country's economic deterioration. However, after 1967, a more rapid and dialectical process of abdication and conquest between the legislative and executive branches of government took place. Congressional acquiescence before presidential indifference to constitutional guarantees and institutions constituted a major failure in the exercise of legislative oversight of the executive branch. In part it resulted from the feeling of helplessness by the democratically accountable leadership before the intractability of the country's problems. The temptation, therefore, to give the executive branch free rein in the pursuit of solutions was almost irresistible. But it soon resulted in a dramatic shift in the balance of power between the two branches that, when finally challenged by the congressional leadership, resulted in the closing of Congress itself. The Uruguayan case provides a potent lesson of the dangers of congressional abdication of its constitutional authority.

Another important lesson the Uruguayan case provides is the danger of authoritarian responses by democratic leaders to an armed and violent opposition. The government's decision permitting the military to dispense with constitutional procedures and guarantees in the struggle against the Tupamaro guerrillas constituted an abnegation of civilian supremacy over the armed forces and an erosion of the integrity of the constitutional system. It was, ironically, a major step toward the Tupamaros' objective of discrediting and overturning the constitutional regime. Furthermore, it advanced the process of military encroachment on political decision making. This process was more incremental than planned. It reflected a changing consensus within the military on its national role, as civilian leaders turned increasingly to it for help in resolving political problems. It ultimately forged a consensus within the military and much of society on the ineffectiveness of civilian constitutional rule.

Annotated Bibliography

Gillespie, Charles. "The Breakdown of Democracy in Uruguay: Alternative Political Models," Working Paper no. 143, Latin American Program, Washington, D.C.: The Wilson Center, 1984. In a very useful article, Gillespie analyzes and criticizes several models of the Uruguayan political system, as well as interpretations by different authors of events leading up to the 1973 breakdown. He also provides his own hypotheses of the breakdown of democracy in Uruguay, drawing on theoretical work by Juan Linz.

Kaufman, Edy. *Uruguay in Transition: From Civilian to Military Rule*. New Brunswick: Transaction Books, 1979. This book examines the several facets of the gradual dissolution of civilian government in Uruguay.

McDonald, Ronald H. "Electoral Politics and Uruguayan Political Decay," *Inter-American Economic Affairs* 26 (Summer 1972): 23–45. In this article McDonald advances the notion that Uruguay's political system underwent a process of political decay (or deinstitutionalization) during the 1950s and 1960s. His article is highly useful for highlighting the institutional roots of the breakdown of the Uruguayan regime, and, read in tandem with the next article, provides a balanced picture of that process.

McDonald, Ronald H. "The Rise of Military Politics in Uruguay," *Inter-American Economic Affairs* 28 (Spring 1975): 23–45. In this article McDonald provides an analysis of the incremental process of the military taking control of Uruguay's political system, particularly during the period from 1967 to 1973.

Weinstein, Martin. *Uruguay: The Politics of Failure.* Westport: Greenwood Press, 1975. Weinstein provides one of the few book-length treatments in the English language of politics in Uruguay from the days of Batlle y Ordóñez to the breakdown of democracy in 1973. Weinstein pays particular attention to the role of ideology in shaping the Uruguayan political system, to the dynamics of institutional development, and to their interrelation with class and political power in Uruguay.

ARGENTINA, 1976: The Limits of Charismatic Authority

Chronology of Key Events

MAY 1969: Massive antigovernment demonstrations and riots in the city of Córdoba weaken the three-year-old military government of General Juan Carlos Onganía and start a long process of transition to constitutional government.

OCTOBER 1972: Juan Perón returns briefly to Argentina, after eighteen years in exile, to prepare the groundwork for Peronist strategies in upcoming presidential elections.

MARCH 1973: Peronist candidate Hector Cámpora wins the presidential election. Less than two months later he resigns from the presidency to open the way for new elections with Perón as a presidential candidate. Political violence intensifies.

OCTOBER 1973: Juan Perón is sworn in as president.

JULY 1974: Juan Perón dies in office. His vice-president, Isabel Perón, is sworn in as president. Violence, particularly between Peronist factions, escalates dramatically.

MID-1975: Following intense pressure from labor and the Congress, Isabel Perón abandons her austerity program and removes her close advisor, José López Rega, from office. She requests a temporary leave of absence from the presidency, but returns shortly thereafter.

MARCH 1976: The armed forces overthrow the Peronist government.

Introduction

The March 1976 overthrow of the constitutional government of Isabel Perón met with little effective opposition from Argentine society. The unifying power of General Juan Perón's charismatic authority had failed to lay the foundations for democratic governance. In large measure this was due to the violent polarization of Argentine society, which made conciliation and compromise through institutional channels almost impossible. Yet it was also in large measure due to the failure of the constitutional leadership to strengthen the mechanisms of democratic decision making during the brief period of consensus prior to Perón's death. The assault on constitutional procedures effected by the chaotic government of Isabel Perón completed the delegitimation of the constitutional regime.

General Perón's personalistic style of rule prevented such democratic institutions as the Congress and political parties from playing a meaningful role in the political process, and prevented these institutions from becoming sources of civilian authority that could provide continuity for the regime after Perón's death. Perón's disappearance created a power vacuum in the government and led to a significant escalation of political violence. The government's own involvement in the violence, both through its association with right-wing paramilitary groups and its abdication of supervision over the armed forces' campaign against the guerrilla opposition, severely eroded the legitimacy of the democratic regime. Also, the manifest incompetence of the president, her reliance on antidemocratic elements for support, her government's inability to put an end to the political and economic chaos, and the lack of an obvious democratic alternative created widespread support for the overthrow of the democratic regime by the Argentine armed forces.

Prelude to the Peronist Government

Prospects for the consolidation of a democratic regime in the early 1970s were clouded by institutional and normative weaknesses in Argentina's democratic policy. Eighteen years of Peronist political proscription and military intervention had severely delegitimized democratic procedures and the elites associated with them. The installation of constitutional government in 1973 was thus less a result of public clamor for democratic rule than it was of the general desire for the return of the harmony, progress, and authority of the early Peronist era.

Those eighteen years had also eroded the role and influence of political parties. They prevented parties from gaining experience in governing and mediating the conflicts of civil society and placed them under the control of a detached, aging elite, prone to conspiracy-mongering and military intrigue.

Finally, political parties had played a very limited role in the transition from military-authoritarian rule. The pressures that led to the military's departure came from highly activated groups in civil society—labor, student groups, violent opposition groups. The military's departure was also marked by intense popular mobilization, most of which lay beyond the control of political party elites. The locus of political initiative during the transition lay outside the party system: in civil society and in secret negotiations between Perón and military leaders. The elites committed to the country's formal democratic institutions played almost no role in the events leading to the breakdown of the regime.

Juan Perón in Power

An interesting feature of the Peronist party that came to power in 1973 was that its most important factions were disloyal, or, at best, semi-loyal, to democratic forms of government. Also, these factions—labor, *montonero* youth/guerrilla organizations, and right-wing groups—possessed the bulk of the Peronist movement's power resources. Political party leaders, after years of proscription, had little actual influence in the movement. Under such conditions, the task of democratic consolidation required the formal subordination of all sectors to the party leadership and the strengthening of the legislature's role in the policymaking process. However, specific decisions by President Perón and his style of government prevented a transfer of authority to the regime's formal democratic institutions.

Perón's choice of his politically inexperienced wife as his vice-presidential running mate exposed both a lack of confidence in his political party and a preference for personalistic politics over the building of a viable democratic regime. Given his age and poor health and the availability of relatively qualified individuals from his political cadre, his selection was particularly injurious to the party and the regime. It further eroded the party leadership's prestige within the movement, and prevented it from providing democratic continuity to Peronist rule after Perón's departure. Equally important, it consigned a highly volatile country to rule by an ill-equipped and inexperienced president in the likely event that Perón would not survive till the end of his term.

Perón's governing style also hampered the consolidation of democratic institutions. Most important policy decisions were made by the old *caudillo*. There was little consultation with the leadership of the party or the legislature. Interparty collaboration in the policymaking process was largely limited to the close personal relationship that developed between Perón and the leader of the Radical Party, Ricardo Balbin. This relationship was not reflected in meaningful collaboration at the congressional level between officials of the two parties.

Juan Perón sought to restore unity and order to Argentine society through the forging of a multiclass coalition known as the *Pacto Social*. While this device succeeded in producing a temporary consensus between management and labor and in reducing inflation and restoring economic growth, its major flaw was that its sole unifying force was the charismatic authority of Juan Perón. The Peronist party played almost no role in the *pacto social*. As a result no common institutional arena for conflict resolution and negotiation between diverse social sectors had been created to provide continuity for the goals of the *pacto social* after Perón's death.

Another decision by Perón that would cause serious problems for the democratic regime was his preelectoral strategy of encouraging the growth of the violent *montonero* movement. While the *montoneros* were a useful power resource against the military and non-Peronist opposition, they became a serious liability to Perón in office. Their political agitation and guerrilla activities (which Perón condemned once he took office) intensified the climate of violence and instability. They were a major destabilizing force during the tenure of the government of Isabel Perón, and they generated violent countermeasures by the state and by right-wing paramilitary groups.

The Breakdown of the Regime

The vacuum left by Perón's death unleashed a violent struggle in the Peronist movement for control of the government. The erosive effect this had on the stability of the democratic regime was compounded by the visible ineffectiveness of the president, and by the government's own indifference to constitutional procedures.

Shortly after Perón's death the office of the presidency came under the control of right-wing authoritarian elements of the movement, led by Social Welfare Minister José López Rega. They made full use of paramilitary squads to assassinate their opponents in political society, the labor movement, and other sectors of civil society. The government also granted *carte blanche* to the military in its war against the guerrilla opposition. That decision formed part of a larger strategy of organizing the armed forces as a pillar of support for the government—support that would counter opposition from an activated labor movement and a weak yet recalcitrant party leadership. A pro-Peronist officer was appointed chief of staff of the armed forces, and another was elevated to the cabinet.

These decisions, however, ultimately led to the fall of the government. Congressional action taken against López Rega's prominence in the government, coupled with protest from labor and other sectors, forced his removal and left the president politically isolated. Furthermore, the blatant attempts to politicize the armed forces sparked a rebellion by "professionalist" elements in the military that led to the removal of military officers from the government and the appointment of a new military chief of staff, General Jorge Rafael Videla. The military subsequently withdrew from all involvement in political affairs. It was to maintain that posture until the government's loss of power and the disintegration of the political process had reached the stage where a majority of the population welcomed the restoration of order by a military regime.

Conclusion

The breakdown of Argentine democracy in 1976 provides an example of the difficulty of establishing democratic legitimacy under conditions of social violence and polarization. Yet an ironic element in this case is that the regime was inaugurated under the highly unifying and charismatic leadership of Juan Perón. It thus possessed an advantage that few new democracies have had the privilege to enjoy: the loyalty of large segments of the population to the head of government during the first difficult stages of democratic consolidation. However, Perón failed to impart the authority and legitimacy of his leadership to the nation's democratic institutions. This would have been a critical requirement for Argentina's democratic consolidation in the early 1970s and the only prospect for a democratic outcome to the political conflicts of the period. Perón's personalistic style of rule and his neglect of the party and the country's formal democratic institutions ensured that almost no authority would be vested in those sectors with an interest in the continuation of democratic rule after his death. In a sense, the Argentine experience from 1973 to 1976 provides important lessons in how the dynamic personal leadership of a head of state can hinder the consolidation of democratic procedures and institutions. These are lessons that should not be lost on the leadership of future democratic regimes in Argentina.

While Juan Perón had been instrumental in hindering the development of firm democratic foundations in Argentina, his wife's government ensured that the process of democratic delegitimization would complete its course. Her weakness as a chief executive contributed to a major loss of public support for the regime. Furthermore, her government's obvious disregard for constitutional procedures and guarantees, and its gradual takeover by authoritarian elements within the Peronist movement, added an air of illegality to ineffectual rule. By March 1976 the government had lost all legitimacy, and the democratic leadership in political society lacked any power to resolve the crisis through constitutional means. This left a void that was quickly and effectively filled by the armed forces.

Annotated Bibliography

Cavarozzi, Marcelo. *Autoritarismo y Democracia, 1955–1983*. Buenos Aires: Centro Editor de América Latina, S.A., 1983. This book provides a short analytical treatment of Argentine politics after the 1955 overthrow of Perón. Cavarozzi analyzes the evolving patterns of military intervention, the authoritarian tendencies in Argentine civil society, and the difficulties of consolidating the norms and institutions of democracy in Argentina.

Crawley, Eduardo. *A House Divided: Argentina 1880–1980*. London: C. Hurst and Company, 1984. Crawley provides a detailed and enjoyably written journalistic account of Argentine politics over the last century.

De Riz, Liliana. *Retorno y Derrumbe: El último gobierno peronista*. Mexico: Folios Ediciones, S.A., 1981. This is a book-length treatment of the rise and fall of the second Peronist government. De Riz provides a strong focus on the intersectoral conflict that contributed to the breakdown of the regime.

Rouquié, Alain, and Jorge Schvarzer, eds. *¿Cómo renacen las democracias?* Buenos Aires: Emecé Editores, 1985. This is a collection of essays focusing extensively on Argentine politics and the problems of democratic consolidation. Of particular interest is Ricardo Sidicaro's essay on the erosion of Argentina's party system over the last twenty years, entitled "¿Es posible la democracia en Argentina?"

GRENADA, 1979: The Ouster of Personalistic Rule

Chronology of Key Events

MARCH 1951: The Grenada People's Party (later changed to the Grenada United Labor Party), led by Eric Gairy, wins 71 percent of the vote in legislative elections and captures six of eight seats on the Legislative Council.

MARCH 1973: The New Jewel Movement (NJM) is formed by the merger of the Movement for Assemblies of the People, founded by Maurice Bishop, and Joint Endeavor for Welfare, Education, and Liberation (JEWEL).

NOVEMBER 1973–JANUARY 1974: Widespread anti-Gairy strikes and demonstrations are held on the eve of Grenadian independence from Great Britain. Uprisings are crushed by Gairy's police forces.

FEBRUARY 1974: Grenada becomes an independent nation with Eric Gairy as prime minister.

DECEMBER 1976: Maurice Bishop is elected to Parliament and becomes the leader of the opposition.

MARCH 1979: Maurice Bishop and the New Jewel Movement seize power in a coup. Shortly thereafter the suspension of the 1974 constitution is announced.

Introduction

The 1979 overthrow of the government of Eric Gairy by Grenada's New Jewel Movement represents a rare instance of regime breakdown in the English-speaking Caribbean. Grenada shares with the other British West Indian Islands a historical legacy of affiliation with English forms of constitutionalist government. It also shares with many of those countries a history of personalistic leadership by populist figures who have led their people from colonial rule to independence. Eric Gairy introduced Grenada to the era of mass politics. He built a strong base of support among the poor and disenfranchised that gave him decisive electoral majorities and solidified his control over the Grenadian polity. However, his increasingly repressive, corrupt, and inefficient rule alienated many in the middle and educated classes. His ability to legitimize and perpetuate his rule through such democratic mechanisms as elections discredited parliamentary procedures among his opponents, who were unable to compete with him in the electoral arena. Furthermore, it convinced his more radical middle-class opponents, particularly in the New Jewel Movement, of the need to develop alternative political structures to mobilize the masses and to build new bases of support for their leadership. These young opposition leaders successfully utilized the few functional elements of Grenada's formal democratic system to make their case against Gairy and to crystallize support for an alternative to his authoritarian rule. Yet they quickly and easily dispensed with these democratic elements upon assuming power, and they sought instead to establish a new revolutionary order.

The Emergence and Decay of Personalistic Rule

Prior to Eric Gairy's emergence on the political scene, Grenadian politics was largely restricted to the activities of a small group of "parties of notables." The franchise excluded much of the uneducated majority, and political leaders made little effort to reach the mass of poor, mostly dark-skinned blacks that worked on plantations or scratched out an existence on small plots of land. Gairy launched his political career in Grenada as a trade union organizer. In 1950 and 1951 he organized a series of strikes and demonstrations that produced major wage increases for factory and estate workers. In 1951, with the introduction of universal suffrage, Gairy's political party swept the legislative elections, which gave him majority control of the legislative council. Thus was inaugurated a prolonged period of almost complete dominance of Grenadian political life by Eric Gairy. Peasants and plantation workers, previously ignored by the political leadership, would constitute the key to his political power. They would grant him an immense advantage over other middle-class political leaders who, unsuited to the imperatives of mass political mobilization, would provide him with little effective electoral competition.

The emergence of Gairy's personalistic leadership paralleled that of other West Indian leaders, such as Eric Williams of Trinidad. However, Gairy's leadership differed from that of his West Indian counterparts in one crucial respect. In over two decades in power, he did not institutionalize his rule through systematic organization or ideology, but relied instead on direct personal appeal. Toward the latter half of his rule he was to resort increasingly to repression against his opponents, particularly through the instrument of the "Mongoose Gang," a police force personally loyal to him.

Gairy's personalistic and repressive style of rule gradually alienated many in the middle classes who were excluded from the political process and suffered from his corrupt and inefficient economic management. Yet organized opposition to Gairy consisted of small circles of disaffected intellectuals and an aging and uninspiring political leadership that lacked the means to remove him from office constitutionally. This fact was dramatized by elections held in 1972, when Gairy soundly defeated an alliance of traditional and radical political forces.

Disaffection with Gairy in the middle class was vividly manifested by large antigovernment strikes and demonstrations in late 1973 and early 1974, on the eve of Grenadian independence. The uprisings were brutally crushed by Gairy, and this accelerated the radicalization of the opposition, particularly the youthful leaders of what would become known as the New Jewel Movement (NJM).

Gairy's rule also led ultimately to a deep discrediting of parliamentary forms of government among many of his most dynamic opponents. His systematic abuse of constitutional procedures, and the lack of any real constitutional alternative to his government, gave opposition forces little faith in parliamentary procedures as a way of redressing the country's deep injustices. The fact that Gairy was able to use his support among the poor majority to legitimize and perpetuate his rule through electoral procedures intensified their disdain for those procedures. This was particularly the case among Gairy's youthful opposition in the New Jewel Movement. The NJM's leaders, mainly middle-class in origin, were heavily influenced by the black power and antiwar struggles in the United States and Europe, and by the efforts of Third World leaders to build socialist alternatives to liberal democracy and capitalism. Gairy's electoral hold over the poor majority to which the NJM's leaders sought to appeal convinced them of the need to build alternative political structures to reach the masses and mobilize them into a new base of support for their leadership.

However, it is important to note that the ability of the NJM's leadership to build a strong base of support among the middle and educated classes in the mid-1970s was in large measure a result of the political space provided by the existence of formal democratic institutions that remained functional under Gairy's despotic rule. These institutions included the court system and the legislature.

Grenada shares with other West Indian countries a common appeals court system. This arrangement assured that, even under Gairy, Grenada would have a relatively independent judiciary. The NJM's leaders, many of them trained and highly skilled barristers, repeatedly used the court system to embarrass and attack the Gairy government. The independent judiciary became an important weapon for the NJM and its allies in the struggle against Gairy.

In the 1976 elections a coalition headed by the NJM won several legislative seats and formed for the first time an effective minority opposition in the legislative council. Maurice Bishop, a charismatic leader within the NJM, became the leader of the parliamentary opposition. The legislative council became a highly effective forum for Bishop and the NJM to make their case against the Gairy government, and the council was eventually critical to the NJM's strategy of generating public support for Gairy's removal. By 1979 Gairy's repression, corruption, and growing proclivity toward mysticism had eliminated most of his support among the middle classes. Also, in contrast to previous periods, the formal opposition now provided the Grenadian public with an attractive alternative to Gairy's rule in the New Jewel Movement. In March 1979, while Gairy was on an official overseas visit, the New Jewel Movement seized power. The coup was greeted with widespread support and celebration. In spite of assurances by the new leadership of a quick return to constitutional rule, the constitutional system was disbanded and a new revolutionary order was established in its place.

Conclusion

Although Eric Gairy ushered in the era of mass politics in Grenada, his style of rule prevented its evolution into a stable democratic order. The tight control he exercised over political power excluded many in the educated middle class from the political process. Deprived of the possibility of influencing political decisions either through an institutional structure led by Gairy or as a loyal opposition, the more dynamic elements moved into a position of disloyalty to the constitutional regime. Also, Gairy's strong electoral hold over the poor majority created resentment among his middle-class NJM opponents, who intended to appeal to that majority, and who came to view the parliamentary system as a mere instrument of demagogic control of the masses.

The ease with which the New Jewel Movement dispensed with the country's democratic institutions in a region strongly influenced by a common constitutional heritage attests to the erosive effect of Gairy's rule on Grenada's polity. His failure to institutionalize his charismatic leadership stands in contrast to the record of other personalistic leaders in the region who helped to consolidate viable democratic systems.

Nevertheless, the Grenada case also demonstrates the power of democratic institutions to provide political space to oppositions in their struggles against an authoritarian ruler. In the Grenadian case the NJM eventually used that space to overturn the constitutional system. Yet its lessons should not be lost on democratic oppositions laboring under authoritarian conditions where some elements of democratic procedure continue to exist.

Annotated Bibliography

Dunn, Peter, and Bruce Watson, eds. *American Intervention in Grenada: The Implications of Operation "Urgent Fury."* Boulder and London: Westview Press, 1985. This is a collection of essays, widely focusing on the origins, execution, and implications of the U.S. military intervention in Grenada. It also contains a number of essays on the internal dynamics of Grenadian politics during the period of NJM's rule and the period preceding it.

Sandford, Gregory, and Richard Vigilante. *Grenada: The Untold Story.* New York: Madison Books, 1984. This book provides a conservatively biased yet detailed interpretation of Grenadian politics before and during the NJM revolutionary period. Much of its primary resource material consists of documents captured by U.S. forces during the U.S. intervention.

O'Shaughnessy, Hugh. *Grenada: Revolution, Invasion and Aftermath.* London: Hamish Hamilton, 1984. O'Shaughnessy provides a critical yet generally sympathetic portrait of Maurice Bishop, as well as a negative assessment of the U.S. invasion of the island in this book-length treatment of Grenadian politics before and during the revolution.

Singham, A. W. *The Hero and the Crowd in a Colonial Polity.* New Haven: Yale University Press, 1968. Singham provides an interesting examination of Grenadian politics under colonial rule as a case study of political development in colonial polities.

Also of interest to Singham are the dynamics of charismatic leadership in such polities and Gairy's personalistic appeal in particular.

Notes

1. The concepts of "loyal" and "disloyal" oppositions are taken from Juan Linz, *Crisis, Breakdown, and Reequilibrium.* (Baltimore: The Johns Hopkins University Press, 1978). Other references to Linz are from this work.

2. Ibid., pp. 33–34.

3. Robert Potash, *The Army and Politics in Argentina, 1945–1962* (Stanford: Stanford University Press, 1980), p. 364.

4. Gary Wynia, *Argentina in the Post-War Era: Politics and Economic Policy Making in a Divided Society* (Albuquerque: University of New Mexico Press, 1978), p. 120.

5. Alain Rouquié, *Poder militar y sociedad politica en la Argentina* (Buenos Aires: Emecé Editores, 1978), p. 247.

6. Alfred Stepan, *The Military in Politics: Changing Patterns in Brazil* (Princeton: Princeton University Press, 1971).

7. Paul E. Sigmund, *The Overthrow of Allende and the Politics of Chile, 1964–1976* (Pittsburgh: University of Pittsburgh Press, 1977), p. 170.

8. Linz, *Crisis, Breakdown, and Reequilibrium.*

Nine Cases of Transitions and Consolidations

PHILIP MAUCERI

COSTA RICA, 1948–1970: Consensus Politics

Chronology of Key Events

FEBRUARY 1948: In presidential elections, Dr. Rafael Angel Calderón Guardia (PRN) is narrowly defeated by Otilio Ulate (PUN). Claiming that fraud marred the election results, the PRN-controlled Congress voted 27 to 18 to overturn the results and to declare Calderón Guardia the winner.

MARCH 1948–APRIL 1948: Opposition candidates José Figueres Ferrer (PSD) and Otilio Ulate (PUN) form an alliance and an army to defeat Calderon. With civil war conditions prevailing in San José, President Picado resigns and a second republic is declared by *Liberacionista* forces.

MAY 1948–NOVEMBER 1949: A *junta* is established with Figueres as president. Constituent Assembly elections result in Ulate's forces controlling the assembly. An invasion by PRN forces from Nicaragua is defeated. The new constitution abolishing the armed forces is adopted, and Ulate assumes the presidency.

JULY 1953–JANUARY 1955: Figueres and his newly formed PLN win the presidency with 65 percent of the vote. A reform program involving new taxes and wage increases is enacted. In early 1955 remnants of Calderón's forces invade Costa Rica with four hundred men and support from Somoza. The invasion fizzles after the United States and the OAS condemned it.

JULY 1958: Mario Echandi (PUN) is elected president with 46 percent of the vote. The PLN remains the largest party in the Legislative Assembly with twenty seats, though a Calderón-Ulate alliance gives control to the government.

JULY 1962–1966: Presidency of Francisco Orlich Bolmarcich (PLN).

JULY 1966–1970: Presidency of José Joaquín Trejos (PUN).

JULY 1970: José Figueres Ferrer (PLN) is elected president for a second time with 55 percent of the vote.

Introduction

Costa Rica is distinguished by a long history of democracy after the 1948 Revolution. Only one previous breakdown of democracy occurred in Costa Rica in this century (in 1917) and in the country's entire history, only some forty years of the postindependence period were spent under dictatorships. After the 1948 breakdown, a transitional *junta* was established for one year to oversee the disbanding of the armed forces, the holding of elections, and the drawing up of a new constitution. Since 1949, ten peaceful transfers of presidential power have occurred.

"Revolution" of 1948

In the elections of February 1948, the leftist-populist Dr. Rafael Angel Calderón Guardia attempted to capture the presidency, which he had held during the period from 1940 to 1944. When election returns showed Otilio Ulate (PUN) a center-rightist candidate had won, Calderón and the then-President Teodoro Picado, also of the PRN, implored the Congress to nullify the elections. With the majority of seats on their side, the Calderón-Picado forces declared the elections void due to fraud and corruption, a charge that the autonomous electoral tribunal denied.

By early March, José Figueres Ferrer, a center-leftist who had also sought the presidency, joined in a political pact with Ulate's forces and formed an Army of National Liberation. Fighting between *Liberacionista* and government forces was sporadic but bloody. The government relied on a force of fifteen hundred communist *Vanguardia Popular* militiamen to complement the five-hundred-man Costa Rican army. During the fighting, reports of an invasion from Somoza's Nicaragua and of U.S. intervention were rampant; however, it appears that both sides deliberately avoided escalating the conflict to a regional level by not requesting outside assistance.

At the end of April, President Picado resigned and a *junta* was declared with Figueres as president. Though the surrender agreement negotiated through the U.S. ambassador and the Church called for the protection of the lives and property of the Calderón-Picado forces, the new *junta* moved swiftly to dismiss from office, imprison, or exile most of the key previous leaders.

The Junta *and Transition*

During the period of *junta* rule (from May 1948 to November 1949), the democratic norms that had governed Costa Rica over the previous half-century reasserted themselves. The *junta's* eleven members, consisting of Figueres, Ulate, and their supporters, scheduled Constituent Assembly elections for December. The assembly was charged with the task of writing a new constitution. Election results gave Ulate's PUN a landslide: thirty-three of the forty-one contested seats. Calderón's PRN was not allowed to participate in the elections.

Following the elections, the *junta* announced the dissolution of the armed forces. The decision was in keeping with the *junta's* stated goal of reducing the powers of the executive, which were seen as having been excessively enlarged during the Calderón and Picado administrations. Moreover, there was a lingering resentment at the military for having openly taken the side of Calderón-Picado. Surprisingly, there were few protests of the decision from any sector of society. The fact that Costa Rica's army traditionally had been minuscule, and that the nation had just suffered a rare eruption of violence that many attributed to a military-minded executive, played an important part in this reaction. Nevertheless, shortly after the announcement, forces loyal to Calderón crossed the border with Nicaraguan troops in an apparent attempt to seize power. It was only after vigorous protests from the UN, the OAS and the United States that the troops withdrew peacefully.

Not all the provisions of the new constitution met with the approval of the *junta,* though they were respected. The *junta* had been urging a greater emphasis on socioeconomic rights, a position the assembly rejected. Article 12 of the new constitution did institutionalize the *junta's* prohibition of a military. In its place, a civil guard was established to exercise police functions and border patrol. In keeping with the *junta's* concern for reducing executive authority, the assembly curtailed the president's power to issue decrees and to veto legislation. In addition, the bureaucracy was given greater autonomy from the executive.

Both the Supreme Electoral Tribunal and the judiciary were given new independent powers.

Aside from its legacy of democracy, Costa Rica's redemocratization also benefited from the consensus and deference shown by leading politicians during the transition. Thus, Figueres, a Social Democrat, continued as president of the *junta* even after Ulate's forces had swept the assembly elections. Considering that Ulate had been rightfully elected president in the 1948 elections, his deference to Figueres was an extraordinary example of the willingness to compromise between the two leaders.

Consolidation

The day after the new constitution was inaugurated in November 1949, Otilio Ulate assumed the presidency as the legitimately elected head of state. Ulate's term in office (from 1949 to 1953) witnessed economic prosperity and two armed revolts by Calderonistas. The latter were then permitted to participate fully in the democratic system. More importantly, the political alliance forged between Figueres and Ulate during the revolution collapsed. In 1951 Figueres formed a new party (PLN) and attacked Ulate's increasingly conservative economic policies. In the 1953 elections, Figueres won with the largest electoral margin in Costa Rican history. During his administration (from 1953 to 1958), a series of major socioeconomic reforms was enacted. Significantly, he renegotiated the share of profits to be handed over to the government by the United Fruit Company (from 15 to 35 percent), while the latter was engaged in bitter disputes with the Guatemalan government over a similar issue. He also doubled the income tax on top income brackets and increased the minimum wage in a drive toward his stated goal of social equity.

The political rancor caused by these moves was, however, soon overshadowed. In January 1955 a force of four hundred men, under the command of ex-President Picado's son, invaded Costa Rica from Nicaragua. The invasion was openly aided and supported by Anastasio Somoza as well as by the Dominican Republic's Rafael Trujillo and Pérez Jiménez of Venezuela, all of whom were angered by Figueres' outspoken denunciations of them and by his domestic reform program. Rather than a quick victory, the invasion triggered an outpouring of support for Figueres, who portrayed it as a "Somocista plot" against Costa Rican democracy. Costa Rica appealed for assistance to the OAS, which sent an investigating committee. In addition, the United States made P–51 fighter jets available. Open U.S. support for Figueres was based on an assessment of him as a moderate reformer acting as a bulwark against communist-influenced Calderonistas. This support and widespread condemnation from other Latin American nations deterred an escalation by Nicaragua, and the attack soon fizzled.

In the decade following Figueres' administration, alternating party control of the executive proved to be the norm. While the PLN controlled the executive and legislative branches during Figueres' rule, a rapprochment occurred between the bitter enemies of 1948—Ulate's PUN and Calderón's PRN (now the PR). In the 1958 elections, both parties joined forces to support the winning conservative, Mario Echandi. Calderón's party after 1955 purged itself of its leftist factions and moved to adopt a centrist position. Though the PUN–PR alliance split in the 1962 elections, when both Ulate and Calderón sought the presidency for themselves, it reemerged victorious in 1966. The PLN meanwhile succeeded in 1962 and again in 1970, when Figueres recaptured the presidency.

The failure of any one party to dominate the electoral game contributed to the competitive nature of politics. Yet, despite this competitiveness, Costa Rican politics during this period was also governed by consensus on a wide range of issues. The policy of not maintaining an army was supported by all parties. President Echandi went so far as to rename the civil guard barracks "police stations" and to abolish remnants of the Defense Ministry.

Several factors contributed to the narrow policy range of Costa Rican politics during the period of consolidation. A crucial aspect was the lack of extreme parties and organizations on either the left or right. The three main parties were generally centrist, with labor unions and business associations closely tied to individual parties. Political moderation had evolved over the course of Costa Rican history and extremes were assimilated (for example, the PRN) or else defeated, as was the communist *Vanguardia Popular* in 1948. But political moderation was also the result of a socioeconomic climate that lacked extremes of wealth and privilege. Ethnically, the nation is relatively homogeneous, without major racial cleavages. Moreover, large latifundia have never dominated Costa Rican rural society, and income levels are not sharply unequal. A sizable middle class exists.

Annotated Bibliography

Ameringer, Charles D. *Democracy in Costa Rica*. New York: Praeger Press, 1982. A basic overview of modern Costa Rican history with an emphasis on post-1948 events. The analysis focuses on the reasons for the persistence of democracy, including economic, cultural, and political factors, as well as a review of critiques of Costa Rican democracy. Costa Rica's role in light of Central American turbulence is also assessed.

Bird, Leonard. *Costa Rica: The Unarmed Democracy*. London: Sheppard Press, 1984. The period since 1948 is reviewed, mostly with extensive quotations from U.S. and Costa Rican newspapers. Special attention is given in two separate chapters to the dissolution of the armed forces. The appendix covers speeches by Costa Rican presidents extolling the virtues of an unmilitarized society.

Denton, Charles F. *Patterns of Costa Rican Politics*. Boston: Allyn and Bacon, 1971. The emphasis here is on assessing the role of parties, the economic environment, and political institutions with a view toward explaining democratic stability. The ability of the system to adapt and absorb new political demands is seen as a key component of this stability. Throughout the book, a "systems analysis" approach is employed.

Zelaya, Chester, ed. *Costa Rica Contemporanea*. Tomo 1, 2da Edicion. San José: Editorial Costa Rica, 1982. While volume 2 covers the culture and demography of Costa Rica, the first volume contains a series of essays reviewing political parties, elections, foreign policy, and the economy through the 1970s. The essay on elections gives complete figures on most major elections and assesses electoral rules, while the essay on parties reviews the political programs of all major parties.

COLOMBIA, 1956–1974: The National Front

Chronology of Key Events

JULY 1956: The Declaration of Benidorm is issued by Liberal leader Alberto Lleras Camargo and Conservative Laureano Gómez, acknowledging joint responsibility for the breakdown of democracy.

MARCH 1957–MAY 1957: The Civic Front Manifesto is issued by the two parties opposing a Rojas candidacy and vowing to present a single candidate. Rojas is deposed and a military *junta* installed.

JULY 1957–MARCH 1958: The Pact of Sitges is signed, pledging both major parties to bipartisan cooperation over a twelve-year period. In a national plebiscite, the National Front agreements are overwhelmingly ratified. In congressional elections, Liberals outpace Conservatives 58 to 42 percent, though seats are divided equally.

MAY 1958–OCTOBER 1958: In presidential elections, Liberal Alberto Lleras Camargo is elected with 85 percent of the vote. The constitution is amended to include the National Front agreements, now extended to sixteen years. General Rojas is tried and convicted on charges of corruption.

MAY 1962: Guillermo León Valencia (a Conservative) is elected president, with 62 percent of the vote.

MAY 1966: Carlos Lleras Restrepo (a Liberal) is elected president, with 71 percent of the vote.

MAY 1970: Misael Pastrana (a Conservative) is elected president in a close four-way race. He is declared the winner over Rojas in a ruling by the Supreme Electoral Court. Following the elections a state of siege is declared, because rioting and protests occur in reaction to the election.

MAY 1974: Alfonso López Michelson (a Liberal) is elected president, while Rojas's ANAPO vote share declines to 10 percent.

Introduction

The transition following the collapse of the Rojas Pinilla dictatorship, which ruled from 1953 to 1957, was characterized by a deliberate attempt to structure political institutions and competition in a way that would avoid the breakdown conditions of 1948–53. For sixteen years, Colombia would be governed by political accords forged during the transition by the two major parties, the

Liberals and the Conservatives. Those accords guaranteed a monopoly on holding elective office for the two parties during that period, a prescription for constructing democracy that within the last decade has been increasingly questioned.

Authoritarian Breakdown and Party Pacts

During his rule, General Gustavo Rojas Pinilla attempted to create a popular movement—the Third Force—to support his increasingly personalistic regime and to challenge the dominance of the traditional Colombian parties. His efforts, however, met with resistance not only from the parties but from the military itself. The military as an institution was reluctant to commit itself to a permanent political role that would exclude the parties. To a large exent, this unwillingness resulted from the military's history since independence of obedience to party dominance of the political system. Rojas's attempts to challenge traditional party rule also had the effect of uniting the dominant parties against this common threat. The growing realization that this threat was the result of the vicious divisions between the parties contributed to the forging of political pacts between them between 1956 and 1958. As early as 1954 former President López urged that Liberals and Conservatives join together to reform political institutions.

The first formal agreement emerged in July 1956, when Liberal leader Alberto Lleras and Conservative Laureano Gómez signed the Declaration of Benidorm, pledging to cooperate in a return to democracy. In addition, they acknowledged that both parties had contributed to the *violencia* and shared responsibility for the breakdown of democracy. After Rojas declared that he would be a candidate in the scheduled 1958 elections, both parties issued the Civic Front Manifesto in March 1957 opposing his election and vowing to present a single candidate.

Faced with strong pressure from newly cooperative party leaders and the prospect of extended authoritarian rule under a corrupt and personalist leader, the military deposed Rojas in May. A transitional *junta* led by General Gabriel Paris was installed and declared its readiness to cooperate with party leaders, now joined under the rubric of the National Front. Within two months of Rojas's fall, Lleras and Gómez had signed their most important agreement yet, the Pact of Sitges. It called for bipartisan cooperation over a twelve-year period, with alternating party control of the presidency and equal representation in the Congress and bureaucracy. A commission was to be appointed to ensure that the agreements were incorporated into the constitution, and a plebiscite seeking public approval was to be held. Although it was agreed that a Conservative would be the first president, choosing a Conservative proved to be difficult.

The first in a series of factional disputes arose when Gómez objected to the choice of Guillermo León Valencia as a candidate because the latter belonged to the faction led by Mariano Ospina Pérez, which had given early support to

General Rojas. The dispute was resolved through the Pact of San Carlos, which let the Congress settle the selection process.

Transition and Elections

With the fall of Rojas, the political initiative once again returned to the political parties. The National Front pacts were overwhelmingly approved in a December plebiscite. In March 1958 congressional elections were held. Though Liberals won 58 percent to the Conservatives' 42 percent, seats were divided equally. Among Conservatives, the Gómez faction outdistanced Ospinistas, thereby vetoing the choice of Valencia as president. After extensive negotiations it was agreed that the first president would be a Liberal and that the National Front accords would be extended to sixteen years, so as to give both parties an equal number of presidential terms.

One of the first acts of the new Congress was to ratify the accords as constitutional amendments. In addition to the power-sharing arrangements, key changes included stipulations prohibiting parties other than the Liberals and Conservatives from seeking office for sixteen years, legalizing the period of military rule, and requiring a two-thirds majority for the passage of legislation. Moreover, Catholicism was acknowledged as the national religion, ending a dispute over the Church's role in society that had contributed to the breakdown of democracy. It should be noted that the Church itself had significantly changed, attempting to distance itself from politics toward the end of the Rojas regime. In 1958 a new archbishop was appointed, Luis Concha Córdoba, who was known as a political moderate. Two months after the congressional elections, the Liberal leader Alberto Lleras Camargo was formally elected president of the republic.

The New Rules of the Game

By institutionalizing the National Front accords, the Liberal and Conservative leaders argued, excessive partisan strife would end and a democratic consensus could take hold. Yet factionalization of the party system was an important feature of this phase of consolidation, beginning during the Lleras administration (from 1958 to 1962). The prohibition against third-party candidates ensured that factional groups remained within the two parties rather than forming their own parties and losing access to political power.

Conservatives divided into three factions (led by Alzatistas, Ospinistas, and Laureanistas), while the Liberals split into two, an official wing and a wing led by López Michelson (the MRL). With the exception of the MRL, all the factions supported the National Front arrangements. As a result of these divisions, coalition-building became essential, especially in light of the two-thirds majority required for passing legislation. At first Lleras relied on his alliance with Gómez. However, after the 1960 congressional elections gave a majority to the newly formed alliance between the Alza and Ospina forces, Lleras forged a coalition with these latter Conservatives.

Despite the provisions against third-party candidates, other parties were permitted to run candidates on Liberal or Conservative lines. This loose interpretation was allowed to a large extent because it afforded a degree of control over the other parties, primarily the Communists, the Christian Democrats, and the Rojista ANAPO. When Rojas returned from exile in October 1958 he was tried and convicted on charges of corruption, deprived of his political rights (later restored), and deprived of his military title and pension. Because the period of military rule had been legalized by the constitution, these moves appeared directed against Rojas personally and specifically at the political threat he might pose to the National Front through his new party. Nevertheless, the "tolerant" interpretation of the accords can be seen in the fact that both Rojas Pinilla and López Michelson were permitted to seek the presidency in the 1962 elections, even though the accords stipulated that a Conservative was to be the next president. As it turned out, León Valencia, an Alza-Ospina Conservative, won by a wide margin.

Throughout the National Front period, a surprising degree of policy continuity developed. A new emphasis on apolitical "technical solutions" to economic problems was initiated with the creation of the Planning Commission during the Lleras administration. Economic stability and diversification rather than distribution were the stated goals of all the National Front administrations, and no major agrarian or labor reforms were instituted. Overall, the economy achieved a slow growth rate with modest inflation.

An important element in both increasing technical expertise and providing external credits was the Alliance for Progress. The impetus of most foreign assistance was the need for developed and autonomous public sector agencies to engage in economic "planning." Viewed as a democracy and as a nation with a pro–U.S. policy, Colombia soon found itself one of the largest recipients of the U.S. aid program. Throughout the 1960s it received an average of $200 million a year.

The first serious threat posed to the National Front was by the ANAPO. After the 1966 congressional elections gained that party a surprising number of seats under the Conservative banner, it came increasingly to be viewed as the opposition to the National Front. In the presidential elections later in the year, ANAPO gained nearly a third of the votes, even though the official Liberal candidate Carlos Lleras Restrepo won most of the remaining votes. However, in a four-way race in the 1970 elections, Rojas, running as a Conservative, gained 39 percent of the vote, and he claimed that only fraud prevented him from capturing the presidency, which went to Conservative Misael Pastrana. ANAPO's support was largely based on the urban poor, on whom Rojas concentrated most of his populist appeals.

With the Pastrana presidency (from 1970 to 1974), the National Front officially came to an end. The rapid escalation of political violence during the 1970s and 1980s has been increasingly associated with the frustration several groups have felt with being excluded from active participation in political life during the National Front. The M19 guerrilla group, for example, was formed after the 1970 elections by Rojas supporters claiming that the elections were fraudulent. This frustration became all the more acute in light of the fact that the norms and rules of the accords continued in operation long after their official termination in 1974. If the consensus and limited competition of the National Front smoothed the way for the transition from military dictatorship, the inability of the system to compromise with new political groups and demands may have significantly limited the scope and ultimately the stability of democracy in Colombia.

Annotated Bibliography

Berry, Albert, Ronald Hellman, and Mauricio Solaun, eds., *Politics of Compromise: Coalition Government in Colombia*. New Brunswick: Transaction Books, 1980. A series of essays evaluating political institutions and public policies since the *violencia* period. Among the topics covered are the military (Ruhl), electoral participation (Losada), industrial policies (Berry) and the Church (Wilde).

Dix, Robert H. *Colombia: The Political Dimensions of Change*. New Haven: Yale University Press, 1967. A comprehensive review of the Colombian political system since the mid-forties. Analyses of the Church, military, labor, and interest groups are included. A separate chapter covers the origins and unfoldings of the *violencia*. Overall, the case of Colombia is seen as a classic case of modernization by elites.

Lara Bonilla, Rodrigo, et al. *Los Partidos Políticos Colombianos: Presente y Futuro*. Bogota: Pontificia Universidad Javeriana, 1983. An up-to-date survey of the history and current role of political parties in Colombia. The internal organization and factionalization of parties is given special emphasis. In addition, the statutes of the four major parties—Liberal, Conservative, Christian Democratic, and Communist—are included.

VENEZUELA, 1957–1973: Democracy and Party Pacts

Chronology of Key Events

DECEMBER 1957–JANUARY 1958: A meeting in New York among Venezuela's three major party leaders leads to agreement on cooperating for a transition to democracy. This is followed by the publication of a "Declaration Concerning the National Political Situation" in which business leaders urge an end to the dictatorship. In late January the regime of General Pérez Jiménez is overthrown and a transitional *junta* is installed.

JULY 1958–OCTOBER 1958: Two coup attempts by forces loyal to the former dictator are thwarted. The Pact of Punto Fijo, in which the parties vow to cooperate during the consolidation period, is signed.

DECEMBER 1958–NOVEMBER 1960: Rómulo Betancourt of Acción Democrática receives 49.2 percent of the vote in the presidential elections and leads a coalition government of AD, COPEI, and URD. An agrarian reform law is enacted. Splits in AD over the Cuban issue lead to urban rioting and eventually to a domestic insurgency.

DECEMBER 1963: Raúl Leóni (AD) is elected president with 32.8 percent of the vote; he governs with COPEI cooperation.

DECEMBER 1968: Rafael Caldera (COPEI) is elected President, and power is transferred peacefully for the first time. The insurgent groups are largely defeated and given the option of entering the electoral system, which most accept.

MAY–DECEMBER 1973: The presidential candidacy of former dictator Pérez Jiménez is barred by constitutional amendment. Carlos Andrés Pérez is elected president with 48.6 percent of the vote.

Introduction

Venezuela's stable democratic regime rests on a strong multiparty system that promotes the sharing of democratic norms and regulates conflict in society. Not only were the transition and consolidation phases characterized by a political pact among the major parties, but the parties have remained key players through their access to political and economic resources. The military has effectively abstained from politics, while until recently oil revenues have provided the resources to meet the demands of key social actors. Venezuela has since 1958 maintained its democracy through six peaceful transfers of presidential power.

Authoritarian Breakdown and Party Pact

The leader of the *junta* that seized power in 1948 was General Marcos Pérez Jiménez. His rule was arbitrary, corrupt, and increasingly personalistic, relying on public works and other welfare measures to gain popularity. Not only did this lead to rising dissatisfaction within the military, but to a reevaluation among the major social actors of their respective political strategies. This took concrete form when the leaders of the three major parties—Rómulo Betancourt (AD), Rafael Caldera (COPEI), and Jovita Villalba (URD)—met in New York in December 1957 to discuss coordinating antiregime activities and cooperating in a transition to democracy.

The meeting was followed by sharp denunciations of the regime by prominent business and civic leaders. In January 1958 Pérez Jiménez was overthrown and a provisional *junta* was established consisting of three military officers and two businessmen. The period between the end of the dictatorship and the December elections witnessed two significant coup attempts by right-wing military factions. As a demonstration of support for the transition, mass demonstrations were held.

The most significant event of this period came, however, in October 1958, when the three major parties signed the Pact of Punto Fijo. The pact was an explicit recognition of the lessons learned from the breakdown of democracy during the *trienio* (1945–48). The extreme polarization and intense partisan conflicts of that period were seen as having provided the basis for the military's intervention. The pact denounced the use of violence and demagoguery, and recognized the existence of parties representing diverse points of view as a necessary and legitimate condition. In addition, the parties pledged their adherence to a common program of governance that would be implemented by a coalition government after the elections. This coalition was to be formed regardless of the outcome, though it would be led by the winner. It is important to note that the parties agreed to consider the election as a vote of confidence for the democratic system and that should a party split from the coalition, its opposition should not be viewed as opposition to the democratic system.

Parties and Social Conciliation

The consolidation period following the election of Betancourt coincided with a significant fragmentation of the party system and a growing leftist insurgency. A key question evolved around the position of Cuba in the hemisphere. In part, the hard line taken against the Castro regime reflected an unwillingness to further antagonize the Eisenhower administration after the rioting that occurred during Vice President Nixon's visit. This in turn alienated Castro sympathizers in AD who split off to form what would later become a guerrilla movement. The URD, also facing internal factionalization, also left the coalition in 1960.

Continued divisions in AD resulted in factional splits in 1962 and again in 1967. These divisions, combined with a general decline in its popular support, meant that AD lost the position of electoral dominance it had enjoyed during the *trienio*. This was an important factor in promoting the electoral game as a viable means to achieve political power. By the time of the 1968 elections, factional disputes had crippled AD enough so that COPEI and Rafael Caldera could capture the presidency. Yet Caldera would continue the tradition of governing through a multiparty consensus and compromise.

Efforts at conciliation with groups that had played a significant role in the breakdown of democracy also characterized the consolidation phase. Since the last attempt at revolt in 1966, the military has not intervened in political affairs. Yet it increased its own institutional prerogatives with the founding of a national war college in 1976 and with the establishment of military-run enterprises that maintain and manufacture weapons.

More recently, former military officers led by Arnaldo Castro Hurtado have formed an "antiparty" party called New Generation. During the Betancourt administration (from 1959 to 1964), a purge of interventionist officers was combined with improved benefits for military personnel. Moreover, the pro-

Cuban leftist insurgency that developed strengthened the government's argument that without cooperation a Cuban-style disintegration of the military as an institution would occur.

Betancourt had already cracked down on the revolutionary left by closing its presses and expelling its labor leaders. By the late sixties, however, the insurgency had clearly collapsed, as the inapplicability of the Cuban model of revolt became apparent. Most of these groups were by the mid-seventies reintegrated into the democratic process. The crackdown on the groups in revolt and the willingness to readmit them into the system appear to demonstrate the primacy the Venezuelan system places upon observing the "rules of the game."

Efforts at reconciliation were also directed at the Church, business, and agrarian interests. The Church, which had bitterly opposed AD's educational policies during the *trienio*, tempered its opposition as leading Catholics were given a role in government under the sponsorship of COPEI, and a concordat with the Vatican was signed during the Leóni administration (from 1964 to 1969). In a similar fashion, land reform was carried out only after extensive consultations had taken place and the most radical peasant leaders had either been coopted or removed. Labor relations followed a pattern that likewise emphasized deradicalization. Ties between unions and parties were strengthened through a new system of proportional representation. In addition, the right to strike was further curtailed.

Stable Competition

The elections of 1968 that brought Rafael Caldera to the presidency with only 29 percent of the vote nonetheless marked an important watershed in the consolidation phase. It represented the first time in Venezuelan history that an opposition party had taken power through the power of the ballot box. Indeed, by the 1973 elections, when AD's Carlos Andrés Pérez won, it was obvious that the Venezuelan party system had evolved into a two-party dominant system. Both major parties began employing foreign, particularly U.S., media experts and spending large sums of money and a good deal of time electioneering. The leftist parties continued to be plagued by factionalism. Efforts to form a unified leftist slate have remained incomplete. Moreover, the fortunes of the URD declined considerably since it left the governing coalition.

A key resource that contributed to the durability of Venezuela's most brutal dictatorship, that of Juan Vicente Gómez (from 1908 to 1935), has also been critical to the maintenance of Venezuela's democracy. Oil has been the major source of foreign exchange but also a cause of external pressure. Yet despite demands during the first decade of democracy for an immediate nationalization of this important sector, Venezuela's leaders moved cautiously through incremental and carefully negotiated steps. The first significant step toward nationalization did not come until the Petroleum Reversion Law of 1971. Nationalization itself was not fully completed until 1976. Venezuela therefore avoided major external financial and political pressure during its transition and consolidation phases.

By the late seventies the oil industry was contributing nearly 70 percent of national revenues. Oil revenues have until very recently helped to prevent sharp swings in the economy and have provided the financial resources that have benefited all segments of society. The extraordinary growth of the state sector, which has been tied to oil, has provided significant employment opportunities in an otherwise stagnant economy. For the two major parties, this has enhanced their patronage power. In keeping with the "rules of the game," both parties respect the right to use this economic resource to provide political benefits in the form of employment and services to their supporters. In turn, this has fostered the mediating role of parties between the state and society in Venezuela.

Annotated Bibliography

Blank, David E. *Venezuela: Politics in a Petroleum Republic.* New York: Praeger Publishers, 1984. A review of the historical and cultural setting of the Venezuelan political system. Attention is given to the special role that oil has played in setting the political agenda during this century.

Gil Yepes, José Antonio. *The Challenge of Venezuelan Democracy.* New Brunswick: Transaction Books, 1981. An assessment of the trade-offs involved in maintaining Venezuelan democracy. An evaluation of what is viewed as the balance between group autonomy and political access is given. The role of business, students, and unions is reviewed.

Levine, Daniel H. *Conflict and Political Change in Venezuela.* Princeton: Princeton University Press, 1973. An analysis that focuses on the dynamics that led to the formation of the party pact and have sustained the rules of the political game. Special attention is given to the role of the Church and student groups.

Martz, John D., and David J. Myers, eds. *Venezuela: The Democratic Experience.* New York: Praeger Publishers, 1977. Probably the most comprehensive examination of the Venezuelan system available in English. The essays cover such topics as attitudes toward the democratic system (Baloyra), the Church (Levine), education (Ruscoe) and civil-military relations (Bigler). A concluding essay by Martz and Myers suggests possible lessons for other Latin American nations in their pursuit of a democratic order.

DOMINICAN REPUBLIC, 1961–1978: The Transition "From Without"

Chronology of Key Events

MAY 1961–DECEMBER 1962: General Rafael Trujillo is assassinated; a council of state prepares for elections. Juan Bosch is elected with 59.5 percent of the vote.

SEPTEMBER 1963: Bosch is ousted by a coup led by Colonel Wessin y Wessin; a ruling triumvirate is installed.

APRIL 1965–AUGUST 1965: Young army officers revolt for a return of Bosch. A military *junta* is installed as fighting begins between loyalist and constitutionalist forces. U.S. Marines land at the request of the *junta* and take up positions to defend loyalist troops. An OAS mission is sent. After heavy fighting, an agreement is reached. Héctor Garcia Godoy is to become a provisional president, followed by elections in a year.

JULY 1966–SEPTEMBER 1966: Joaquín Balaguer narrowly defeats Juan Bosch for the presidency. The last contingent of U.S. Marines is withdrawn.

MAY 1970: Balaguer is reelected: His party captures 60 of the 74 Chamber of Deputies seats and all but one of the Senate seats.

NOVEMBER 1973: Bosch quits the Dominican Revolutionary Party (PRD), which moves to the center under Antonio Guzmán and José Francisco Peña Gómez.

MAY 1974: Balaguer is elected to a third term as three out of the four opposition parties abstain from the elections.

JUNE 1975: A major crackdown on the opposition is launched as strikes and demonstrations increase. Two hundred and fifty labor and party leaders are arrested.

MAY 1978: Vote counting is halted, but after pressure from the United States and others, the vote counting resumes and Antonio Guzmán (PRD) is declared president.

Introduction

The transition to democracy in the Dominican Republic that began after the assassination of General Rafael Trujillo was punctuated by a breakdown, civil war conditions, and direct foreign military intervention. Through its actions, the United States ended the nation's political stalemate and altered the perceptions and resources of the groups competing for power. From the military intervention in 1965 to the crucial political intervention during the 1978 elections, the United States has helped direct the course of Dominican democracy.

Authoritarian Relapse and Disintegration

The nine-month government of Juan Bosch, who was elected in December 1962, antagonized a large number of traditional groups, including the Church, business, and landed interests, with its reformist policies. In addition, the security forces continued to be dominated by officers loyal to the former dictator Trujillo. The ouster of Bosch and his PRD in September of the following year did not, however, result in a stable conservative coalition. Following the coup that was led by Colonel Wessin y Wessin, a ruling triumvirate of three businessmen was installed in power. The first public disagreement arose when the president of the triumvirate, Dr. Emilio de los Santos, resigned in protest at the repression then being carried out. Meanwhile in Puerto Rico, the leaders of several leftist parties including the PRD signed the Pact of Rio Piedras, pledging to cooperate to restore democracy.

A significant rift in the armed forces occurred in April 1965 when a group of young army officers revolted in favor of a restoration of democratic rule. As a "constitutionalist" government was declared, the triumvirate resigned. Taking up positions in the central business district of Santo Domingo, loyalist troops led by Colonel Wessin y Wessin fought the constitutionalist forces. The loyalists installed a military *junta* to replace the triumvirate. By mid-April the conflict appeared to have degenerated into a civil war. It was at this point that both sides escalated the conflict to break an apparent deadlock. Constitutionalist forces, and particularly the PRD, began to arm civilians, and the *junta* appealed for U.S. military support.

United States Intervention

President Lyndon Johnson had recognized the triumvirate in December 1963, reversing the nonrecognition policy of the Kennedy administration. Economic aid was also restored, including the release of a $25 million International Monetary Fund (IMF) loan. The primary motivation for this pro-regime policy was increased apprehension over the strength of the left, particularly that of a guerrilla movement that raised fears of "another Cuba." The rapid disintegration of the regime as well as the arming of civilians in mid-April of 1965 led the United States to accept the *junta*'s appeal for military support. On 28 April the first contingent of what would total twenty thousand marines landed. They immediately created an International Security Zone around the embassy district, dividing the constitutionalist's military positions.

After committing the United States to a full-scale unilateral intervention, President Johnson sought international mediation through the OAS. An OAS negotiated settlement was finally reached at the end of June, after U.S. troops and rebels had engaged in heavy fighting. The Institutional and Reconciliation Acts called for a provisional presidency led by Héctor García Godoy, a centrist and a former PRD member, to be followed in a year by elections. In return, constitutionalist forces would surrender and pledge loyalty to the new president. The agreement came in obvious recognition that the presence of U.S. forces had turned the ground situation decisively against the rebel forces. Yet it did not represent a restoration of the conservative coalition. The fighting and intervention had split the 1963 coalition. The military *junta* led by General Imbert resigned, while business leaders and the Church (which had played a negotiating role through the papal nuncio) approved the agreement.

The United States continued to play an important role even after the withdrawal of the marines in September 1966. Economic aid was significantly increased. The sugar quota was raised for the Dominican Republic, providing an extra $70 million a year. Moreover, the U.S. embassy, with a staff of nine hundred, became the second largest in the hemisphere. During the 1966 electoral campaign, the United States was accused of using its influence through such channels as the Voice of America to take pro-Balaguer positions and to discredit Bosch.

Precarious Consolidation

The period following the inauguration of Joaquín Balaguer and his Reformist Party (PR) government witnessed serious efforts designed to neutralize his opponents, particularly those in the military and among business and labor. Balaguer continued García Godoy's policy of "exiling" prominent loyalist military leaders like Wessin y Wessin by means of diplomatic assignments. Others were reassigned to posts outside of the Santo Domingo or else were simply retired. In the first major challenge to his regime from the left, the transport workers strike of 1969, Balaguer demonstrated a harsh resolve to face down his opponents. The strike, organized to protest austerity measures such as the wage freeze, was also supported by student groups and Marxist parties and was seen as a test of Balaguer's strength. The government declared a state of emergency and hired "veterans" of the armed forces to replace the workers and break the strike.

Balaguer's tough labor policy was not sufficient, however, to guarantee him support from right-wing groups. His policies encouraging foreign investment, a patronage-laden bureaucracy, and his increasingly personalistic rule alienated important sectors of the elite. In the 1970 elections, former loyalist leader Wessin y Wessin and his newly founded party, the PQD, joined with their formerly bitter enemies, Bosch's PRD, in boycotting the elections. Nevertheless, with the open support of army commander General Enrique Pérez y Pérez, Balaguer won a sweeping electoral victory. The campaign was marked by a series of assassinations and charges of sedition and corruption on both sides.

The 1970 elections initiated a period of intense polarization between the government of Balaguer and the opposition that would culminate with the 1978 elections. A revival of guerrilla movements led to the instituting of new security measures and a sharp crackdown on the PRD. The PRD itself had moved closer to the center of the political spectrum, especially after Bosch quit the party and created a splinter group. The 1974 elections, which saw Balaguer elected to a third term, were marred by charges of fraud and by abstention rates as high as 70 percent. Three of the four opposition parties, including the PRD, signed the Santiago Agreement, abstaining from the elections and denouncing the Balaguer administration as oppressive. In his third term, Balaguer increasingly used the military and emergency decrees to suppress the opposition.

Labor and opposition party leaders were arrested and controls on the press were increased. Clashes often turned violent, as with the student protests of March-April 1975 at the Universidad Autonoma de Santo Domingo.

The patronage machinery and personal alliances with the military that had supported Balaguer in office for over a decade collapsed during the 1978 elections. Opposition groups coalesced around the centrist candidacy of the PRD's Antonio Guzman. However, as it appeared that Guzman would win, military troops entered the electoral commission's headquarters and stopped the counting. It remains unclear who ordered these moves. Nevertheless, within a day the Carter administration let it be known that aid would be cut off if the vote counting was not allowed to continue on a fair basis. Protests also came from Latin America's democracies, as well as from groups in the Dominican Republic, particularly the Church, business leaders, and all political parties (including Balaguer's own PR). The armed forces were apparently divided on the possibility of staging a coup. In any event, within forty-eight hours the army withdrew and Balaguer promised to honor the election results. Antonio Guzman was subsequently declared the new president.

In the period since 1978, democracy in the Dominican Republic has faced a series of challenges. Hurricane David in 1979 and a sharp fall in sugar prices produced rising unemployment and inflation. Moreover, the government has had to confront demands that it impose austerity measures from the IMF. Both Antonio Guzman and his PRD successor, Salvador Jorge Blanco (from 1982 to 1986) faced large-scale protests from business and labor over economic policy. The most serious challenge occurred in mid-1984 when rioting caused by food price increases resulted in renewed rumors of a military coup. Balaguer was elected to the presidency again, in 1986.

Annotated Bibliography

Gliejeses, Piero. *The Dominican Crisis.* Baltimore: Johns Hopkins University Press, 1978. An analysis that focuses on the overthrow of Juan Bosch and the U.S. intervention. Particular attention is paid to the decision-making process in the United States that led to the sending of the marines and to the policy background for that decision.

La Torre, Eduardo. *Política Dominicana Contemporanea.* Santo Domingo: Instituto Tecnologico de Santo Domingo, 1979. A comprehensive evaluation of the period from Trujillo's last days until the early seventies. The political tactics and alliances of the Dominican military, and what is viewed as the persistence of personal caudilloism, is emphasized. The author suggests that until "personalism" is removed from politics, Dominican democracy is endangered.

Wiarda, Howard J., and Michael Kryzanek. *The Dominican Republic: A Caribbean Crucible.* Boulder: Westview Press, 1982. An attempt is made to evaluate the Dominican experience with democracy in light of its historic, social, and cultural environment. The review of the postintervention period is similarly helpful. The nation's socioeconomic structure and the dominance of traditional groups are viewed as important impediments to democratization.

BRAZIL, 1974–1987: The Transition "from Above"

Chronology of Key Events

JANUARY 1974–NOVEMBER 1974: General Ernesto Giesel is inaugurated as president and initiates policy of *abertura* ("political opening"). In congressional elections the opposition party MDB captures sixteen of twenty-two contested Senate seats.

APRIL 1977–AUGUST 1977: The "April Package" is announced by Geisel, recessing the Congress and increasing restrictions on the opposition. This is followed by protests and demonstrations throughout the summer months.

DECEMBER 1977: The Institutional Acts that have governed Brazil since 1964 are replaced with new laws. The reform of the party system is also announced.

JANUARY 1978: João Figueiredo takes office as president.

NOVEMBER 1982: In elections, the opposition parties gain ten of twenty-two governorships, while the regime maintains its majorities in Congress and the state assemblies.

JANUARY 1984–APRIL 1984: A major push for direct presidential elections includes a demonstration of two hundred thousand in São Paulo, the largest in several years. An amendment demanding direct elections is defeated in the regime-controlled Congress.

JANUARY 1985–MARCH 1985: Tancredo Neves, the leader of the opposition party (PMDB) is elected president in electoral college by a 450–180 margin. After the death of Tancredo, his vice-president José Sarney is sworn in.

FEBRUARY 1986: President Sarney announces "Plan Cruzado," a heterodox economic program designed to tackle persistent inflation.

Introduction

The distinctiveness of democratization in Brazil rests on the fact that it has been directed by a strong central state, responding as much to the internal conflicts of the military as to the weak and fragmented opposition. The process began with President Geisel's policy of liberalization (*abertura*) from 1974 to 1979, and culminated in the 1985 presidential elections. In the interval, the military government defined the parameters of political conduct both for itself and the opposition. Despite the elections, the Brazilian military has maintained the vast institutional prerogatives it has accumulated over the course of its twenty-year rule.

Military Politics and Abertura

The selection of General Ernesto Geisel in 1974 as the official presidential candidate represented neither a consensus nor a conscious choice by the military as an institution to move toward liberalization. Though General Geisel had a direct link to the legal-constitutionalist tradition of former president Castello Branco (who served from 1964 to 1967), his reputation as a good administrator seems to have been the main reason for his selection. Geisel, along with his chief political advisor and former leader of the National Intelligence Service (SNI), General Golbery do Couto e Silva, were to move away from the grand public works projects and serious human rights abuses of the Costa e Silva and Medici periods (from 1967 to 1974).

The first major challenge to the new administration came with the 1974 congressional elections. Having allowed a relatively free campaign, the regime found itself confronting a strong showing by the opposition party. To a large degree, the results came as a reaction against the worsening economic situation. The oil shock of 1973–74 had put the economy into a recession and seemed to suggest an end to the "Brazilian Miracle." Despite pressure from hardliners, the regime honored the election results. Yet Geisel did not hesitate to use his powers, including the suspension of political rights, against those who appeared to challenge the government excessively.

That the pace of liberalization was completely at the discretion of the regime was reaffirmed with the "April Package" put forth in 1977. After the Congress resisted the regime's initiatives, Geisel declared it in recess. He then announced the replacement of direct gubernatorial elections in 1978 with indirect elections through the regime-controlled electoral college. In addition, he extended the presidential term to six years, prohibited electioneering on radio and television, and created additional senate seats to be selected by pro-regime state assemblies. These measures were followed by the arrest of opposition leader Alencar Furtado after he had sharply attacked the regime.

The reaction to what appeared to be a reversal of the liberalization process was pronounced. Protests were widespread in the summer of 1977, and they came from a wide array of groups including the Church, students, business, and labor. Some have suggested that what appeared to be a crackdown was in fact an attempt to goad opposition groups into action. In this way, Geisel and Golbery hoped to demonstrate to hardliners that the only alternative to liberalization would be unprecedented mass repression. The events of late 1977 seem to support this Machiavellian interpretation.

In late October, Geisel dismissed the minister of the army, General Silvio Coelho da Frota. By dismissing a leading critic of liberalization, Geisel asserted his own firm control and adherence to *abertura*. This was followed in December by his announcement that new legislation would be enacted to replace the institutional acts that had been used by the military to govern since 1964. Moreover, the party system was to be reorganized and given greater leeway.

Perhaps most importantly, it was announced in January that Geisel had chosen the leader of SNI, General João Figueiredo, as his successor. Although he had ties to conservative factions in the military, Figueiredo was seen as a supporter of liberalization.

Opposition

The acceleration of liberalization had the effect of reactivating the opposition groups in the society. The regime always had to cope with opposition, including by guerrillas in the late sixties and early seventies. The Church, as the only nonmilitary institution with a claim to national legitimacy, was, however, probably the regime's most persistent source of opposition. The Conference of Bishops (CNBB), strongly influenced by liberation theology, made perhaps its strongest statement against the regime in a November 1976 pastoral communication denouncing the use of torture, censorship, and corruption. It also condemned the lack of land reform and inadequate programs for the poor. The creation of Basic Christian Communities helped encourage people to defend their rights and make claims.

Another source of pressure on the question of human rights proved to be the United States. A State Department report criticized human rights abuses in 1977 and President Carter publicly referred to Brazil as a violator of human rights. The Brazilian response was to end its military assistance treaty with the United States.

The labor movement, by contrast, was a divided and effectively repressed opposition. It therefore came as a surprise when the metalworkers union led by "Lula" (Luis Inacio da Silva) achieved what was viewed as a strike victory in May 1978. But the same tactics failed in subsequent years, and a strike in 1980 that garnered widespread support, resulted in Lula's arrest. Although the private sector applauded the regime's stand on labor, it also supported the policy of liberalization. In 1978 and in 1983, leading business groups issued statements supporting moves to democracy.

Elections and Transition

As Figueiredo took office in 1979, the economy again felt the shocks of oil price rises and world recession. He signaled the continuation of *abertura* by retaining several of Geisel's advisors, including General Golbery. A crucial test for the regime came with the November 1982 elections. Most of the governorships as well as a large part of the Congress, state assemblies, and municipal posts were to be elected.

The results gave off mixed signals. The government retained its majorities, but lost important governorships, such as those of São Paulo, Minas Gerais, Rio de Janeiro, and Parana to leading opposition figures, including Leónel Brizola (PDT), Tancredo Neves (PMDB), and Franco Montoro (PMDB). The elections proved to be an important turning point. The opposition was provided with the resources that accompany state office. This included a new sense of legitimacy for leaders and parties that only a few years before had been viewed by the government as enemies. Yet because the new opposition had a wide base of support and was thus seen as being responsible, they could provide a bulwark against the radical leftist opposition that the military truly feared. The deepening economic crisis and a general trend toward democratization on the rest of the continent also contributed to the growing sense that the military lacked a sufficient legitimate reason to continue ruling.

Though the ability of the military to control the scope and pace of change made *abertura* a nine-year process, the aftermath of the 1982 elections significantly altered these dynamics because the military lost much of its vaunted capacity for control. The period from 1982 to 1985 can therefore be properly considered the transition phase. By mid-1983, the progovernment Social Democratic Party (PDS) was divided, with the liberal factions gaining strength. Figueiredo's decision not to nominate a successor also contributed to a scramble among possible contenders.

The public campaign, which began in January 1984, to hold direct elections to the presidency the following year, similarly proved decisive in splitting the pro-regime forces. Some in the PSD, such as Vice-President Aureliano Chaves, openly supported direct elections. The issue also galvanized the opposition parties into holding a public dialogue and mass demonstrations. Nonetheless, when a vote on a constitutional amendment for direct elections arose in the Congress, President Figueiredo declared a state of emergency and exercised sufficient pressure to secure its defeat.

The defeat of the amendment accelerated the defection of liberal PDS factions to the opposition. PDS governors and congressmen openly supported the candidacy of Tancredo Neves over that of Paulo Maluf. Tancredo had created a broad center coalition from the PMDB, PDT, and factions from the PT and PDS. His own background was as a moderate coalition-builder. Figueiredo's only condition for the civilian candidates was that there were to be no prosecutions for actions taken by the military during its rule and that the military retain control of the arms industry. Both conditions were accepted by the candidates. On 15 January 1985 Tancredo was elected by the electoral college, becoming the first civilian president elected since 1960.

Uncertain Consolidation

The death of Tancredo came as a shock, but it did not significantly affect the final outcome of the transition. His vice-president, José Sarney, former head of the PDS and a compromise figure, was duly sworn in as president. However, much of the initial enthusiasm that accompanied the transfer of executive power dissipated in the next two years as a weak economic recovery was followed by yet another downturn. Within a year of the February 1986 announcement of the heterodox "Plan Cruzado," Brazil's new democracy was facing an economic and political crisis. Persistent high inflation, large external debts, and growing labor unrest led to a PMDB sweep of the November 1986 congressional elections. The magnitude of the vote and the increasing willingness of opposition leaders to challenge executive authority, especially in debates over the constitution, considerably weakened Sarney's position. With the military maintaining many of its self-defined prerogatives and its capacity to veto attempts to curtail them, the outcome of Brazil's democratic experiment remains uncertain.

Annotated Bibliography

Mainwaring, Scott. "Transition to Democracy in Brazil," *Journal of Inter-American Studies* 28, 1 (Spring 1986): 149–79. A comprehensive analysis of the move toward democracy in Brazil, with an emphasis on the post–1982 events. The author suggests that the regime's declining capacity to control the transition was rooted in internal divisions as well as coalition-building among the opposition.

Moreira Alves, Maria H. *State and Opposition in Military Brazil.* Austin: University of Texas Press, 1985. An examination that focuses on the nature of the opposition in a "national security state." The ways by which the state and various opposition groups affect each other's views of their role in society is emphasized. A review of armed groups, the Church, parties, and grass-roots organizations is included.

Roett, Riordan. *Brazil: Politics in a Patrimonial Society,* 3d ed. New York: Praeger Press, 1984. An attempt to evaluate the Brazilian political system in terms of its social and historical experiences. In addition to an historical review, parties, the economy, and foreign policy are analyzed. A section on the "patrimonial" state examines the relations between the state and social groups such as labor and business.

Stepan, Alfred, ed. *Democratizing Brazil.* Princeton: Princeton University Press, 1988. A series of essays that give a comprehensive overview of the democratization process in Brazil. F. H. Cardoso, F. Weffort and M. Keck are among the contributors, examining such varied themes as Brazil's economic problems, democratizing the military, and grass-roots movements.

ECUADOR, 1975–1986: Institutional Deadlock and Fragile Coalitions

Chronology of Key Events

SEPTEMBER 1975–JUNE 1976: An attempted coup led by General González Alvear promising a return to democracy is defeated. In January, General Rodríguez Lara is replaced by a military triumvirate, which announces plans to oversee a transition to democracy.

JANUARY 1978: By a plebiscite, a new constitution is selected to replace the 1945 constitution.

JULY 1978–MARCH 1979: In the first round of voting, Jaime Roldos Aguilera leads with 31 percent of the vote but he must face second-place Sixto Durán Ballen (a Social Christian) in a run-off election. An official recount by the Supreme Electoral Tribunal is punctuated by renewed threats from the military and rightist groups to halt the electoral process.

APRIL 1979: Jaime Roldós Aguilera is elected president with 70 percent of the vote.

AUGUST 1979–JUNE 1980: Roldós's legislative program is stalled in the Congress by a Bucaram-rightist alliance.

MAY 1981–MAY 1982: Jaime Roldós is killed in an air crash. He is succeeded by Vice President Osvaldo Hurtado, who introduces the first of a series of austerity measures and forges a center-leftist majority in the Congress.

MAY 1984: León Febres Cordero, a Social Christian leader, defeats Rodrigo Borja (ID) by one hundred thousand votes for the presidency.

OCTOBER 1984–JUNE 1985: Febres's legislative program and Supreme Court nominations are stalled in the Congress. An alliance with the opposition is negotiated to break the deadlock.

MARCH 1986: An attempted coup led by Air Force General Frank Vargas is thwarted.

Introduction

Sharp institutional conflicts, party fragmentation, and political polarization have all been key aspects of the Ecuadorean political system since democratization was initiated. The transition phase, which began in 1976 with the removal of the reformist General Guillermo Rodríguez Lara, culminated in the 1979 presidential elections. Though the transition occurred in a period of relative economic prosperity, successive democratic governments both of the left and the right have had to confront a serious economic decline as well as continued threats of an authoritarian relapse.

Authoritarian Breakdown

The military regime that came to power in 1972 strongly emphasized its interest in promoting structural changes, much in the manner of its military neighbor to the south, Peru. However, unlike the latter, the Ecuadorean military lacked both the institutional commitment and administrative capacity to institute major reforms. In September 1975 an attempted coup by General González Alvear was launched, promising a return to democracy, and it was defeated only after heavy fighting. Rodríguez's rule was further shaken by a successful general strike in November, leading to charges from business and the military that the government could no longer control the nation. In January 1976, Rodríguez Lara was replaced by a military triumvirate led by Admiral Alfredo Poveda, who announced his intention to oversee a transition to democracy. Five months later, after consulting the parties and business, the regime unveiled its transition mechanism. It appointed three commissions to draft a constitution and draw up rules for parties and elections. A referendum was to be held in January 1978 to choose between a revised version of the 1945 constitution and a completely new document.

Transition and Elections

By mid-1977 the commissions had completed their work and the parties began campaigning for the referendum. Both the center-left parties (CFP, ID) and the Marxist left (united in a Broad Front) urged adoption of the new constitution, which called for a unicameral legislature and gave the Congress and the president the right to call plebiscites. By contrast, the rightist parties (the Liberals and Conservatives) urged retention of the old constitution. The referendum was therefore viewed as a preliminary test of strength for the first round of presidential elections, scheduled for July. When the new constitution won with 43 percent of the vote, it was taken as an indication of the left's strength, and in particular, as a boost for the candidacy of Assad Bucaram, the CFP leader. An old-style populist whose 1972 candidacy helped spark the military intervention, Bucaram was a traditional foe of business interests in Guayaquil, Ecuador's second largest city. When an anti-Bucaram coalition collapsed after the referendum, the military *junta* intervened in the transition by decreeing that a presidential candidate's parents had to have been citizens of Ecuador, eliminating Bucaram, whose parents were Lebanese.

With their leader disqualified, the CFP turned to Jaime Roldós Aguilera, whose youthful charisma and moderate rhetoric distinguished him from his mentor. In an attempt to forge a broad center-left coalition, Roldos chose as his running-mate a political scientist and Christian Democratic leader, Osvaldo Hurtado. To the surprise of most, the Roldós-Hurtado ticket outdistanced two major rivals, the Liberal Raúl Clemente Huerta and the Social Christian Sixto Durán, but not by a wide enough margin to avoid a run-off against the second-place Durán. Moreover, the Supreme Electoral Tribunal announced that it would take at least four months to complete a recount and to initiate the second round of voting.

In the months between the two elections (August 1978 to April 1979), new threats to democratization emerged. Both the Minister of Government General Bolívar Jarrín Cahuenos and the Commander of the Army General Guillermo Durán were known to favor ending the elections. After the first round, a rightist party, which had close ties to the Guayaquil business community, warned that the election of Roldós would pose a danger to democracy.

León Febres Cordero, then president of the Guayaquil Chamber of Commerce, called for the cancelation of the elections and the institution of a constituent assembly to select a president. Most importantly, the chairman of the electoral tribunal, Dr. Rafael Arizaga Vega, claimed on national television that the elections should be canceled due to fraud, in a clear attempt to strengthen the position of hardline factions in the military. These moves in turn precipitated efforts to mobilize support for elections by Roldós and his supporters, as well as by labor unions, which launched strikes in support of elections.

The United States, through the commander of U.S. forces at Panama, also strongly warned against an attempt to end the transition. By the end of 1978, Admiral Poveda and the ruling triumvirate had reiterated their support for the transition, set a definite date for the transfer of power, and appointed a new electoral tribunal to continue the recount. In the end, sharp internal military divisions, U.S. pressure, and renewed concern over border disputes with Peru appear to have prevented an authoritarian relapse. Toward the end of the campaign, talks between Roldós and the military produced an agreement that there would be no prosecutions of military figures and that key military interests would be preserved.

In the April 1979 elections, Jaime Roldós was overwhelmingly elected, winning all but one province. The results from the congressional elections were perhaps the most surprising, because the traditional center-right parties captured a mere fifteen of the sixty-nine seats.

Conflict and Fragile Coalitions

The factionalization and institutional conflicts that have characterized Ecuador since 1979 began almost immediately after the August inauguration. During the campaign, Roldós had distanced himself politically from Bucaram. Following the elections, Bucaram negotiated a deal with the conservative parties to ensure his election as president of the Congress. Roldós's reform program was stalled in the Congress throughout 1980 by the Bucaram-conservative alliance. Both sides exchanged threats, with Roldos asserting he would call a plebiscite to pass his reforms, while the Congress began impeachment proceedings against several ministers. By June 1980 the pro-Roldós forces had forged an alliance with center-leftists to form a majority. The break with Bucaram became final in December, when Roldós formed his own party.

The tragic death of Jaime Roldós in a May 1981 air crash did not alter the political dynamic begun by growing party fragmentation. Vice-President Hurtado, who succeeded Roldos, was immediately confronted with a crisis when a leftist group withdrew from the governing coalition. Hurtado also faced the new challenge of a severe economic decline. The price of oil, which accounts for some 60 percent of Ecuador's export income, declined precipitously.

In November 1981 the first of a series of austerity measures was adopted. Price rises had already sparked protests, and in early 1982 serious rioting erupted while strike activity by a leftist labor confederation led to renewed rumors of military intervention. Nevertheless, the 1982 congressional elections did not change the balance of power in the Congress. During this period, however, Hurtado was able to forge a new coalition with Bucaram's party after he died. Symptomatic of the frequent changes in allegiance on the part of the parties, Roldós's party then went into opposition.

By early 1983 the political parties began to jockey over positions for the following year's presidential elections. The rightist parties, whose influence had declined, formed a National Reconstruction Front (FRN) under the leadership of Social Christian León Febres Cordero. In contrast, the left was highly fragmented with half a dozen candidates. But Rodrigo Borja of the Democratic left (ID) did succeed in narrowly outdistancing Febres Cordero in the first round, only to lose the May 1984 second-round balloting. Significantly, the FRN was not able to alter the balance of power in the Congress, which remained controlled by the center-left. This situation was at the core of the 1984–85 political stalemate.

The Febres Cordero administration moved quickly to implement its conservative economic program, including ending price controls and reducing protection for domestic industry. In June 1985, Ecuador amended its adherence to Decision 24 of the Andean Pact, which requires that foreign firms sending 80 percent of their products abroad be nationalized or enter into mixed enterprise arrangements with the state. Febres's free market policies and his breaking of relations with Nicaragua in late 1985 were particularly well received by the Reagan administration, which adopted a lenient attitude toward the Ecuadorean debt. An agreement in late 1985 allowed the postponement of 1985–89 debt service payments for a twelve-year period.

Yet Febres's conservative policies also resulted in a year-long deadlock with the leftist-controlled Congress over such diverse issues as the minimum wage and Supreme Court nominations. According to the Ecuadorean constitution, legislative disagreements are to be settled by a special constitutional tribunal. However, because seven of the eleven tribunal members were of the left, Febres refused to recognize their jurisdiction in most disputes.

The institutional deadlock of 1984–85 was only settled when Febres negotiated support from the CFP and its new leader, Averroes Bucaram. In return for legislative support, Bucaram received FRN endorsement in his successful bid to head the Congress. In January 1986, Febres proposed several institutional reforms to reduce the influence of the left in the Congress, including allowing independents to run for legislative office. His planned use of the plebiscite to enact these measures led to opposition charges of Febres's "dictatorial power."

Ecuadorean democracy confronted its severest test, however, three months later, when General Frank Vargas seized the Manta air base, accusing Defense Minister General Luis Pinieros and Army Chief General Manuel Albuja of corruption. The dispute appeared to be settled when Febres promised to investigate the alleged corruption. Yet two weeks later, Vargas seized the Quito air base, claiming that he was betrayed by Febres. When Vargas threatened to seize power, Febres used the army to seal off the area and Vargas surrendered. Febres managed to complete his term and oversee a fair election in 1988, which was won by Rodrigo Borja.

Annotated Bibliography

Handelman, Howard. "Ecuador: A New Political Direction?" in *Military Government and the Movement Toward Democracy in South America,* ed. Howard Handelman and Thomas Sanders. Bloomington: Indiana University Press, 1980. An essay that focuses on events during the transition (1975–79). The shifting party alliances and the threats made by business interests to halt the process are given special attention. Nonetheless, the process is seen as a step away from the militarism-populist cycle that has characterized Ecuador in this century.

Hurtado, Osvaldo. *Political Power in Ecuador*. Albuquerque: University of New Mexico Press, 1980. (Spanish Edition: *Poder Politico en el Ecuador*. Quito: Universidad Catolica, 1977). A comprehensive analysis of the Ecuadorean political system, with a particular emphasis on the socioeconomic and cultural factors that have historically shaped its politics. The special role of the Guayaquil oligarchy as well as the recurrence of militarism and populism are seen as impediments to democratic development.

Martz, John D. *Politics and Petroleum in Ecuador*. New Brunswick: Transaction Books, 1987. An up-to-date analysis of Ecuadorean politics with particular attention given to the historical role that the booms and busts, brought about by the country's reliance on oil, have had on the stability of the political system.

PERU, 1975–1987: The Legacy of a Radical Experiment

Chronology of Key Events

AUGUST 1975: General Francisco Morales Bermudez replaces General Juan Velasco Alvarado in a bloodless coup d'etat.

JULY 1976–FEBRUARY 1977: An abortive coup by conservative General Bobbio Centurion follows weeks of rioting and strikes. Plan *Tupac Amaru* is announced. It includes an austerity program and sets a timetable for elections.

JULY 1978–JULY 1979: The constituent assembly is elected. APRA gains thirty-seven seats, the left combines for thirty-four seats, while the right totals twenty-nine. AP abstains from the vote. A constitution is drafted and enacted.

MAY 1980: Fernando Belaúnde Terry is elected president with 45.4 percent of the vote, defeating a divided opposition.

MARCH 1981–DECEMBER 1982: A sharp rise in guerrilla activity is noted; 310 attacks are registered in nine months. Neoliberal economic policies and tough antiterrorist laws are enacted by Belaúnde.

NOVEMBER 1983: Opposition candidates sweep the municipal elections. Marxist Alfonso Barrantes becomes mayor of Lima, and human rights groups criticize the army's antiterrorist tactics.

MAY 1985: Alan García Pérez is elected president with 47 percent of the vote.

JANUARY 1986–JULY 1986: Stimulative economic policies including debt ceiling payments are enacted. Prison uprisings result in a massacre and rumors of a military coup.

Introduction

Peru's return to democracy occurred in a context of unprecedented social mobilization and a fragmented party system, and in the presence of a formidable insurgency. The transition began with the election of a constituent assembly in 1978 and culminated in the return of Fernando Belaúnde Terry to the presidency, the office of which he had been deprived by the 1968 coup d'etat. With the election of Alan García Pérez in 1985, Peru's consolidation phase took a decidedly leftist-nationalistic turn, uncommon in the most recent democratization efforts of Latin America.

Authoritarian Breakdown and Economic Pressures

The authoritarian regime of General Juan Velasco Alvarado, which took power in 1968, has been described as "populist," "modernizing," and "radical." But as commitments to increased public expenditures confronted a depressed market for Peru's primary product exports, and international creditors demanded fiscal austerity, the military's social experiment began to falter. Velasco's declining physical health added a sense of uncertainty to the possibility of continuing the regime's reformist policies.

By mid-1975, a coalition of moderate and conservative officers had already formed around General Francisco Morales Bermudez, Velasco's prime minister. In August of that year, an Institutional Manifesto was issued by the nation's five regional army commanders declaring Morales Bermudez president of the republic. Although they pledged continued support to the "revolution," it soon became apparent that Morales Bermudez's "second phase" was to be far more conservative than Velasco's "first phase."

Within a year, an austerity program was announced providing for budget cuts, sharp increases in consumer prices, and a devaluation. The reaction was swift. Strikes and three days of rioting were followed by the declaration of a state of emergency. Popular organizations created by Velasco to foster corporatist control among peasants and workers formed a Front for the Defense of the Revolution to coordinate antiregime activities. Thus, ironically, the very organizations created to support authoritarianism in Peru were being used to bring about its collapse.

Labor unions were to play a significant role in this opposition, and strikes increased dramatically between 1974 and 1978. Similarly business groups exerted pressure for an end to the regime, although their concern was primarily with dismantling the reforms of the Velasco era. Pressure on the regime came not only from these societal groups, but also from within the military. An attempted coup by the conservative General Bobbio Centurion was thwarted in June 1976. Partly to placate the right wing of the armed forces, most remaining generals associated with Velasco were moved. Some, such as Leonidas Rodríguez and Tantalean Vanini, went on to form or to join opposition organizations. By the end of 1976, the military as an institution had lost any semblance of a consensus on how to rule the country.

In February 1977 the regime unveiled Plan *Tupac Amaru*, a plan for democratization with economic measures designed to reduce social spending, encourage decentralization, and allow greater foreign investment. The impetus for much of the regime's economic austerity in this period came from external pressure, particularly from the International Monetary Fund. Indeed, much of the 1977–79 period involved a cycle of austerity followed by riots, and then relaxation followed by renewed IMF pressure. That pressure culminated in the cut-off of Peru's access to IMF funds in 1978.

There is little doubt that creditor-induced austerity greatly added to the regime's unpopularity. The plan also announced elections for a constituent assembly the following year. That assembly was to provide an opportunity for all parties to help write a new constitution to take effect when power was transferred to civilians in 1980.

Transition and Electoral Shifts

The scheduled elections significantly changed the dynamics of the transition, and parties began taking a leading role in setting the political agenda. The number of parties had dramatically increased from five parties in the last elections (held in 1963) to thirteen in 1978. Moreover, nearly all of the new parties were on the left. Aside from this shift to the left, the party system was highly fragmented, with many parties that were little more than coalitions of local or regional organizations.

Before the elections took place, the first general strike in half a century was called. It was designed not only as a repudiation of the military regime, but also as a demonstration of the left's new-found strength. This was confirmed by the election results: the left won thirty-four seats, while Peru's oldest party, The American Popular Revolutionary Alliance (APRA) gained thirty-seven seats. Four rightist parties won twenty-nine seats. But the election results were marred by the absence of Fernando Belaúnde Terry's Popular Action Party (AP). His decision to abstain appeared to be a calculated risk, but one that paid off handsomely.

By not participating in the assembly, AP maintained its status as a party in opposition, while the other parties were seen as participating in the military's final days and engaging in petty partisan jockeying over the constitution. Belaúnde's ability to rise above the fray was enhanced by his stalwart opposition to the regime since his own overthrow. Unlike many of the parties, including APRA, which had achieved a modus vivendi with the regime, Belaúnde's position justified his claim in the 1980 elections of being the candidate least associated with the military's twelve-year rule.

Democracy, Insurgency, and Populism

During the Belaúnde presidency (from 1980 to 1985), neoliberal economic policies and a severe recession combined to produce a dramatic fall in wages and rising inflation. By 1983, a widespread financial crisis had resulted in the collapse of numerous banks and many rumors of official corruption. Moreover, it was during this period that the Maoist guerrillas *Sendero Luminoso* emerged, launching a violent campaign of bombings and assassinations. Led by a provincial university professor named Abimael Guzman, it has used a fanatical ideology and secret cells to capitalize on the discontent of peasants and the urban poor. The number of attacks consistently increased between 1980 and 1986, spreading beyond the rebels' initial base in Ayacucho into Lima and as far north as the jungle regions of Alto Huallaga.

In December 1982, the government declared Ayacucho under military control, giving all power to a military governor. The increased use of the military was, however, also accompanied by growing charges of human rights abuses. The massacre of journalists at Uchuraccay by apparently progovernment peasants and the discoveries of mass graves seemed to substantiate these charges.

Amid rising concern over the militarization of the countryside and the severe recession, the United Left (IU) coalition made substantial gains in the 1983 municipal elections. The left's reemergence under Alfonso Barrantes in 1983 along with its strong showing in 1978 seemed to indicate that for a significant portion of Peru's new electorate, the Marxist left has now become a viable governing option.

During this same period an important realignment was occurring in the APRA party. A new generation of leaders led by Alan García Pérez entered into key leadership positions. Recalling APRA's early radical roots, they adopted a leftist-nationalist program, attempting to appeal to the new radical electorate. The election of García to the presidency in May 1985 marks an important turning point for Peru's democracy. It is only the second time this century that power has been transferred between two elected presidents, and it is the first time in its sixty-year history that APRA has gained the presidency.

Using his popularity, García initiated several important social and political changes. Attempting to curtail the power of the security forces, he reorganized the police forces, which were widely viewed as abusive and corrupt, and introduced a defense ministry and cut military budgets. His heterodox economic program met with surprising success in its first two years, reactivating an economy that could seemingly only lurch from one recession to another, generating little growth. Nevertheless, with the continued growth of terrorism, the economic downturn, and the sharp decline in García's popularity after the nationalization of the banks in July 1987, Peru's democracy could not be considered consolidated.

Annotated Bibliography

DeGregori, Carlos Ivan. *Sendero Luminoso*. Working Papers No. 4 & 6. Lima: Instituto de Estudios Peruanos, 1985. Probably the single best analysis on the origins and growth of this unusual insurgent group. The author focuses on the economic environment of Ayacucho, Peru's poorest region, and the growth of radical, including Maoist, groups in the area as they formed around a new university.

Gorman, Stephen, ed. *Post-Revolutionary Peru: The Politics of Transformation.* Boulder: Westview Press, 1982. A collection of essays that traces the roles of key actors in the transition phase (from 1975 to 1980). An emphasis is placed on how the authoritarian regime changed the resources and perceptions of these groups. Overviews of the military, labor unions, parties, and peasant organizations are included.

McClintock, Cynthia, and Abraham Lowenthal, eds. *The Peruvian Experiment Reconsidered*. Princeton: Princeton University Press, 1983. These essays attempt to evaluate the legacy of military reforms primarily on the social and economic structures of the nation. They offer an opportunity to place the experience of a "radical" military in historical perspective and assess its long-term implications.

EL SALVADOR, 1979–1986: Transition Amid Internal Warfare

Chronology of Key Events

OCTOBER 1979–DECEMBER 1979: Junior military officers overthrow General Carlos Humberto Romero and install a revolutionary *junta*, which includes moderate and leftist politicians. Land reform and official disbanding of paramilitary organizations (ORDEN) enacted.

JANUARY 1980–MARCH 1980: Center-left politicians, including Guillermo Ungo and Rubén Zamora, resign from *junta* and form *Coordinadora*. Rightist leaders also organize. Political assassinations, including of Archbishop Oscar Romero, increase sharply.

MAY 1980–NOVEMBER 1980: Rightist leader Roberto D'Aubuisson is arrested in coup plot, though he is later released. The hardline position in the *junta* solidifies with removal of Colonel Majano. An escalation of guerrilla activities take place.

DECEMBER 1980–JUNE 1981: José Napoleón Duarte, leader of the Christian Democrats (PDC), is chosen president by the *junta*. U.S. military assistance is suspended after the murder of four American nuns. Nonlethal military aid is resumed in January. The Reagan administration issues a special report linking Salvadoran guerrillas to Cuba and Nicaragua. Sharp increases in aid are requested by Reagan, though Congress conditions aid on an improved human rights situation.

MARCH 1982–MARCH 1984: Constituent Assembly elections are held. The right wins a working majority, but a moderate apolitical businessman, Alvaro Magaña is selected interim president. The constitution is enacted in mid-1983, and annual U.S. military aid surpasses $30 million.

MARCH 1984–NOVEMBER 1984: José Napoleón Duarte is elected president with 53.6 percent of the vote, defeating ARENA's Roberto D'Aubuisson. Meeting with guerrillas at La Palma results in little progress.

MARCH 1985–JANUARY 1986: Elections give the PDC a majority of thirty-three seats in the Legislative Assembly, and 200 of 262 contested municipal posts. Guerrillas adopt low intensity warfare tactics.

Introduction

The most recent effort to achieve democracy in El Salvador was initiated with the 1979 coup d'etat. In its aftermath, violence accelerated from both the disloyal left and right, while modest attempts at socioeconomic reform were made. The resources of key actors have been significantly affected by the changing policies of the U.S. government. This external factor and the continued violent polarization has made democratization in El Salvador a tenuous and highly reversible process.

Authoritarian Breakdown and Reaction

Under the hardline rule of General Carlos Humberto Romero (from 1977 to 1979), the military regime established close relations with landowners and rightist paramilitary forces such as ORDEN. On the other hand, nascent guerrilla groups also accelerated their activities, assassinating government officials and bombing industrial plants and offices. The conservative coalition forged by Romero had a weak base of support and was soon shattered by internal bickering.

Under severe pressure from the United States, the Church, and international organizations, the Public Order Law, which had given virtually unrestricted authority to the military, was repealed in early 1979. In August, opposition organizations formed the *Foro Popular* to urge a "popular democratic" government. The *Foro* was notable because it included diverse groups, such as the Christian Democrats (PDC), center-left parties, the Ligas Populares (LP-28), and several trade unions. Nonetheless, the opposition could not successfully challenge the overwhelming force of a regime that could not distinguish an opposition from subversion. Thus, the regime's collapse in October resulted from an internal coup rather than from opposition actions.

Motivated to a large degree by the decline in the military's institutional integrity and growing corruption, which was attributed to the alliance that had been forged with conservative interests, the new "Provisional Revolutionary Government" promised to adopt a reformist program. Land reform, free elections, and respect for human rights were proclaimed as being the goals of the new regime. The *junta* brought into the government moderate politicians from the *Foro,* including Guillermo Ungo, and moderate elements from business.

Yet the military as an institution was far too fragmented to implement all of the proposed reforms, although some measures such as the raising of the minimum wage and the limitation of landholdings to one hundred hectares were enacted. The *junta* was particularly divided over how to deal with the left, Colonels Guillermo García and Nicolás Carranza were far more committed to a hard-line approach than Colonel Adolfo Majano. Moreover, the army could not control the security forces—the National Police, the Treasury Police, and the National Guard—that still maintained contacts with right-wing paramilitary groups. For its part, the extreme left used mobilization tactics to pressure the *junta* for more radical reforms and for a clear accounting of those who had disappeared, neither of which the government could produce.

In January 1980 most of the Social Democratic politicians abandoned the government, citing their inability to overcome obstruction from the right on a variety of issues. Later in the month, a new *junta* was formed that relied more heavily on Christian Democratic leaders. It was at this point that violent polarization intensified. Various leftist organizations formed the *Coordinadora Nacional* and called for revolutionary struggle. Two key leaders on the right, Major Roberto D'Aubuisson and José Alberto ("Chele") Medrano, joined forces in the National Democratic Front (FDN). In late February 1980 the Attorney General Mario Zamora was assassinated, and on 30 March Archbishop Oscar Romero was gunned down.

Overall, the first three months of 1980 witnessed 689 political assassinations, mostly carried out by right-wing "death squads." The Christian Democratic (PDC) strategy amid the increasing violence was to create a credible center, with the support of moderate officers and the United States. What the PDC lost in terms of its reformist image by participating in the *junta*, it hoped to gain by creating a viable political space within which it would have an initial advantage. It had already used the little power it had in the regime to push an admittedly limited agrarian reform and bank nationalizations.

United States Influence and Elections

In early May, forces loyal to Colonel Majano seized D'Aubuisson with documents supposedly describing a coup. In the weeks that followed, D'Aubuisson was released and Majano was exiled, an indication of the strengthening of the hardliners' position in the regime. To a large extent the escalation of the guerrilla war had discredited the position of the progressive officers who had argued for rapprochement with the left, and it improved the position of those who saw the "dirty war" as a tactic against subversion. Already by April dissident factions of the PDC led by Héctor Dada broke ranks with Duarte, claiming that the *junta* was not interested in reform or democratization.

The apparent shift to the right by the *junta* was accompanied by increasing rightist confidence that a Reagan victory in the U.S. elections would result in U.S. approval for a rightist takeover. Throughout 1980, the Carter administration warned D'Aubuisson that the United States would not support a right-wing coup, and that conspiracies should be ended. The United States supported the regime that came to power in 1979, but only on condition that it fulfill its promise of reform and free elections.

In December 1980, after the murders of four American Maryknoll sisters and public outrage in the United States, the administration suspended all new military assistance until the murders were clarified. As a result of increased U.S. pressure and the discrediting of D'Aubuisson, a new *junta* was organized in mid-December in which José Napoleón Duarte would be appointed president. Hardliners in the *junta* clearly suffered a setback, as they were forced to disassociate themselves from the disloyal right and D'Aubuisson's plotting.

The United States increasingly focused on the deteriorating position of the Salvadoran army and the links between the guerrillas and Cuba and Nicaragua. Guerrilla forces had formed a united front (FMLN) in late 1980, and they stepped up their activities in the countryside. In January 1981, the Carter administration announced shipments of "nonlethal" military aid to the Salvadoran army.

With the arrival in office of the Reagan administration, the military aspect of the situation received new emphasis. Yet it was confronted by a reluctant Congress and public opinion fearful of any U.S military intervention. By the end of the year, U.S. rhetoric had been toned down, though assistance was accelerated. In March 1982 elections were held for a constituent assembly that was to select an interim president and design a new constitution. The results gave the right a working majority in the assembly, as D'Aubuisson's ARENA forged coalitions with other rightist factions. After much infighting and U.S. pressure, a moderate, Alvaro Magaña, an apolitical banker, was chosen interim president.

The Constituent Assembly period (from March 1982 to March 1984) was characterized by rightist efforts to roll back land reform and by an intensification of the guerrilla war. The economy continued to deteriorate, with unemployment and underemployment affecting over two-thirds of the population. U.S. aid dramatically increased, though at lower levels than those requested by the Reagan administration.

The Duarte Administration

The election of José Napoleón Duarte to the presidency in March 1984 was a crucial turning point in El Salvador's democratization. Duarte brought improved credibility to the process, particularly abroad. As a result, aid from the United States as well as from Western Europe increased. His government moved quickly against the disloyal right, reorganizing the security forces such as the Treasury Police and sending rightist officers abroad. The Reagan administration continued to warn against a rightist coup, and indicated that it fully supported Duarte's policy of creating a centrist coalition. The military with the assistance of U.S. advisors also stepped up activities against the FMLN, emphasizing counterinsurgency tactics to win the loyalties of local populations. Human rights violations in particular declined from their 1980–82 levels.

Nonetheless, facing grass-roots pressure from within the PDC and a recognition that a prolonged war could only further weaken a war-torn economy, President Duarte invited the guerrilla leaders to negotiate an end to the conflict. For their part, the guerrillas' increasing difficulties against a better-equipped and trained Salvadoran army, and their declared willingness to negotiate, combined to produce a meeting with the government at La Palma in November

1984. Surprisingly, most groups supported Duarte's efforts, though the military emphasized that the 1983 constitution was nonnegotiable. What was not surprising was that an agreement was not immediately reached. Guerrilla demands for immediate incorporation into the government would have violated the tenuous understanding Duarte had reached with powerful social groups, such as the military and business. To secure at least the tolerance of the right, Duarte acknowledged the inviolability of the 1983 constitution and slowed the pace of reform. Similarly, he assured the military that prosecution for human rights abuses would not be pursued, and that the military would receive the equipment and training it deemed necessary.

In the period since the La Palma meeting, the Duarte government faced renewed challenges from the FMLN, which launched a "low intensity war" that emphasized assassinations, kidnappings, and urban violence. Nevertheless, divisions between the FDR leaders and the FMLN appeared to grow over the new tactics. Several FDR leaders began to return to El Salvador in early 1986. The kidnapping of Duarte's own daughter in September 1985, which appeared to harden his position, may also have contributed to the renewed tensions in the guerrilla camp.

Although the PDC won a majority of the Legislature in March 1985, the four subsequent years of war and economic deterioration caused a division within the PDC. In the presidential election in March 1989, the Salvadoran people chose the rightist candidate Alfredo Cristiani of ARENA.

Annotated Bibliography

Baloyra, Enrique A. *El Salvador in Transition*. Chapel Hill: University of North Carolina Press, 1982. A comprehensive review of the Salvadoran political system, with special emphasis on events from the mid-seventies until the 1982 elections. U.S. policy, the role of parties, and the internal dynamics of the military are evaluated. Important appendices include figures on the 1982 elections, political violence, and agrarian reform.

Karl, Terry L. "After La Palma: The Prospects for Democratization in El Salvador." *World Policy Journal* 2, 2 (Spring 1985): 305–330. An evaluation of the policies of President Duarte. The negotiation initiative is viewed as a reaction to a deteriorating economy, grass-roots pressure in the PDC, and fear that the political space opened up by elections would be closed by the military or the guerrillas. The attitude of the United States in the aftermath of the talks and U.S. options are explored.

Pastor, Robert. "Continuity and Change in U.S. Foreign Policy: Carter and Reagan on El Salvador," *Journal of Policy Analysis and Management* 3, 1 (Winter 1984): 175–90. An assessment of the similarities and differences between Carter's and Reagan's policies and their effect on El Salvador.

Sharpe, Kenneth. "El Salvador Revisited: Why Duarte is in Trouble." *World Policy Journal* 3, 3, (Summer 1986): 473–94. An analysis of the most recent events in El Salvador. Duarte is evaluated in terms of being a "prisoner of war," unable to accomplish most of his goals and barely tolerated by the right. Moreover, the Reagan administration views him primarily as a conduit for U.S. military aid. Worsening of the situation, it is said, is especially seen in the government's unwillingness to encourage returning FDR rebels.

ARGENTINA, 1981–1987: Authoritarian Breakdown and Military Defeat

Chronology of Key Events

MARCH 1981–JULY 1981: General Roberto Viola assumes the presidency after sharp infighting over political and economic strategies. Viola's overtures to the opposition result in the formation of the *Multipartidária,* or party alliance, to negotiate a return to democracy with the regime.

DECEMBER 1981–MARCH 1982: Viola is replaced by hardline factions in the *junta* and General Galtieri is named president. He imposes an austerity program and ends talk of a transition that is not "directed from above." Antiregime demonstrations begin and the parties harden their positions.

APRIL 1982–JULY 1982: Argentina invades the Falkland (Malvinas) Islands. The British naval force arrives and surrounds Argentine troops, who surrender at Port Stanley. Galtieri resigns and is eventually replaced by General Bignone.

SEPTEMBER 1982–DECEMBER 1982: Demonstrations and strikes increase as an election timetable is announced.

OCTOBER 1983: Raúl Alfonsín wins the presidency with 52 percent of the vote. This is the first defeat of the Peronists in a presidential race.

JUNE 1985: *Plan Austral* is unveiled by President Alfonsín to control inflation and increase economic confidence. Austerity includes a new currency, wage and price freezes, and budget cuts.

MARCH–APRIL 1987: A series of rebellions by junior military officers takes place, protesting prosecutions for actions taken during the military regime.

Introduction

Argentina's road to democracy was conditioned by deep cleavages in the military and among political parties, as well as a decisive military defeat. The transition phase began in early 1981 when moderate factions led by General Roberto Viola assumed the presidency. Though he was later ousted, his overtures to civilian groups helped set the stage for an expected return to democratic rule. The War of the Malvinas in early 1982 accelerated the disintegration of authoritarianism and paved the way for elections the following year and for the democratic government of President Raúl Alfonsín.

Authoritarian Breakdown

The military government led by General Jorge Videla that came to power in 1976 maintained its unity through its pursuit of social and economic "efficiency," which the military as an institution diagnosed as being lacking in modern Argentina. It was during this period (from 1976 to 1981) that the worst of the human rights abuses occurred, as the regime attempted to eliminate "subversives." In addition, a neoliberal economic program similar to that being pursued in Pinochet's Chile was adopted. By early 1981, however, the military consensus had been shattered as inflation had again reached 100 percent and the economy had entered a recession. Middle-class and business groups, many of whom had supported the 1976 coup, were especially hard hit by the lowering of protection for domestic industries.

The designation of General Roberto Viola as president in March 1981 was an attempt to increase political support for the regime while signaling the possibility of a return to democracy. He appointed conciliatory figures to his cabinet, with seven of the thirteen cabinet positions going to civilians. His new Interior Minister, General Horácio Tomás Liendo, openly called for a dialogue with political parties that would include the Peronists. In July, the principal political parties formed the *Multipartidária,* an alliance whose purpose was to negotiate a return to democracy with the regime. These moves toward reconciliation that were aimed at gaining a wider base of support among the middle classes and even labor led hardliners in the regime to issue warnings against a return to "populism and anarchy."

The hardline factions of Generals Leopoldo Galtieri and Cristino Nicolaides finally overthrew Viola in December 1981 and promised a return of "national reorganization." With General Galtieri as president, a new austerity program was announced. He also announced that a return to democracy would take place only if the process were controlled by the regime. The reaction of the *Multipartidária* was divided between those urging moderation, led by the Radicals (UCR) and Peronists, and those urging a harder position and greater social mobilization (left-wing Peronists).

The unwillingness of the regime to negotiate a timetable for elections and the increasing harshness of orthodox economic policies soon led to a general hardening of the opposition's position. This also coincided with a rise in labor protests against the regime. The Peronist unions staged the largest antigovernment rally since 1976 at the end of March 1982, which was brutally broken up by police and army troops.

The Malvinas War and the Opposition

President Galtieri ordered an invasion of the British-controlled Falkland Islands on 2 April 1982, an obvious effort to end internal divisions in the military and rally nationalist support from the public. Argentina also gained wide support from other Latin American nations, although the Reagan administration, which had developed a conciliatory policy toward the regime, backed Great Britain in the conflict. Though Galtieri achieved his goal in the short term, the quick defeat of seventy-five hundred Argentine troops at Port Stanley in June 1982 deepened the regime's crisis. Divisions in the military services now asserted themselves over who had "lost" the Malvinas, with cleavages being drawn between the different services.

Similarly, the nationalist fervor that the regime's propaganda had whipped up among the public turned into disenchantment and then anger, as demonstrators ridiculed a military regime that could not win a war. By July, General Galtieri had been replaced by General Nicolaides as an interim president, while both the air force and navy withdrew from the governing *junta*. In essence, this left the army in control of the regime. At the end of the month, a retired general from the engineering corps, Reynaldo Bignone, was chosen president by Nicolaides.

Despite the internal disintegration of the regime and its delegitimation in the eyes of most sectors of society, there were few initiatives from opposition groups. Though demonstrations and strikes increased toward the end of the year, there was little apparent coordination or consensus among the opposition. In December 1982 the first general strike since 1976 was led by the Peronist unions, with little government response. General Bignone's announcement that elections would be held in October 1983, therefore, appeared to be less a response to massive opposition than the last groping act of a regime that had run out of ideas. In any event, the announcement of elections left the parties scrambling for partisan advantage. As the campaign got under way, both the Radicals and Peronists refrained from the mass mobilization tactics characteristic of previous Argentine elections. The decision to refrain from such tactics seemed to be motivated by a recognition that they had proved destabilizing in the past.

As the campaign got under way in early 1983, the Peronists had the advantage of being Argentina's dominant party. Yet in the period before the elections the party had been plagued by factional jockeying, as leaders contended for the mantle of Perón. The old union leadership, led by the conservative populist Herminio Iglesias, developed strong ties to the Church and the army. The party's final presidential candidate, Italo Luder, built up a network of provincial support and finally negotiated the support of the Iglesias faction. More importantly, the regime had begun a dialogue with the Peronists, offering their support in return for a grant of amnesty covering the period of military rule.

This was to prove a political liability that the Radicals fully used to link the Peronists to the military. For their part, the Radicals had chosen the leader of a new reformist faction to be their candidate. Raúl Alfonsín not only used the Peronist dialogue with the military as a campaign issue, but he also pointed to the political power plays in the Peronist party as an example of the type of politics that had led the military to take over in 1976. This was in keeping with a future-oriented campaign that emphasized the value of democracy and the punishment of the military. As it turned out, the Alfonsín campaign was in step with the public mood and the Radicals handed the Peronists their first ever presidential defeat.

Consolidation

In the period since Alfonsín was inaugurated president of the republic in December 1983, he has moved to reform the economy and purge those responsible for the "dirty war." The *Plan Austral* introduced in June 1985 was an attempt to control runaway inflation and revive a stagnant economy. In addition to a new currency (1 austral = 10 million pesos), wage and price freezes and budget cuts were enacted.

While meeting with early success in lowering inflation, the *Plan Austral* provoked rising labor militancy in the face of a lowering of real wages. In his first three years, Alfonsín confronted six general strikes called by the Peronist labor confederation. This opposition was strengthened by the Peronist sweep of the September 1987 elections, where they captured sixteen of twenty-two governorships.

The most persistent danger to the consolidation of Argentine democracy has remained the military. The prosecution of military officials for human rights violations stands in contrast to other recent transitions where the military has managed to negotiate its immunity from prosecution. Life imprisonment sentences have been imposed on General Jorge Videla and Admiral Emilio Massera for their part in the disappearances of an estimated ten thousand persons. Former Generals Leopoldo Galtieri and Basilio Lama Dozo and Admiral Jorge Anaya, though cleared of charges arising from the "dirty war," were court-martialed and imprisoned for their role in the Malvinas/Falklands war.

The proposed extension of prosecutions to lower-ranking officers led to a series of military rebellions in 1987 and 1988. The rebellions forced the government to back down on prosecutions. Under a new law *(obediencia debida)*, officers who held ranks below lieutenant colonel during the regime cannot be prosecuted for their actions. The decline of the economy and the growth of the Peronist Party around Carlos Saúl Menem, a charismatic governor of the remote province of La Rioja, led to Menem's victory in the presidential election on May 14, 1989.

Annotated Bibliography

Debat, Alejandro, and Luis Lorenzano. *Argentina: The Malvinas and the End of Military Rule.* London: Verso Press, 1983. An attempt to evaluate the significance of the Malvinas to Argentina historically and to the military *junta* in particular. The *junta's* decision to occupy the islands and the views of various social groups in Argentina toward the war are reviewed. Special emphasis is given to the effects of the war on leftist factions and on the continuing legacy of the conflict.

Fontana, Andrés. *Fuerzas Armadas, Partidos Políticos y Transición a la Democracia en Argentina.* Buenos Aires: CEDES, 1984. A short evaluation of the transition process during the 1981–83 period. The internal alliances of the military and the political strategies of parties are given special attention. The author suggests that although the military were the most powerful actors, they could not control their own disagreements or the economy.

Makin, Guillermo. "The Argentine Process of Demilitarization: 1980–1983." *Government and Opposition* 19, 2, (Spring 1984): Special Issue: Transitions in Brazil and Argentina. A review of the reasons for the militarization of Argentine politics since 1930 and of the possibilities of strengthening civilian institutions. Overall, reform of the military is viewed as key in ending the cycle of coups in Argentina.

Rouquié, Alan, ed. *Argentina Hoy.* Mexico D.F.: Siglo Vientiuno Editores, 1982. A series of essays that examines the social and historical background of modern Argentina. Essays by Aldo Ferrer and Peter Waldman on the post-1976 military regime are especially useful. Particular emphasis is given throughout on the difficulty of achieving consensus among various groups, including workers, landowners, and the military.

Bibliography

Almond, Gabriel A. and Sidney Verba, eds. *The Civic Culture Revisited*. Boston: Little, Brown and Company, 1980.

Arias Calderón, Ricardo. "The Christian Democrats in Latin America: The Fight for Democracy." *Caribbean Review* 11, 2(1982): 34–37.

Baloyra, Enrique. *Comparing New Democracies: Transition and Consolidation in Mediterranean Europe and the Southern Cone*. Boulder: Westview Press, 1987.

Berger, Peter L. "Democracy for Everyone?" *Commentary*, September 1983.

Caldera, Rafael. *International Social Justice and Latin American Nationalism*. Caracas: Seminarios y Ediciones, 1974.

Dahl, Robert A. *Polyarchy: Participation and Opposition*. New Haven: Yale University Press, 1971.

———. "The Democratic Mystique." *The New Republic*, April 2, 1984.

Diamond, Larry, Juan J. Linz, and Seymour Martin Lipset, eds. *Democracy in Developing Countries*. 4 vols., Boulder, Colo.: Lynne Rienner Publishers, 1988 and 1989.

Diamond, Larry, "Beyond Authoritarianism and Totalitarianism: Strategies for Democratization." *Washington Quarterly* (Winter 1989): 141–160.

Drake, Paul W. and Eduardo Silva, eds. *Elections and Democratization in Latin America*. San Diego: Center for U.S.-Mexican Studies, 1986.

Gardner, Lloyd C. *Safe for Democracy: The Anglo-American Response to Revolution*. New York: Oxford University Press, 1984.

Gastil, Raymond D. "The Importance of Ideas: How Democratic Institutions Become Established." In *Freedom In The World, 1978*, ed. Raymond D. Gastil, New York: Freedom House, 1978.

Hirschman, Albert O. "On Democracy in Latin America." *The New York Review of Books*, 10 April 1986.

Huntington, Samuel P. *Political Order in Changing Societies*. New Haven: Yale University Press, 1968.

———. "Will More Countries Become Democratic?" *Political Science Quarterly* 99 (Summer 1984): 193–218.

Huntington, Samuel P. and Joan M. Nelson. *No Easy Choice: Political Participation in Developing Countries*. Cambridge: Harvard University Press, 1976.

Lijphart, Arend. *Democracy in Plural Societies: A Comparative Exploration*. New Haven: Yale University Press, 1977.

Linz, Juan J. *The Breakdown of Democratic Regimes: Crisis, Breakdown, and Reequilibration*. Baltimore: Johns Hopkins University Press, 1978.

Linz, Juan J. and Alfred Stepan, eds. *The Breakdown of Democratic Regimes: Latin America*. Baltimore: Johns Hopkins University Press, 1978.

Lipset, Seymour Martin. *The First New Nation*. New York: W. W. Norton, 1979.

Lodge, George C. *Spearheads of Democracy*. New York: Harper and Row, 1962.

Mainwaring, Scott and Eduardo J. Viola. "Transitions to Democracy: Brazil and Argentina in the 1980's." *Journal of International Affairs* 38 (Winter 1985): 193–219.

Malloy, James M. and Mitchell A. Seligson, eds. *Authoritarians and Democrats: Regime Transition in Latin America*. Pittsburgh: University of Pittsburgh Press, 1987.

Manglapus, Raúl. "Human Rights are not a Western Discovery." *Worldview,* October 1978.

Martz, John D. and David S. Myers, eds. *Venezuela: The Democratic Experience.* New York: Praeger, 1986.

McCoy, Jennifer. "The State and the Democratic Compromise in Venezuela." *Journal of Developing Societies* 4:1 (1988): 85–104.

Moore, Barrington, Jr. *Social Origins of Democracy and Dictatorship.* Boston: Beacon Press, 1966.

Needler, Martin. *The Problem of Democracy in Latin America.* Lexington: Lexington Books, 1987.

O'Donnell, Guillermo. *Modernization and Bureaucratic-Authoritarianism: Studies in South American Politics.* Berkeley: Institute of International Studies, University of California, 1973.

O'Donnell, Guillermo, Philippe C. Schmitter, and Laurence Whitehead, eds. *Transitions from Authoritarian Rule.* Baltimore: Johns Hopkins University Press, 1986.

Pastor, Robert A., "Securing a Democratic Hemisphere" *Foreign Policy* 73 (Winter 1988–89): 41–59.

Paz, Octavio. "Latin America and Democracy." in *Democracy and Dictatorship in Latin America.* New York: Foundation for the Independent Study of Social Ideas, 1983.

Peeler, John A. *Latin American Democracies.* Chapel Hill: University of North Carolina Press, 1985.

Porter, Charles O. and Robert J. Alexander. *The Struggle for Democracy in Latin America.* New York: The Macmillan Company, 1961.

Powell, G. Bingham, Jr. *Contemporary Democracies: Participation, Stability, and Violence.* Cambridge: Harvard University Press, 1982.

Rustow, Dankwart A. "Transitions to Democracy." *Comparative Politics* 2, 3 (1970): 337–63.

Samuels, Michael A. and John D. Sullivan. "Democratic Development: A New Role for U.S. Business." *The Washington Quarterly* (Summer 1986).

Schaposnik, Eduardo C. *La Democratización de las Fuerzas Armadas Venezolanas.* Caracas: Fundacion Nacional Gonzalo Barrios, 1985.

Schwartz, Stephen, ed. *The Transition: From Authoritarianism to Democracy in the Hispanic World.* San Francisco: Institute for Contemporary Studies, 1986.

Serafino, Nina. "Defining Democracy." *Foreign Policy* 70 (Spring 1988): 166–82.

Silvert, Kalman H. "Turning Ideals into Reality: Democracy in Latin America." *The New Republic,* 22 March 1975.

Stepan, Alfred, ed. *Democratizing Brazil: Problems of Transition and Consolidation.* New York: Oxford University Press, 1988.

Stepan, Alfred. *Rethinking Military Politics: Brazil and the Southern Cone.* Princeton: Princeton University Press, 1988.

U.S. Department of State. *Democracy in Latin America and the Caribbean: The Promise and the Challenge.* Washington, D.C., 1987.

Valenzuela, Arturo. *The Breakdown of Democratic Regimes: Chile.* Baltimore: Johns Hopkins University Press, 1978.

Wesson, Robert. *Democracy in Latin America: Promise and Problems.* New York: Praeger, 1982.

Wiarda, Howard. "At the Root of the Problem." in *Central America: Anatomy of Conflict,* ed. Robert Leiken. New York: Pergamon Press, 1984.

List of Commentaries and Memoranda Prepared for the Consultation

(Copies are available from the Latin American Program, The Carter Center of Emory University, 1 Copenhill, Atlanta, Georgia 30307)

Commentaries

Comments on the Issue of Defining Democracy:

Daniel Oduber, former president of Costa Rica. "Latin America's Definition of Democracy."

George Price, former prime minister of Belize. "The Social Dimension of Democracy."

Sergio Ramírez, vice president of Nicaragua. "A Nicaraguan View of Democracy."

Jim Wright, former speaker of the House of Representatives. "Democracy and Liberty."

Comments on the Issues of Breakdown, Transition, and Consolidation of Democracy:

Fernando Belaúnde Terry, former president of Peru. "Terrorism and Its Consequences for Democracy."

William D. Rogers, former undersecretary of state. "The Role of Outsiders: The Kennedy Years."

Edgardo Boeninger, vice president of the Christian Democratic Party of Chile. "Why Do Civilians Invite Military Dictatorships?"

Rafael Caldera, former president of Venezuela. "The Roles of the Governing Party and the Opposition During the Democratic Transition."

Teodoro Petkoff, Venezuelan Socialist leader, former revolutionary. "The Rebel and the Importance of Negotiations."

Karl Deutsch, professor of political science of Emory University. "Lessons from Other Regions."

Vinicio Cerezo, president of Guatemala. "Replacing Ideology with a Spirit of Compromise: Consolidating Democracy in Central America." Edited transcript of discussion on human rights, terrorism, and the fragility of political transitions among the participants at the Consultation in November 1986.

Comments on How to Reinforce Democracy

Richard Lugar, U.S. senator, former chairman of the Senate Foreign Relations Committee. "Debt, Economic Growth, and U.S. National Interests."

Luiz Bresser Pereira, former Brazilian minister of finance. "Industrialization and Democracy."

Errol Barrow, former prime minister of Barbados. "The View of Democracy from the English-speaking Caribbean."

Raymond Burghardt, former director of Latin American Affairs on the National Security Council. "Defining Grounds for Intervention."

Pierre Elliott Trudeau, former prime minister of Canada. "Social and Economic Democracy."

Carlos Andres Pérez, president of Venezuela. "What Can Latin American Governments Do to Reinforce Democracy?"

Country Memoranda

(1) Chile
    Alejandro Foxley, CIEPLAN (Chile) and University of Notre Dame. "A Note About Political Dilemmas in Chile."

(2) The Caribbean: Suriname, Guyana, and Cuba
    Anthony Maingot, Florida International University. "A Logic of Democracy Approach to Cuba, Guyana, and Suriname."

(3) Mexico
    Lorenzo Meyer, El Colegio de Mexico. "Mexico: The Democracy of the Crisis."

(4) Argentina
    Natalio R. Botana, Director, Centro de Investigaciones Sociales, Instituto Torcuato Di Tella. "Social Pact and Political Traditions in Argentina."

(5) Haiti
    Leopold Berlanger, President, Haitian International Institute for Research and Development. "Haiti's Transition to Democracy."

(6) Colombia
    Juan Carlos Pastrana Aranga, Fundación Simón Bolívar. "Democracy and Guerrilla Violence in Colombia."

(7) The Andean Transition
    Julio Cotler, Director, Instituto de Estudios Peruanos. "Democracy in Peru: Problems and Possibilities."

(8) Paraguay
    Domingo Laino, President, Authentic Radical Liberal Party.

(9) Brazil
    Luiz Orlando Carneiro, Director, Jornal do Brasil, Brasilia. "A Note About the Press and Democracy in Brazil's Transition."

(10) The English-Speaking Caribbean
    Oliver Clarke, Editor and Managing Director, Gleaner. "A Caribbean Perspective."

(11) U.S. Foreign Policy
    J. Brian Atwood, President, National Democratic Institute for International Affairs. "Proposals for Democratic Development."

Carl Gershman, President, National Endowment for Development, and Christopher Barton. "Strengthening Democracy in the Americas."

Abraham F. Lowenthal, University of Southern California. "Converting Barriers into Bulwarks."

Ambassador Viron Pete Vaky, Carnegie Endowment for International Peace. "Should the U.S. Promote Democracy? How?"

Issue Memoranda

The Military

Virginia Gamba, former director of the Strategic Studies Course of the Joint Chiefs of Staff in Argentina. "The Role of the Military in the Transition Process."

Ricardo Arias Calderón, president of the Christian Democratic Party of Panama. "Reasserting Civilian Authority Over the Military."

Edgardo Mercado Jarrín, retired general of the Peruvian Army, currently president of Instituto Peruano de Estudios Geopoliticos y Estrategicos in Lima. "What Changes Will Be Necessary in Military Institutions to Insure the Transition and Consolidation of Democracy?"

Elections

Larry Diamond and Seymour Martin Lipset, Hoover Institution. "Ensuring Free, Fair, and Peaceful Electoral Competition."

Larry Garber, director of the Election Observer Project of the International Human Rights Law Group. "A Proposal to Establish an Inter-American Commission on Elections."

Labor Unions

William Doherty, director, American Institute of Free Labor Development. "The Role of Unions in the Development of Democracy."

Economic Issues

Albert Fishlow, chairman of the Department of Economics, University of California, Berkeley. "Democracy and Economic Performance in Latin America."

Church

Rev. Xavier Gorostiaga, director, *CRIES/INIES*, Managua. "Proposals for the Creation of Democracy in Central America."

Contributors

Raúl Alfonsín was elected President of Argentina on 30 October 1983 for a six year term as the leader of the Unión Cívica Radical party. He graduated from the Liceo Militar General San Martin and then studied liberal arts and law at the National University of La Plata, earning his doctorate in 1950. President Alfonsín is the author of several articles and books, including: *The Argentine Question: Now, My Political Proposal;* and *What is Radicalism?*

Nicolás Ardito Barletta was President of Panama from 1984 to 1985. He was Vice President of the World Bank for Latin America and the Caribbean from 1978 to 1984, and Panama's Minister of Planning from 1973 to 1978. Dr. Ardito Barletta also served as Director of Economic Affairs at the OAS and President of the Latin American Export Bank. He has a B.S. and M.S. degrees from North Carolina State University and a Ph.D. in economics from the University of Chicago.

Jimmy Carter was the thirty-ninth President of the United States (1977–1981). He attended Georgia Southwestern College and the Georgia Institute of Technology and graduated from the United States Naval Academy (1946). He is the author of *Keeping Faith: Memoirs of a President* (1981) and *The Blood of Abraham* (1985). In April 1982, he accepted appointment as Emory University Distinguished Professor, and in September of that year the Carter Center of Emory University was established.

Tom J. Farer is Professor of Law and Director of the Program in Law and International Relations at The American University. He received his LL.B. from Harvard University in 1961. Mr. Farer was Special Assistant to the Assistant Secretary of State for Inter-American Affairs, and later was a member of the Inter-American Commission on Human Rights, serving as President from 1980–1982. He is the author of *The Future of the Inter-American System.*

Edward Gibson received his B.A. from Clark University and is completing his Ph.D. in Political Science at Columbia University. His dissertation is on *Conservative Power and Political Action in Argentina.*

Samuel P. Huntington is Eaton Professor of Government and Director of the Center for International Affairs at Harvard University. He is a former President of the American Political Science Association and served as Coordinator of Security Planning for the National Security Council (1977–78). He has authored numerous articles and books, including *No Easy Choice: Political Participation in Developing Countries* (co-author, 1976) and *Political Order in Developing Countries.* Professor Huntington received his B.A. from Yale University, his M.A. from the University of Chicago, and his Ph.D. from Harvard.

Osvaldo Hurtado was President of Ecuador from 1981 to 1984. He is now President of CORDES, a research group. He founded the Christian Democratic Party of Ecuador in 1964 and was President of the Christian Democratic Organization of the Americas in 1985. President Hurtado received his M.A. in Political/Social Sciences (1963) and Ph.D. in Law (1966) from the Catholic University of Ecuador. He is the author of many articles, essays, and other publications, including *Political Power in Ecuador* (1977).

Juan Linz is Pelatiah Perit Professor of Political and Social Science at Yale University. He holds degrees in Political Science, Economics, and Law from the University of Madrid, and in 1959 received a Ph.D. in Sociology from Columbia University. His publications include: *Crisis, Breakdown and Reequilibrium,* an introductory volume to *The Breakdown of Democratic Regimes,* and "Totalitarian and Authoritarian Regimes" in *Handbook of Political Science,* ed. F. Greenstein and N. Polsby.

Philip Mauceri received his B.A. and M.A. from New York University and is completing his Ph.D. in Political Science at Columbia University. His dissertation is on *Radical Opposition and Political Conflict in Peru.*

Lorenzo Meyer is Professor at the Center for International Studies of El Colegio de México. He received his Ph.D. in History from the University of Chicago, and is the author of numerous books, including *The United States and Mexico* (1985) and *Mexico and the United States in the Oil Controversy, 1917–42* (1972), both written in Spanish, but also published in English. Dr. Meyer is the winner of Mexico's National Prize in the Social Sciences. He is a regular columnist on Mexican politics in the newspaper *Excelsior.*

Guillermo O'Donnell is Helen Kellogg Professor of International Affairs and Academic Director of the Kellogg Institute at the University of Notre Dame. He is also director of *CEBRAP* in Sao Paulo. He is the author of numerous books, including *Modernization and Bureaucratic-Authoritarianism: Studies in South American Politics,* and *Transitions from Authoritarian Rule: Prospects for Democracy* (co-editor). He received an M.A. from Yale, and a Master's Degree in Law from the National University of Buenos Aires.

Robert A. Pastor is Professor of Political Science at Emory University and the Director of the Latin American and Caribbean Program at Emory's Carter Center. Dr. Pastor was the Director of Latin American and Caribbean Affairs on the National Security Council (1977–1981). He received his M.P.A. and Ph.D. from Harvard University and is the author of numerous books, including

Condemned to Repetition: The United States and Nicaragua, Latin America's Debt Crisis (editor), and *Limits to Friendship: The United States and Mexico* (co-author).

Thomas E. Skidmore is Professor of History at Brown University. He was a professor at the University of Wisconsin (1968–88). He received a B.A. from Denison University, an M.A. from Oxford, and a Ph.D. from Harvard in 1960. Dr. Skidmore is General Editor of The Latin American Histories Series for the Oxford University Press, and is the author of *Politics in Brazil, 1930–64* (1969), *Modern Latin America* (1984, co-author), and *The Politics of Military Rule in Brazil, 1964–85* (1988).

Alfred Stepan is Dean of the School of International and Public Affairs and Professor of Political Science at Columbia University. He graduated from the University of Notre Dame and holds an M.A. from Balliol College, Oxford, and a Ph.D. from Columbia. He is on the Board of Governors of the Foreign Policy Association and the National Executive Committee of *Americas Watch*. Dean Stepan is the author of a number of books, including *Rethinking Military Politics, Democratizing Brazil*, and *The Breakdown of Democratic Regimes*, co-edited with Juan Linz.

Laurence Whitehead is Official Fellow at Nuffield College, Oxford. Mr. Whitehead received his B.A. from Magdalen College, Oxford, and his M.A. from Nuffield College, Oxford. He is the co-editor of *The Central American Impasse, The Adjustment Crisis in Latin America*, and *Transitions From Authoritarian Rule: Prospects for Democracy*.

Index

Acapulco Pact, 95*n*

Acción Democrática, 86

Adversity, political processing of, 42–48

AFL-CIO Free Trade Union Institute, 146

Albuja, Manuel, 230

Alfonsín, Raúl, xvii, xix–xxi, 54, 83–84, 242; on economic cooperation, 138, 151; election victory of, 135; on foreign debt, 137; inauguration of, 243; on rebirth of democracy, 133; support of, 152

Algeria, independence of, 124

Allende, Salvador, 185–86, 187–88

Alliance for Progress, 6; call for social reform by, 137; and Colombia, 212; early days of, 116

Alza, 212

American Convention on Human Rights, xv–xvii, 115

American Declaration on the Rights and Duties of Man, 115; Article 20 of, 143

American Revolution, 24

Americas, founding fathers of, 3–5

Americas Watch, 147

Anaya, Admiral Jorge, 243

Andean Pact, 117, 230

Arana, Colonel Francisco, 170

Arbenz Guzmán, Jacobo, 5, 169–71; ouster of, 172–73

Areco, Jorge Pacheco, 189

Arévalo, President, 92

Argentina: authoritarian breakdown and military defeat in, 240–43; bipartisan system in, 98; breakdown of democracy in, 173–78, 194–98; *Conciencia* in, 144–45; democracy in, xix–xx, 151; Frondizi government in, 175–76; Illia government in, 176–77; increased valorization of democracy in, 47; instability of constitutional regime in, 175; Malvinas war, 7, 241–43; military human rights violations in, 136; paramilitary violence in, 59*n;* parliamentary system in, 57; party system in, 135;

Peronists in, 195–97, 241–42; political violence in, 51; restraint of military in, 83–84; transition from authoritarianism in, 62

Arias Plan, 93

Aristotle, 13

Arizaga Vega, Dr. Rafael, 228

Associated states, 129–30

Athens, in Peloponnesian war, 127–28

Austria: interwar depression in, 59*n;* political violence in, in interwar period, 51; socioeconomic efficacy and democratic legitimacy in, 46

Authoritarianism, 16: caudillo-centered, 72–74; collapse of, 63; economic growth in, 19; groups involved in transition from, 64–68; military force in, 22; moral rejection of, 67; revival of society following breakdown of, 34; transitions from, 62–64; view of democracy of, 34–35; welfare benefits of, 20

Autogolpe, 69

Axis, defeat of, 12

Aztecs, 3

Baker Plan, 103, 107

Balaguer, Joaquín, 220–21

Balbín, Ricardo, 175, 196

Bankruptcy, risk of, 102

Barletta, Nicolás Ardito, 137

Barrantes, Alfonso, 234

Basque terrorists, 49, 51

Batista, Fulgencio, fall of, 5

Belaúnde Terry, Fernando, 6–7, 232–33

Belgium, socioeconomic efficacy and democratic legitimacy in, 46

Belize, democracy in, 134

Betancourt, Romulo, 149–50, 214, 216; election of, 215

Betancourt Doctrine, 92; multilateralizing of, 150–51; new, 148–49

Bignone, Reynaldo, 242

Bipartisan systems, 98

Birkelbach Report, 93

253